NAZI PSYCHOANALYSIS

VOLUME II

Crypto-Fetishism

Laurence A. Rickels

FOREWORD BY BENJAMIN BENNETT

University of Minnesota Press
Minneapolis • London

Nancy Barton grants permission to the University of Minnesota Press for the use of the image "Untitled—Testing" in *Nazi Psychoanalysis.*

Every effort was made to obtain permission to reproduce the illustrations in this book. If any proper acknowledgment has not been included here, we encourage copyright holders to notify the publisher.

Published by the University of Minnesota Press
111 Third Avenue South, Suite 290
Minneapolis, MN 55401-2520
http://www.upress.umn.edu

A Cataloging-in-Publication record for this book is available from the Library of Congress.

ISBN 0-8166-3698-2 (hc : alk. paper)
ISBN 0-8166-3699-0 (pbk. : alk. paper)

Printed in the United States of America on acid-free paper

12 11 10 09 08 07 06 05 04 03 02 10 9 8 7 6 5 4 3 2 1

NAZI PSYCHOANALYSIS

VOLUME II

NAZI PSYCHOANALYSIS

VOLUME I

Only Psychoanalysis Won the War

VOLUME II

Crypto-Fetishism

VOLUME III

Psy Fi

CONTENTS

Foreword

BENJAMIN BENNETT

"If God had intended us to fly...," the saying goes, or at least used to go. To be sure, the scope of Laurence A. Rickels's *Crypto-Fetishism,* the second volume of *Nazi Psychoanalysis,* extends well beyond the question of how human beings might be made suitable for flying. Especially the idea of fetishism—in the form of a "techno-mourning ... that mourns even over those merely integrative moments in works of mourning and substitution"—both receives and reveals unexpected significance.

> As techno-mourning, fetishism isn't about the identifiable or identified-with body. For one, it's not about couples. And it's not about losing, just because you lost. It is about winning, like a winner and not like a victim; it's about some power of emergency propulsion that gets us past the totalization and paralysis of loss to the wide open and outer spacing of what in a more couplified era or moment of mourning could only be seen as closed and enclosing delusional states that were the determining limit and dead end of failed mourning.

Radical transformation is the matter here, something like a turning of the world inside out, or perhaps rather a disintegration of the whole "couple" inside/outside in a new space of "greater psychoanalysis" where the internal (intrapsychic) and external (technological, gadget-loving) aspects of fetishism are no longer strictly distinguishable. And yet the question of flying is not merely a metaphor in this context. There is, in fact, no longer any such thing as a "mere" metaphor in the neither internal nor external (nor even spatial) space that opens between our world wars, a space we traverse, if at all, on wings no god ever dreamed of. We can gain perspective on this situation, I think, by first stepping back a quarter millennium or so.

To the extent that a main point exists, the main point of Johann Georg Hamann's *Aesthetics in a Nutshell* (1762) is probably that scripture and history, and indeed nature itself, are all versions of a single text, a single divine writing, and that the purport of that writing depends radically on how the reader approaches it, which in turn never fails to involve the question of who the reader really is. These last two ideas are set forth with perfect clarity, toward the end of Hamann's text, in a pair of quotations, the first in Latin from St. Augustine, the second in German from Luther. But rather than call Augustine by name, Hamann cites him as "the Punic church father," with a footnote mark on the word "Punic." And if one follows that lead, if one descends here into what Laurence A. Rickels likes to call the text's "footnote underworld," one is dragged further and further away from anything like a main point. That "Punic" refers to Augustine's Carthaginian origins, Hamann doesn't bother to tell us; we're supposed to know. Instead, he begins with a reference to Johann David Michaelis's condescending remarks about Augustine's Latin style, and then jumps, via a pun (what else?) on the word "Punic," to the idea of "punning" as developed in an early-eighteenth-century English treatise (necessarily English, since "pun" in German is merely "Wortspiel") that is variously attributed to Swift and Sheridan, and jumps from there.... You see what I'm getting at, and if you have looked at the main text of the present book, you probably see something of my reasons for starting with Hamann and punning. Like Hamann, Rickels has important points to make, about the structure and growth of psychoanalysis, and in general about the impossibility of marking off areas in modernity that are somehow sheltered from Nazi contamination. And like Hamann—who must at all costs deny systematic Lutheran theology access to his texts, lest his thought be co-opted into reinforcing exactly the postlapsarian division between scripture and nature against which it is directed—Rickels has excellent reasons for what he terms his "user-unfriendly" procedure. Psychoanalysis, as Rickels means it, is not, strictly speaking, susceptible to being written or known "about." The pretense of possessing an objective or innocent verbal instrument with which to take hold of psychoanalysis violates the discursive implications of the subject matter in exactly the same way that Hamann's Christianity is violated by theological systematics.

Does it follow, then, that the present work is accessible only to strict insiders, only to psychoanalysts? In fact, psychoanalytic literature abounds with formulations of the peculiarly evasive quality of its core discipline; perhaps the best known is Jacques Lacan's remark that what the unconscious "is" cannot be disentangled from the circumstances of its discovery and the person of its discoverer. The theory of psychoanalysis, we are told, is never fully detached from its object, never in command of it, but always itself a self-relativizing instance of analytic procedure; in Rickels's arguments, specifically, it is the analytic mechanism of transference that turns out repeatedly to be operative, on a large public scale, in the history of the discipline. Everything is provisional or heuristic in psychoanalysis; there is no level of abstraction at which the discipline might in principle stand wholly revealed to the gaze of pure intelligence. (We think of the aspirations of Hamann's Wolffian contemporaries.) Understanding is never distinct from practice, and to "understand" a work such as Rickels's is therefore always in some sense to be a practitioner. But in exactly what sense?

The parallel case of Hamann continues to help us here. To be an insider with respect to Hamann means to be the adherent of a special kind of transtheological Christianity, or at least to recognize its presence as an analogue in one's own philosophical practice. Therefore it is not hard to imagine why Hegel and Kierkegaard should be among Hamann's prominent admirers. But to find Goethe in this group, the older, "classical," self-consciously heathen Goethe, is a bit startling. And yet it is true that Goethe, who was in possession of some interesting manuscript material, for a long time considered actually editing Hamann. In book 12 of *Dichtung und Wahrheit,* he characterizes Hamann as follows:

> When a person speaks, he must become for the moment one-sided; there is no communication, no written doctrine, without particularity. Since Hamann, however, was once and for all opposed to this sort of separation, and since he desired to speak in the same all-embracing manner in which he felt, imagined, and thought, and since he demanded the same of others, he stood in opposition to his own style and to everything that others could produce. In order to accomplish the impossible, he therefore lays hands on all conceivable elements of writing.

This does not read like unequivocal praise, and in fact, a few lines later, Goethe speaks of a historical "darkness" into which Hamann's writings descend. But then, toward the end of the same long paragraph, we hear that if we take the trouble to look up some of Hamann's references, we encounter

> an ambiguous double illumination which strikes us as highly agreeable, as long as we resolutely avoid requiring what one would usually call an "understanding" of it. Such pages therefore deserve to be called "sibylline," because one cannot take them in and for themselves, but must wait for the occasion when one is specially moved to seek refuge in their oracular quality.

Surely, when he speaks of "seeking refuge" in Hamann, Goethe is not referring to any specific religious content. What he means can only have to do with Hamann's attempt at an impossible "all-embracing" form of writing. Hamann's texts, I mean, are a place where one seeks refuge *as a writer,* as a practitioner of writing, as a struggler with the "one-sidedness" of writing—not because Hamann in any degree solves the problem of writing but because, by straining its limits, he *situates* that problem, thus profiles it for us and offers us a "scene of writing" in which our particular performance, though still indelibly marked with futility, makes a kind of quasi-dramatic and historical sense after all.

And by alluding to Derrida's essay "Freud and the Scene of Writing," I mean of course to make the connection with psychoanalysis and Rickels. The kind of practitioner implied as the reader of Rickels's trilogy, I contend, is a *writer,* in the sense obliquely suggested by Goethe for Hamann.

> Freud [writes Derrida] *performed for us the scene of writing.* But we must think of this scene in other terms than those of individual or collective psychology, or even anthropology. It must be thought in the horizon of the scene/stage of the world, as the history of that scene/stage. Freud's language is *caught up* in it.

The "one-sided" move of the writer—which Goethe vaguely calls "separation," whereas Derrida would relate it to *différance*—not only is imposed by the world but also in a sense *establishes* the world as a "scene" (and how else would it become "world" in history?) by performing it. Derrida suggests that in writers like Freud, this quality of performance lies closer to the surface than elsewhere. But writers like Hamann—and Rickels—still constitute a special class, in that their performance is informed by a depth of resistance (a "user-unfriendly" stance "in opposition") that strains the boundaries, and thus marks them, and so *sets* the scene of writing. Not permanently, not once and for all: if this were possible, then "one-sidedness" would not be a necessary attribute of writing after all. Rather, as a moment of respite or "refuge," a kind of breathing space. This does not mean that one must "actually" be a writer to read Rickels with profit. But one does have to be able to adopt a writerly point of view, to read without falling into the comfortably dependent relation of consumer to a presumed producer, to manage one's handling of the text so that there is in the end no strict "user" for anyone to be unfriendly to. One must approach Rickels not in terms of "the oppositions sender-receiver, code-message" (these "coarse instruments," Derrida calls them), but rather so as to engage (Derrida again) "the *sociality* of writing as *drama.*"

To be less cryptic about it, one can in fact formulate as a proposition the basic implications of Rickels's difficult style. His use of wordplay and allusion and quotation insists constantly on the point that neither knowledge itself nor the objects of knowledge can reasonably be said to exist in a manner that is strictly prior to, or at all independent of, the discursive acts and techniques by which they are shaped, the verbal garments in which they make their appearance to us. Which means, in turn, that there is no way of describing a clear division between the referential and logical structure of argument on the one hand, and, on the other, the structure of relations (the arbitrarily grammatical as well as the associative and allusive) that constitute the general verbal horizon in which we happen to be operating. Rickels's particular talent as a stylist is his ability to keep this proposition in the foreground of his presentation, even while suggesting a large number of specific and cohesive interpretive arguments on another level. And just this foregrounding, in turn, is crucial in relation to the subject matter, including the inseparability of theory and practice in psychoanalysis, and the impossibility of establishing a strict division between the two concepts in the work's main title. Foregrounding, however, is the form in which this point appears in Rickels, not formulation; for formulation (including the one I have just suggested) automatically offers its reader the safe, separated position of a consumer (we recall Goethe on "separation"), which contradicts exactly the point being formulated. Formulation requires understanding as a response. But as Goethe says of Hamann, "understanding" is out of place here. How can this be? What do we *miss* in the present text by "understanding" it?

Rickels answers this question when he speaks of his project as the "excavation" of material and the maintenance of its "materiality." The trouble with systematic argument in general, and our understanding of it, is that it (so to speak) dematerializes its material, imposes on the material an order that supplants the structure of the experience of finding it more or less unprepared. This is not to say that either Rickels or we are trying to preserve cultural-historical material in something like an "original" state—a state of the sort that can in fact never reasonably be said to exist. Nor can either we or Rickels reliably reproduce the more or less immediate experience of seeing our not-seeing psychoanalysis. (The ocular metaphor in the pun "Nazi = not-see" produces a contradiction for the understanding here, but not a material impossibility in experience.) Nor, finally, does Rickels ever actually avoid systematic argument. Rather, by the use of balance or tension between argumentative and associative structures, Rickels positions his reader—constantly, from sentence to sentence—so as to enable him or her to go as far as possible (whatever that means in each particular case) toward recovering the materiality of the work's material, without ever losing hold of its (argumentatively established) significance. Materiality, moreover, is also the key to Rickels's use of quotation. A style based heavily on quotation, once a certain density is arrived at—as in Rickels (or Hamann)—begins to body forth the understanding that meaning in language is never really anything *but* quotation, that *langue* and *parole*, in other words, the governing linguistic system and the mass of actual instances, are not really distinct, that language, even in that aspect that is systematized in grammars and lexica, is entirely constituted by the accumulation of material in the form of particular utterances. Indeed, Rickels's fondness for pop-cultural quoting establishes this point at a more immediate level of linguistic practice than, for example, Hamann's quoting mainly from scripture and classics plus commentaries and glosses.

To the extent that a main point exists, the main point of *Nazi Psychoanalysis* is probably that Nazism cannot be isolated in the structure of modernity, that no element of modernity can be thought adequately without thinking its Nazi component. "That's right, it's about facing the continuity that was there: Nazi psychoanalysis, Nazi Marxism, Nazi deconstruction." But this is not a point that can be "understood" in the normal sense of the word, for understanding it would produce a detached critical perspective for the understander, hence an element of modernity (precisely the intellectual juncture at which this understanding takes place) that is thoroughly purged of any Nazi contamination after all. The point, rather, as Rickels suggests, must be "faced" in all its immediate material undigestibility. Or seen from a different angle, it must be *performed*, as Rickels's style performs the identity of meaning and quotation. If you want theory, you go to Derrida, who in fact produces what is in essence a neat theory of "greater psychoanalysis" in his argument on how the opening of Freud's discourse "to the theme of writing results in psychoanalysis being not simply psychology—nor simply psychoanalysis." But in Rickels, what you get is better termed, if not perfectly termed, performance.

For this reason, finally, I will not attempt to do more than Rickels himself does, in the matter of summarizing the present volume, when he indicates that all the material here is connected, at whatever remove, with the idea of air war, as seen either from aloft or from below. Instead I will simply point the reader toward one or two of what strike me as the most interesting pieces of material. The chapters "Cyber-Lacan" through "On Turing," for example, create an exceptionally dense fabric by which Lacan's difficulty with melancholia and his cybernetic meditations are related to his attendance at the Berlin Olympics, whence the idea of "games" supports an extension of the associative web to Ernst Kris on propaganda, the breaking of the Enigma code, and the electronic battlefield. And a brief mention in a quote at the end of "A Couple of Fetishes" prepares Heidegger—not only his texts but details of his life, as well—for becoming the rabbit pulled out of a hat ("Hi Ya Heidegger") at the end of a section mainly on mummies, whereupon, by way of a neat association with H. Rider Haggard, the matter of Nazi-period psychiatric appreciations of Heidegger is raised.

It is true that some readers will still be bothered by the associative aspect of this writing, by the virtual structural equivalence in it of "real" historical or factual relations and those verbally mediated relations, as it were material puns (the consonantal similarity of "Heidegger" and "Haggard," which trumps Heidegger's own etymological gymnastics), that one is tempted to call "coincidence." But the thing about coincidence in this sense is that it refuses to go away; there is no home for it, no grave, in our filing systems. A strictly real relation gets used up in its reality, and so always gets left behind, disposed of, by any reasonably adequate representation in language. But a coincidence, whose substance is both verbal *and* factual, or at least the sort of pregnant coincidence that is repeatedly brewed up by Rickels's broad knowledge and analytic skill, sticks in the craw of language, so to speak, and confuses the comfortable triangle of producer-consumer-object, as if reality had wrenched the instrument from our hand and were writing itself. The separation between reality and writing, the space of a presumed visibility that hides not-seeing from view—or as Hamann (who else?) would say, the separation between nature and scripture, which makes space for us to accept, for instance (as not-seeingly in the eighteenth century as in the twentieth), the notion of an enlightened politics—this separation is not transcended so much as it becomes, for the time being, in a manner of speaking, hard to swallow.

In other words, as long as you expect Rickels to do something for you—to teach you, to improve you, to take you somewhere—as long as you insist on something "positive," you will be disappointed. Reading, in the age of the novel, is generally understood as the mental equivalent of traveling. When you read—as when you place yourself physically in unfamiliar surroundings—you take a kind of vacation from your identity. This applies not only to the reading of novels, where it is obvious, but also to the reading of expository texts, where you try to be objective or open-minded (which means, not yourself), in order to understand the writing "in and for *it*self." But this attitude is as misplaced with Rickels as Goethe says it is with Hamann. You are never going to have all of this book anyway. The way you in fact are, as yourself, named, scarred, broken, accidental, radically compromised, like modernity *it*self, is how this book wants its reader, and how you, the reader, want the book.

Achtung

A PREFACE TO *NAZI PSYCHOANALYSIS*

> Ruth Eissler reports the successful analytic treatment in a case of acute paranoid delusion. A young woman whose mother is of German ancestry accuses herself of being an "innocent Nazi spy" when her husband, a member of a depreciated minority group, is about to be drafted. In one of his last papers, Freud has asserted that each delusion contains a kernel of historic truth from infantile sources. In Eissler's case, the "truth" is a miscarriage of the mother at the height of the patient's Oedipus complex. The traumatic position was later fortified when a girl cousin died of tuberculosis. She had been closely attached to this girl and employed a secret code in communication with her. This code she unconsciously used in her psychotic episode again, thus getting magically in touch with the dead. In her paraphrenic language, "Nazi" was really "not see"—referring to the magic destruction of the unseen rival.
>
> —FRANZ ALEXANDER AND GERHART PIERS, "PSYCHOANALYSIS"

If we were to list all institutions that supported this project and, on the other side, the many distinguished addresses that could not follow at all, rejected it out of their hands, we would be reminded, more by metonymy I suppose than by any direct reference, that there was, after all, the one side that won the war. I hope this reassurance will in some measure uncanny-proof volume 2 of *Nazi Psychoanalysis*. All you consumer fascist types, you know who you are, cannot be stopped from policing the middlebrow beat to which intellectual discourse was condemned a long time ago. But it is still important to keep up with the symptomatic character of these conspiracies of mediocrity and tag the show of not understanding at all as no more, no less, than resistance.

In interview (*Spex*, October 1997, 52–53), Brigitte Weingart raised the question of an extra dimension in my interrogation of adolescent or group psychology (in addition to the conceptualization and talking about the Teen Age) that is performative or, as I prefer to address it, languistic in nature. My answer: "I have tried to build up a critical language that hovers between diagnosis and performance. A discourse that seeks a connection, one that could be analogized with the case or status of a so-called borderline psychotic, namely, standing between neurosis and psychosis, a connection with all the noise and overhearing coming out of the media, advertising, radio music, headlines. In all our lives this metabolization of the media sensurround goes down visibly and audibly in our teenage languages, in these invented in-group idioms. This process interests me mainly because it represents the first attempt to absorb and control release the impact of our ongoing technologization and group psychologization."

But what may strike some as obstructive in this manner of genealogy or total history is less the style of writing than the insistence on staying with the materials in the juxtapositions in which they can be and have been thought. The book is nonphobic about what comes its way. But most important of all, the space of this tension between low and high, literary and historical, material and interpretation comes right out of the force field of Freud's legacy. It's an allegorical tension that comes down to the unrepresentable gap lying between the in-session experience of the transference and the shorthand of analytic theory. Here we find the materiality of psychoanalysis, through which all concepts continue to pass. The silent but pressing inclusion of this tension in psychoanalytic theorizing was what Freud was listening to when he allowed for a distinction between his science and philosophy. It's what I want you to hear whenever you, dear reader, already a survivor of the collision between "Nazi" and "Psychoanalysis," come across, in the reading that lies just ahead, juxtapositions or even contaminations of seemingly undigested blocks of time or language. Mourning is the model of this work. It's work, all work, that takes the time—the times—it takes to mourn.

In the course of the dig, as they all rose to consciousness, the materials kept on putting through uncanny connections between so many of the split-off, discontinuous segments of our standard tradition or reception of good modernism, good psychoanalysis. The influence we now see come out in the watch of the materials relies on a sense of audience that puts on Freudian ears to listen behind the lines: out of the noisy wear and tear of resistance there emerges one genuine line of influence, the kind that represents real change. A clean transferential cutting in of "the father," say, into the place of the analyst or therapist can promote the immediate cause of healing; but in matters of influence—a matter psychoanalysis alone made an issue of its science, also in the sense that there was no influence until we learned how to interpret for the transference, the resistance, the defense—the intactness of a foreign corpus inside another's identity or identification indeed symptomatizes a host or ghost of issues but does not, finally, give the measure of any influence.

The least likely place to look, therefore, which was where previous studies of the Nazi history of psychoanalysis and the psychodynamic therapies tended to start and stop, is the small band of certified analysts who stayed on in Germany after 1933 (only one "Aryan" analyst felt it was the time to leave with his Jewish colleagues) and formed compromises that, out of context of the big influence, and slipping into and around see-through rationalizations, seem but an abject of study. Even the wider bandwidths measuring the entire eclectic setting of the old analysts back together again with their former competitors, the Adlerians and Jungians, who thought they had split psychoanalysis once and for all, only come in shortwave. There was the obvious prestige and scope of application of psychotherapy with full state support. The backing the German Institute of Psychological Research and Psychotherapy received was given directly, no problem, or it came, in triumph, at the end of another corridor skirmish with bioneuropsychiatry. Psychotherapy openly maintained its outright lead in the contest with psychiatry until after Stalingrad the analytic-therapeutic influence became less public in its broadcasting out to the war effort. But there is evidence that frontline work with schizo soldiers was still being conducted in ways and means compatible with greater psychoanalysis. The corridor wars between analytic psychotherapy and neuropsychiatry, which had already commenced upon Freud's first full entry into the field of psychological interventionism by way of the extremely good rep psychoanalysis received during World War I as treatment of choice for war neurosis, frame the ambiguous status and conflicting verdicts or second opinions that affected the nonreproductive members of Nazi German society. At the therapeutic end of the corridor, homosexuals were under treatment to be healed (with all the other neurotics, including the symptomatizing soldiers); but if the neuropsychiatrists got hold of them, they went the one way of all the other untreatables. This split-leveling of homosexuality occupies the bottom line of projections ultimately held in common and in conflict at all ends of the corridor.

But even the Institute-sized networking of the materials sets a limitation on the ranging of Freud's effects, which were rolled over beyond the jurisdiction of the reunified analytic psychotherapies. Psychotherapeutic standards of correctness and correction, according to which every German was to be given one more chance, were too popular to be contained within the history of one institute. From the close of World War I through the end of World War II, Germany was a pop-psychological culture of all-out healing. Before the baton could be passed to California, the current finish line of eclectic psychotherapy for all, the big splits between the Germanys and between a good German psychoanalysis and a disowned German neoanalytic therapy were all that the Germans, their victims, and their conquerors could do to defend themselves.

Nazi Psychoanalysis reconnects all the outposts of frontline intrapsychic theorization and treatment inside the orbit of the central psychotherapy institute in Berlin. One more jump cut through the material, one that once again doesn't follow Institute guidelines, tunes in the otherwise least likely candidates for analytic influence, military psychologists trained in psychotechnical methods. In particular, their specialized understanding and management of the relations obtaining between pilots and their flying machines reflect a Freudian influence strong enough to receive and transmit between the lines. These psychotechnical relations, which were seen to be always shock-absorbed with what was fundamentally traumatic about artificial flight, follow the intrapsychic model where few analytic thinkers had gone before, right up to the head of the receiving line of Freud's reading of technology. It was this double reading of a Freudian techno-criticism that my first two books, *Aberrations of Mourning* and *The Case of California*, already sought to raise to consciousness from between the lines of Freud's studies of psychosis, melancholia, perversion, and group psychology. In *Nazi Psychoanalysis*, which marks the final installment of my trilogy on "Unmourning," the long haul through tracts on war neurosis, military adjustment, and psychological warfare, all of which had been abandoned, now in the ditches of one world war, now inside the air-raid shelters of the other one, leads to a reconstruction of what can be called to this day "greater psychoanalysis." By World War II, between the air-raid sheltering of the populace in a group-therapeutic mode and the intrapsychic wiring of the pilot to his machine, an axis of technologization was being followed, up through cybernetics (both in Gregory Bateson's sense of feedback and in Jacques Lacan's staging of the rearview mirror) all the way out to the fantasy horizon of science fiction, which is where this book begins again.

What the particular science fiction that was Nazi Germany tried to outfly belonged to the gravity, the grave, of earthbound or limited supplies, which each time marked the spot the German war machine was in when the world came to war. To open up the underworld commentary that runs with the flights of techno-fantasy, focus can be fixed on an ambiguously held term or introject, the German word *Bestand*, in which the notions of reserve supplies and staying power are combined, and which goes by "standing reserve" in translations of Heidegger's use of the word (in his essays on technology). Here we find the melancholic scarcity or lack that through total mobilization was to be transformed, like a wound, as in takeoff, into the miracle of flight all the way to fetish victories of rocket or robot bombing. But the itinerary of flight was all along skipping another beat around the rush for prospects for technologization and group psychologization. It was the master beat of reproductive coupling. By the time of his essay on fetishism, Freud was staying tuned to the impulses of gadget love that we've been jamming with ever since the onset of technologization. Technofantasies or science fictions have, at least since the eighteenth century, special-featured the overcoming of a crisis in reproduction through the self-replicating prospects of immortality now (in other words, without the loss of generation). This is the place of tension to which Freud assigned the fetishist, after first discovering it over the symptomatizing body of the war neurotic: between, on one side, the attractions of splitting or doubling within a borderline zone lying across neurosis and psychosis and, on the other side, the requirements that are still and for the time being with us, the same old ones that only reproduction can keep on fulfilling for the survival of the species. Thus through the fetish future that science fiction holds open and shut, the continuity back then that we're addressing here for the first time can be brought back into real-time proximity with the live or dead issues that currently occupy the media grounds for our existence.

Achtung contains the word of caution but also the word for respect. In the course of gathering all the materials that fit my monster topic, I benefited from many leads given me by the following individuals I think/I thank: Nancy Chodorow, Mark Grotjahn, Werner Hamacher, Elliot Jurist, Friedrich Kittler, Wolf Kittler, Catherine Liu, Peter Loewenberg, Brian McCormick, Ulrike Ottinger, Karl Rickels, Avital Ronell, Lorraine Ryavec, Renate Schlesier, Ursula Schreiter, Lawton Smith, Klaus Theweleit. My project was supported by fellowships from the Alexander von Humboldt Foundation, the Center for German and European Studies (University of California–Berkeley), the Interdisciplinary Humanities Center (University of California–Santa Barbara), and the Academic Senate (University of California–Santa Barbara). It took me more than the two years Freud estimated for the work of mourning to place this book. My *Achtung* has therefore been won in the first place by the University of Minnesota Press. Thanks to William Murphy and Doug Armato for their support of my project.

When I first opened up shop with the materials of Nazi psychoanalysis in 1991, I right away enrolled in a local clinical psychology graduate program and commenced my training as a therapist in the setting of licensure in California. My training in California as just another psychotherapist whose eclecticism remains, by training, stuck on the parts of psychoanalysis that "work" afforded me the next-best thing to being there, at the Nazi German institute of psychotherapy in Berlin. Alongside the archival labors—along for my metabolization of those materials—this field-tripping hands-on portion of my analytic research must be admitted as equally formative in the development of the study of Nazi psychoanalysis.

This study was completed in 1995. Beginning in 1991, I presented papers and published articles advertising my discoveries and their final destination as part of work I was pursuing at book length. Discoveries I had made, for example, in the prehistory of Nazi German investments in psychotherapy that had their primal scene in Freud's World War I reading of war neurosis, among other headlines from the trenches of my dig, were thus fixed in the same space as my name. Nineteen ninety-five remains the cutoff point for my published interest in contemporary accounts of these "same" histories. If a certain first-generation historian of Nazi German psychotherapy, who is given credit for his study in the first volume of *Nazi Psychoanalysis* in the exact amount due, has since 1995 published an "expanded" new edition of his work that suddenly takes another look at the materials by the stolen fire of my work (admittedly reduced to a night-light by the shame of it), then I can only make the referral to Karl Kraus, who had all there is to say about the double failure in journalism and prostitution that leaves the loser only one option by default—the small-change careerism of the academic historian. Perhaps there is an affirmation here, after all, in the way my work goes into others' works and words without saying or commemoration. I am reminded of a most exciting moment in the late 1980s when (I was attending the annual meeting of the International Association of Philosophy and Literature) I watched someone steal the display copy of *Aberrations of Mourning* from the conference book exhibit. There is honor from thieves.

On a clear day you can see psychoanalysis both in the recent primal past and in the future now. The overdetermination of a Freudian influence is not about a responsibility or codependency diagnosis (the deep sitting-stuck fear of the overprotectors). Only the analytic discursivity is in positions to contain the Nazi symptom, for even historically, the symptom we're all still struggling to bust was already highly saturated with psychoanalysis. Another healing, more long term in its scheduling, more long span in the attention that can be given in-session materiality, is still in order, on order, in the works. Let the closure begin.

PART TOO

Time to Remember

In our first installment, *Only Psychoanalysis Won the War,* we followed the spread of psychoanalysis into all the departments and brands of psychological interventionism back to a PR origin in the success stories circulating by all accounts about the analytic healing of shell shock during the Great War. It was the start of what would become all the rage and range of Freud's influence, namely, "Greater Psychoanalysis." This was the main genealogical condition given for the promotion in Nazi Germany of psychoanalysis, even if by many other names, as major component in a blending of psychotherapeutic eclecticism that, as genre, remains to this day the standard of behavioral science.

Thus those who would take interpersonal responsibility for psychoanalysis have been denied a certain agency. But that all the contestants are figures in a transferential setting or force field is at the same time to be underscored. Consider how often, ever since recent and repressed history began returning to consciousness in the mid-to-late seventies, the continued existence of psychoanalysis in Nazi Germany—and thus by the implication of the exclusion of the Jewish colleagues, the collaboration of psychoanalysis with the Nazi regime—has been blamed on Freud.

Because he's all in a state about Wilhelm Reich's 1933–1934 exclusion from psychoanalysis, Bernd Nitzschke holds Freud responsible for pursuing Reich's dismissal in the first place as the act of political cleansing preliminary to the acceptability of psychoanalysis to the Nazi state. He makes fun of Ernest Jones's so-called diplomacy and of all those commentators who would therefore grant him and themselves immunity from general political responsibilities. Klaus Theweleit has taught us moves that allow for another reading of these interpersonal oppositions along given political lines. In such a rereading, diplomacy goes to the art of the issue, the art of the state, or the state of the art, the status in other words of psychoanalysis as an independent state, at least in Freud's own writing, a state that in the thirties was caught in the crossfire between political oppositions. Reich had already broken away from Freud by 1932. His symptom was not to know when time was already up (Orgone) for him to sign on with his new and improved analytic treatments and theories. Priority given to either wing did not serve the interests of analysis, which had its own flight schedule to keep. Plus preference for wings just symptomatized an overestimation of interpersonal or social relations that set a spell of resistance.

The (Helmut) Dahmer story (the story of the editor of *Psyche* who in 1983 reprinted Carl Müller-Braunschweig's forgotten 1933 newspaper article, in which the postwar hero of German psychoanalysis could be caught or read, hands-on, in the act of advertising the compatibility of psychoanalysis with the aims of the Nazi state) is on the same martyr role that Freud diagnosed in Reich. Nitzschke hears volumes when Chasseguet-Smirgel dismisses Dahmer as a sociologist and nonanalyst. But they're not the same volumes that she checked out. But then Chasseguet-Smirgel sets up Dahmer by praise: her free association of all sociologists as interchangeable causes her to take on the Frankfurt school. She is defending the specificity, first, of the shoah and then, second, of National Socialism against the diffusion and generalization unconsciously sought by sociopoliticos. She wonders that German Jews would promote a study of fascism (rather than, specifically, of National Socialism) as a political possibility in a great many settings. Her question is a good one. But it's not, as she intends it, a good rhetorical question. She does, however, manage to demonstrate the transferential backfire she analyzes so well in the heated protests against Freud's passivity or complicity. But: she doesn't think a strike against Adorno or Benjamin also strikes Freud? But then she accepts at faith value (that of her own bad faith) that Marxist sociology inevitably has the upper hand in the discursivity marriage with psychoanalysis that critical theorists proposed from California to Germany.

The ecstatic cling of transference issues gives way to a certain streamlining that attends the destiny of fetishism in greater psychoanalytic thought. After World War I, the greater flexibility Freud was demonstrating in his understanding of psychosis provided the setting for an exploration and a construction all the way to and through World War II of the first cyborg, namely, the pilot, whose psychic space had to admit the pressures of merger with his machine in flight. What was breakdown in the shell shocked had to be remade as user-friendly inside techno-compatible psyches functionally reorganized around the splittings of borderline states. The psyche that was at once borderline disintegrated and low maintenance was what the natural selection of merger with technology required. The psycho-techno developments of the pilot, on all sides of World War II, together with the adjustments, in theory and in therapy, that had to be made by civilian populations under total air war conditions (or in anticipation of the return to their fold of rewired soldier boys, with the pilot series at the front of the line), will fill the contents of installment number two.

Giving Up Which Ghost?

> During my stay in Pierson's Asylum (the "Devil's Kitchen"), von W. held there the position of senior attendant—not as a real human being but, as I thought then and think still, as a "fleeting-improvised-man," that is to say as a soul temporarily given human shape by divine miracle. He was said to have already led a second life as the "Insurance Agent Marx" on some other planet during the process of transmigration of souls.
>
> —DANIEL PAUL SCHREBER, *MEMOIRS OF MY NERVOUS ILLNESS*

Since the fall of the wall (and the San Francisco earthquake on the other side of one bicontinental divide, drift, and slide) there's been time to underscore what I take to be the most grievous side effect of the disappearance of Marxism: the growing disownership of psychoanalysis, even or especially in all the discourses or projects that owe what foundation they have to Freud's science. This double disappearance act seems to me reflective and refractive of a split that emerged most fully perhaps by the 1930s, but which had been in preparation since World War I. I'm referring to the split-leveling between the partners of a momentous marriage into which psychoanalysis and Marxism were shotgunned down, over and over again. It was already our biggest symptom, in theory and in therapy, by the time Marxism was really at a loss to account or prepare for the group psychology that Nazi German psychological warfare had so forcefully reformulated as the prescripiton of ingredients to be mixed and control released along the thin line between inoculation and uncontrollability.

The "hauntology" within which Derrida gave shelter to Marxism's effects so readily scattered among all the warning signals and opportunisms claiming to bury, not to raise, Marx pulled up short before the couple and addressed instead, directly, the corpus of Marxism that was thus home alone with its life and death. The frame of such a decouplified reading would be existentialist or postexistentialist if it were not implicitly advertised instead as the Heidegger aversion, I mean version, that comes, free gift and all, with a certain deconstructive reception (which is syntonic with a Freudian reading of textual symptoms). But as though enlarging a bit on the symptom, the up-front framing of psychoanalysis as out of this picture makes Freud's science out to be just one discourse among several with equal but separate rights to a certain precedence that philosophy, however, will always supersede. Even in matters of media technologization, haunting, and mourning.

Over the issue of Marxism's missingness, deconstruction goes down a second time for the body count of mourning. We remember the first time, the one that was so lasting. Paul de Man's corpus was identified with and assimilated, put to rest by being put to the test of already being deconstruction. Like the ghost or vampire animated by a survivor's split-off mixed feelings, the beloved man returned as Nazi teenager. What was thus brought back, as a necessity for all sentient beings, was a Freudian, nonphobic recognition of the corpus, in all its parts, whether objectionable or not. The work of mourning, the Freudian reformulation that remains the frame of all analytic work, requires that all this resistance, the defense, and the transference be open to interpretation.

But this time, efficient mourning has a better chance. There are no mixed feelings, not about Marxism. Derrida just doesn't like the ism. The resistance here is in the unwillingness to give Bad Marx outright. The defense of dissemination is securely and preemptively in place; the projected enemy is now not the identifiable dead but any identifiable death or ontological mourning, any bereavement bent on absolute ghostbusting, on total success (*Specters of Marx,* 9). No more efficient mourning (except, maybe, after all, by no default of his own, for Marx). The admission of a tension between efficient mourning and the interminability of a mourning that already outlasts the outcome of melancholic shutdown resurrects while eliding a tension that is always there, in the work of mourning, as in (it's the same line of work) the work of transference. What I'm trying to suggest is that even in *Specters of Marx,* Freud's always the spook, or he's spooked out of haunted site, out of haunted mind; in other words or worlds, he's the unidentified object, the ultimate object of identification. How soon we forget that in psychoanalysis there's always a tension—let's call it allegorical—along for every conceptualization: the tension between the shorthand or shortcut of theory and the slow time, the in-session materiality of the transference.

In closing out the ledger of inheritance, Derrida reads Marx's concept of "commodity fetishism" as symptomatic of a certain split reception of, and resistance to, the ghosts that nevertheless crowd Marx's discourse with the bad-styling abandon of too many mixed metaphors (149). This move against and into Marxism's monopoly within the psychosocial study of culture underscores the false or hysterical inflation of next to nothing there that did not, however, stop commodity fetishism from holding the top position. How is it that the commodity version succeeded in obscuring the full range of Freud's intervention in matters of fetishism? Well, there are always greater contexts and questions that psychoanalysis just can't address, owing to its captive audience to a family setting, even or especially to the techno, TV setting of all that's in the family. Both social studies types (Marxists and Deleuzers) and the Heidegger kids head psychoanalysis off at the impasse of a too perfect fit with its objects of study. The familial fit keeps Freud tied to merely projective relations with the outside world; the techno-compatibility of his science zoning-restricts psychoanalysis to being part of the problem and not being party to interrogating the essence of technology. Heidegger, who already came after Marx, was the first discourse meister to be haunted not by the corpus that was history but instead, although at the displaced remove of disownership, by psychoanalysis, even in its social or institutional forms. It might prove too circular to flash back to Heidegger's brother, hospitalized at a psychiatric institute known for its eclectic compatibilities with Freud's science, or forward to the Zollikoner Seminare, which offer substantial documentation of the philosopher's regular superintendence of his influence on, by, within eclectic psychotherapy. More to the point or period is to read Heidegger's emplacement as theoretical and therapeutic modality, one with rights of passage across all corridors, departments, disciplines, in the era of what one can now call "Greater Psychoanalysis."

The rise National Socialism was getting out of its mobilization and metabolization of all the modernist disciplines that worked, including a monumental "reversal of psychoanalysis" that the Frankfurt school theorists were quick to diagnose as the basis of Nazi thought and praxis, provided the most pressing cause for attempting yet another forced marriage. Marxism required its vitalizing supplement in time, big time, for a first emergency of totalitarianism right in the midst of modernism. But Marxism got the free ride in what was supposed to be a dialectical booster or collaboration. Over the issue of fetishism in particular, their union just got in the way. What the partners for all their differences might after all hold in common was to be the compatibility of Freud's group psychology with ideology, even if only as just another ideology subsumable under critique (this was always the Marxist version of the "resistance" defense). But the narcissism of the small difference between group psychology and ideology is, once again, captured in the complete nonrapport between Freud's and Marx's separate takes on fetishism. Thus I come to praise the conclusions of *Specters of Marx*, but on Freud's terms and on his missing behalf: there is in fetishism, according to Freud, both acknowledgment of the ruinous materiality of loss and submission to a greater mourning—let's call it techno-mourning—one that mourns even over those merely integrative moments in works of mourning and substitution. As techno-mourning, fetishism isn't about the identifiable or identified-with body. For one, it's not about couples. And it's not about losing, just because you lost. It is about winning, like a winner and not like a victim; it's about some power of emergency propulsion that gets us past the totalization and paralysis of loss into the wide open and outer spacing of what in a more couplified era or moment of mourning could only be seen as closed and enclosing delusional states that were the determining limit and dead end of failed mourning. A change came over Freud's science by the end of World War I, one that tends to get shortchanged by its confusion with, and commodification as, post-Freudian rereading or critique of Freud.

Keeping Up

Let's catch up with ourselves by keeping up with Ernest Jones. In his 1944 address to the Joint Session of the American Psychoanalytic Association and the American Psychiatric Association, Jones recalls, by way of introduction, how before World War I psychoanalysis or medical psychology passed the Joint to neurology (the field in which pioneers Charcot and Freud were trained). "Soon after the last war medical psychology in this country, led particularly by Dr. Brill, began to move more and more definitely towards the general body of psychiatry, helping thus to restore to the latter term its original signification of 'mental healing'" ("Psychology and War Conditions," 170).

But when by the end of the First World War, American military psychiatry, for example, found itself all revved up with no place to go, its attention didn't fall onto peace, which Germany was in the meantime threatening to win.

> You will remember that the status of American military psychiatry at the end of the last war was higher than that of any other country, though I dare say its activity flagged somewhat in the interval between the two wars. Already in the twenties it seems to have been overtaken by that of Germany, which established in 1929 a special department in the Army entitled Military Psychology. A comprehensive study of this was published in America in 1941, with a bibliography of some 561 German writings on the subject. Very little was done in Britain until the present war was some two years under way. We have a scurrilous saying among us that our War Office begins every war on the basis of the war before last.... One did, it is true, hear stories of how various authorities were determined to purge the Army of the psychological nonsense that had crept in during the last World War and to put all psychiatric illnesses on a proper basis of organic neurology as they had been in the good old days of the Boer War. (171–72)

As Jones looks back on the fast-forward efforts of his British colleagues to catch up with German military psychology, we look forward to this volume's engagement with the innovations made on "Emergency Island." "Military psychiatry in the British Army, when it got going, proved to be particularly enlightened and modern in its outlook. That is to say, it has been extensively influenced by psychoanalytic researches, though for obvious reasons of prudence this taboo word is replaced by the more innocuous term of 'depth psychology'" (172). The importance of military, evolutionary, and psychoanalysis-compatible selection was soon realized in Britain. Fears that psychiatric input on the selection boards would exclude more recruits for otherwise hidden psychological reasons were not confirmed. The psychiatric contribution, in fact, was not to overestimate the significance of certain disturbances or character traits. In certain cases, an eccentric character type could prove particularly syntonic with combat conditions (175). "One might almost say that it does not matter what neurosis he has so much as how he manages it in actual life. The total personality is the central criterion" (176).

In addition to the Jung-based word-association test (which, however, uses phrases rather than isolated words) and the thematic apperception test, which "Hesse introduced . . . in the German Army some fifteen years ago," but which was introduced in Britain via the revised method elaborated by Murray of Harvard, there is one out-of-doors test the British administer that is really new in the field.

> Devised by one of our Army psychiatrists, Major Bion, [the "leaderless group test"] . . . reveals striking psychological insight, and incidentally illustrates the contrast between the British outlook and the German or, more broadly, between the democratic outlook and the totalitarian one. The test that corresponds to it in the German Army is of a double nature, designed to assay the candidate's responses when under command or when in command respectively. Apparently no other situation is envisaged as thinkable than a definitely superior or definitely subordinate one, and indeed this is perhaps a characteristic military point of view which is as averse to the very idea of a group without a leader as it is to guerilla warfare or to mob rule. It has in fact taken some time to inculcate a different idea into the military officers who conduct these leaderless tests. In them a group of ten men are given a military task to perform together, crossing a river or what not, and they are left quite free to make their own plans about it. This task is the quasi real or set problem, but it masks the real problem on which the observing officer concentrates. That is the purely social problem of how each individual reconciles his natural desire to distinguish himself favorably in the eyes of the examiner with the desirability of cooperating in a team spirit with the other members of the group so as to accomplish the set task. (178)

All the distress symptoms that were back with the second total war were (also again) placed on hold for the peace that this time, Jones warns, cannot be allowed to go to pieces. Because the symptomatic soldiers (with the exception, Jones notes, of cases of "exhaustion in the heat of battle") cannot be treated short term enough to meet the military's needs, the field of war neurosis treatment will assume greater importance only after the war. But in the meantime it has been discovered that "various forms of group rehabilitation treatment" have yielded "promising results" (180). The therapeutic relationship, too, was widening.

The group tests in the service of selection were also the brand-new therapy formats for soldiers who just the same broke down. What gets shock absorbed in groups was seen going down in the primary dyad either protecting the child against or projecting into the child traumatizing fear under air war conditions. "Very notable was the adaptation displayed by children, provided their parents showed no neurotic terror. . . . I remember one child whose first word ever spoken was 'bomb,' uttered as he cheerfully pointed up to the sky" (186). In this 1944 lecture (which was first published in 1945), Jones admits a shift in the scale of psychopathology or rather in the range of psychoanalytic reflection and intervention. "Of recent years we have been presented with the startling spectacle of irrational and psychoticlike mechanisms dominating the effective part of whole nations" (191). It is time to accept psychotic traits and mechanisms as omnipresent among normals.

But even with the reformatting of the client focus in the understanding and treatment of inimical forces cutting across society and cutting down scapegoats, psychic disturbance still keeps up the father's end of traumatization. "The basic biological complex," to which (according to psychoanalysis) religion and ideological worldviews make the pitch, is "the father-murder guilt of the Oedipal situation" (192). Jones concludes with the Nazi genocide of the Jews as the overkill example of the same-old, same-old projection economy of father-murder guilt. But how to make even (or especially) this instance of brutality that Nazi Germany succeeded in making ego syntonic for so many participants in the mass of murder a cautionary tail end of the traumatization that comes to an end? "Now it may be doubted whether any but the actual victims have the power of imagining such things with any degree of vividness except those who derive a directly sadistic pleasure from the thoughts or accounts of them" (194). In other words, for those witnesses and bystanders whose minds as a rule recoil (like a gun) from such horrors, the question remains: "How to retain a strong impression that will serve as an adequate spur to action and yet not affect one's mental balance is an as yet unsolved sociological problem. It is in the solving of such a problem and the many other cognate ones that I see a new field opening before psychiatry" (194).

Take Off

> To defeat motorized Germany, the youth of other countries, as well, has to learn like modern centaurs to grow together with their fighting machines into new restless beings of passionate precision.
>
> —ERIK ERIKSON, "HITLER'S IMAGERY AND GERMAN YOUTH"

The pressure that has been on, as a result of the repress releases of "Nazi psychoanalysis," to rewire the transference connections can only rise higher with the psychoanalytic conception of fetishism. What pushes fetishism to the top of the line is, first, that it is a ready-made washing up out of the context that's really a contest between the intrapsychic axis of interpretation and the social study of whatever external force is with interpersonal relations. What seconds the nomination of fetishism for a first forced entry into the uncanny cohabitation with National Socialism is that it's the password for a genealogy of media in which modern group psychology can be tracked through internalization and technologization of trauma.

Our mass mediatization is, bottom line, the reduction of the sensorium to sheer visibility, a reduction program that sheds the limits of the visible, as in the parasurgical zooms and cuts of the projective media. That means that even those media that are audio portion only hold down this portion as their time-share in not seeing. In other words, the most basic expression of fetishism, as we'll see, folds back along the split between to see and not to see (or to "not see"). Fetishism's splitting image, both as theory and as the theory's practice or performance, doubles on contact with every invention of mass mediatization. Which is to say that this doubly performative automatism of the concept is a metapsychological fact.

It is true that most fervently fetishism has been the concept noted most likely to secede from decidability. And yet, at the same time, fetishism, as theory and as the theory's practice or performance, has been fine-tuning our working receptions of the mass media. Along for the side effects of its conceptual performance, fetishism's outer-concept experiences, which even the cultural study of the mass media cannot but promote, line up for a psychology, not of the one-on-one or one-by-one, but of techno-reception and invention in group-effort format. In cultural commentary, fetishism often packs a sex or sexism charge, but since one of the partners in the couplification is always a technical medium, the sex content shifts, and prospects for our technologization open up down lines of identification plugging along into another psychologization, the kind found in groups.

Sometimes a received notion drops by the wayside, way inside a missing context that doubles as rereading invitational. The acupressure applied through reintroduction of Nazi psychoanalysis tunes back both the jammed *and* the drifting receptions of the fetishism concept to the first takeoff of rocketry and cybernetics across intrapsychic airspace. Inside the missing context, then, the reception of the fetishism concept, which elsewhere scrambles for cover, decodes and counts down with the intrapsychic airwaves that wartime psychological research was making. That's right: the aerospace and psychotherapeutic connections are in it together, in the forgotten genre of invention called "psy fi." In his World War I essay on war and death, Freud already warned that every invention (including "attempts at mechanical flight") would stop dead in its tracks if mourning did not mediate the loss of irreplaceable relations (*SE*, 14:289–300). Fetishism, which is not mourning, nevertheless describes a detour taken around the melancholic metabolism that threatens to die on the invention that must go ahead and cut its failures or losses.

In the follow-up treatments administered by Nazi psychoanalysis, the fetishism concept opened onto a psychic (really: psychotic) war economy based on scarcity or lack *and* total mobilization that makes it to an outside, an outside chance, where successful realization of the wished-for aim, in spite of its already accomplished total loss first time around, can be scored. But in the missing place of the continuity that was there, the outside society-wide career of the fetishism concept belonged (according to the Allied-only mix of discourses) to Marxism's sphere of thinking about the commodification of everyday life, which was awarded instant unchecked credit for being the placeholder of Freud's public address system, his analysis of group psychology. Marx's chart of the prehistory of competing claims on fetishism put the commodity in the top position doing the number on sexuality, which comes second. The hold that the commodity (or, at another end of the same difference, ideology) thus has on sex relations is so close to group psychology and mutual mass identification—but so far away. It was into these near-miss relations (within the register that puts self-esteem before sex) between the all-out psychologization of the socius and the equally total sociologization of the psyche (from World War I on down) that the widest range of the psychoanalytic fetishism concept withdrew and expanded.

The exchange value that the Marxist half of the alliance assigned psychoanalysis restricted Freud's fetishism license to the one one-sided side or wing that was leftover. In exchange, therefore, Freud's immediate focus on fetishism belonged in the home or, to translate into the missing context, on the home front. But when it comes to the theorization of fetishism, this joint account or division of labor between the two master discursivities gives way along the dotted line of the air-splitting break Freud made between his intrapsychic view of conflict and the socioeconomic overenrollment of struggle in the classes. In his 1933 lecture tour of worldviews, Freud skywrites the line of irreconcilability between psychoanalysis and Marxism across the genealogy of media wars. That is, Freud goes ahead, skips a couple of classes, and reduces World War I and its Second Coming, coming soon, to "the conquest of the air":

> That does not sound very illuminating, but the first links at least in the chain are clearly recognizable. English politics were based on the security which was guaranteed by the seas that washed her coasts. In the moment at which Blériot flew across the Channel in his aeroplane this protective isolation was breached; and in the night during which (in peace-time and on an exercise) a German Zeppelin cruised over London the war against Germany was no doubt a foregone conclusion. Nor must the U-boat threat be forgotten in this connection. (*SE*, 22:177–78)

These conveyors of velocity and death, which strike psychologically across boundaries before they in fact outflank an enemy's sensorium and go in for the kill, belong to a beating pageant of the media in which the side with the greatest surprise extension dominates. Freud says: forget the other master discursivity's view that social change is an economic-conditions exclusive; the extension pageant is always the way historical change or chance is taken along the front lines of war.

The reading that gets stuck here on the positivism thinking of a machine history of discourses and institutions only libidinizes what we had otherwise already given up on. And that's so nihilistic, or in any event, it's totally unconvincing. Freud's diagnosis of World War I readiness, however, is less about machines in history than it is about the inside-out alternation between internalization and externalization, which doesn't stay put long enough to be composed into a body of evidence or taken into historical account. Instead Freud's reading works the intrapsychic or textual margins where what we call technology begins. That's why psychoanalysis attends to the delay in the invention of new technologies that, when it comes down to their component parts, were already in the ready position for realization at least a couple of centuries before their actual externalization or release (Sachs, 404–24). The invention of TV, for example, which the Nazis promoted in the biggest way, was slowed down by Freud, who kept all reception up to standards of transference, thereby setting a limit to the other set of responses, the television set, on which live transmissions and acting out occupy one short, nontransferential attention span.

Our relations with technology come from the narcissistic side of the psyche. But that means that narcissism was always less about one's own body and more about the relation of control one exercises over absent bodies through omnipotence of thoughts. This is the one power that is flexed in the first place as the death wish: the breast isn't there when I want it; that's all right, because I wanted mother gone, a goner. (Later superego will say: you wanted absent parents: *be* your dead parents.) Freud's diagnosis of World War I readiness is less about machines in history than about the *internal* lead held by technology, a margin along which ego, with no place to go, pulls apart and turns into doubles. Our inevitable interest in technology, in other words, accrues from the narcissistic investments of the psyche. Narcissism is less about one's body, oneself, and more about relations of remote control over missing bodies, and even more about the relation between the ego and its mastery. Once Freud admitted narcissism as a sexual force in its own right, one that did not first require exchange with the vows of object-related sexuality for its own potential (pathogenic or otherwise) to be realized, the conditions for intrapsychic reading were met. And that's why the switchover between the war media and their soldier consumers cannot but proceed with the push-button temporality of inside-out relations. In other words, where the conveyors of war are (as in Freud's inside view of world war), that's where the gadget lovers will be, too.

In the missing-persons reports of adolescent psychology within Freud's science, gadget love comes up for analysis inside its native habitat and favorite haunt on two coasts (California and Germany): the support-group psychology of teen self-esteem. One missing link between the bicoastal workout and this airborne project is *Beach Blanket Bingo* (1965), in which the entire collection of beachside adolescents goes in a heartbeat for the fad of skydiving. There's a Nazi biker group, "the Rat Pack," which remains grounded throughout and off the beach. That these group members appear on the internal screen of the beach movie's projection is as plain as a "No!" to a happy face: the star surfer–sky diver makes fun (and thus libidinizes) the Nazis as "the Mouseketeers." The "fearless leader" of this rodent return reflects back the projection of that other altitude of fetish love in flight: his name is Erich von Zipper.

During the Cold War, U.S. psychological warfare specialist Harold D. Lasswell folded a warning label inside the narcissistic investment that comes

Claus Bergen, *Gegen Engeland* [Against England]. Reprinted from *Die Kunst im deutschen Reich* 4, nos. 8–9 (August–September 1940): 230.

between soldiers and their instruments. Even when subordination of one's own weapon to some larger unit is the official alternative that comes with training, overvaluation of the weapon or vehicle just won't go away.

> Regardless of the physical weapon, or of the personnel devoted to the weapon, there is a vast concentration of understanding and loyalty, the result of which is to magnify the visible role of the weapon in the conduct of war. "Gadget love" is a snare for the unwary in the same way that love of the horse, or the camel, or the elephant appealed to the cavalryman of the past. ("Political and Psychological Warfare," 23)

By any other name, gadget love goes by fetishism. A synonymic and symptomatic reading of the libido fueling planes, bombs, and rockets could quickly be mounted and satisfied. But what was first sent to this front of gadget love belongs to the internal reading of Freud's theorization of fetishism, which at the same time puts the planes, computers, and rockets back where they belong—inside greater psychoanalysis.

Gadget love or fetishism has, since the world wars, given libidinal access to a mass psychology stuck in the groove of a record—the war record, it turns out, of psychoanalysis. But before Gadget goes to war there are steps to be taken that first fall in with Freud's internal reading of fetishism, which rebounds to the two bookends of his thought experiment, the 1887 to 1902 *Project for a Scientific Psychology* and the 1938 sudden take on splitting as the bottom line or borderline of all defense. Between the two (and through his rereading in the meantime of anxiety as signal), Freud caught up with his defense *Project*, which then did compute. In the fifties, editor Strachey resets the trend of analogizing or digitalizing the *Project* with cybernetics to go off inside Freud's approach:

> To take a few instances of this similarity of approach, we may note first Freud's insistence on the prime necessity for providing the machine with a "memory"; again, there is his system of "contact-barriers," which enables the machine to make a suitable "choice," based on the memory of previous events, between alternative lines of response to an external stimulus; and, once more, there is, in Freud's account of the mechanism of perception, the introduction of the fundamental notion of feed-back as a means of correcting errors in the machine's own dealings with the environment. (*SE*, 1:292–93)

Fetish Goes to War

In Freud's theorization, fetishism only stays together as a loner concept as long as we do not see that it has already taken off from itself through the overlapping displacements that go into its formulation, and exchanged its home-alone activities for mascot status within group efforts. In the brief essay on fetishism, in other words, the bottom falls out of the discrete perversion onto disavowal, which then gives way to the defense formulation of splitting. This sliding scale of fetishism's administration of defense also encompasses—that is, gets around—the content points of castration and melancholia. Thus the fixity of boundaries down the psychopathology continuum is along for the slide. First Freud memorializes the fetish as the repeat and reversal of castration, as a substitution, yes, but the kind that only the one who cannot substitute must make. But on second take, we don't have far to go before two cases of virtual melancholia are introduced into what fetishism opens up for colonization or conquest: a newfound outer space between neurosis and psychosis. Fetishism makes it to the front of this borderline right up its internal vicissitudes, beginning with the breakaway concept of disavowal, which it at first contains, a concept that, in its own freer ranging, gives way to the yet wider ranging and more precise notion of splitting of the ego, one that's definitely not contained by fetishistic activities in all the haunts of group-of-one psychology (*SE*, 1:292–93).

Already in the sexological register, the fetishist is the one who gets around the one loss along the original trajectory bound to mother down another pathway that leads not to psychotic breakdown or to the assignment of work of mourning but to the successful realization, just the same, of victories. It is true that the original trajectory is now covered by repression and thus horror: it's what Freud calls the horror of castration that has "set up a memorial to itself in the creation of this substitute" (*SE*, 21:154). But trauma's auto-monumentalization is not, not this time, some horror movie featuring mourning or melancholia. This memorial service is, after all, a substitution (so what if it's simulated and in some other place or cyberspace), one that opens up its own new native habitat, the borderline or no-man's-land between neurosis and psychosis. This other place is the launching pad from which fetishism lifts off to score triumphs. The fetish, the invention that succeeds in the wake of a lost connection, a failed realization, remains, writes Freud, "a token of triumph over the threat of castration and a protection against it" (*SE*, 21:154).

In his wartime essay on death, Freud localized a threat to invention, that of total immobilization, in prewar conditions of failure to substitute for unacknowledged and unmourned loss. Between the wars, fetishism is the name to go by for the other way of getting around loss that world war had only begun to suggest to Freud the first time around. Thus in the 1915 essay Freud, without any form of frontline access, must still restrict his attention to the civilian population and can only point to "changes in the psychology of the combatants" that remain to be gone into (*SE*, 14:291). By the end of World War I those changes would be in place inside psychoanalysis.

With the erection of the fetish, the loss that threatens to traumatize you the first time around can, after all, be written off—as total. This displacing movement, which belongs to the process and progress of invention itself, has the theory of fetishism where it wants it—and leaves it there. The fetish delivers the movement of invention from the shutdown of one approach toward its realization. Which is to say, even though the invention of the fetish was not aimed for, its realizability was all along the focus of the original loss. But you can't decide to go for the fetish. It takes you by surprise when you're at a loss.

That's why, on the inside of Freud's exploration of fetishism, disavowal takes place over fetishism's share in melancholia. Freud brings up two cases in which a father's death goes without the son's realization. But this shutdown of reality or realization did not turn them into melancholy psychos. In the face of evidence running counter to the distinction that he would otherwise draw between neurosis and psychosis, Freud runs for the cover of fetishistic disavowal, which takes off where a grief-stuck metabolism leaves off.

> It was only one current in their mental life that had not recognized their father's death; there was another current which took full account of that fact. The attitude which fitted in with the wish and the attitude which fitted in with reality existed side by side. (*SE*, 21:156)

There are two currents, then, and two attitudes (or altitudes) that together, although as different as wish and reality, tune in, side by side, as what Freud calls fetishism's "oscillation" between psychosis and neurosis. The change in attitude fetishism brought about in Freud pushed neurosis up against the frontier with psychosis, where a borderline economy was now open to negotiation. From National Socialism to all the other science fictions, this in-between place (which expands on contact) was the long distance awaiting colonization for the survival of the species.

Fetishism's disavowal-style overlap with melancholia, the cover they also split between them, takes off with the one direct connection Freud does make—to traumatic neurosis. Following the near miss with melancholia, then, fetishism catches its hardest and fastest analogy with the neurosis that, traumatically enough, could be cracked open for inside viewing only once it was re-presented to psychoanalytic treatment in the form of ready-made war neurosis.

> It seems rather that when the fetish is instituted some process occurs which reminds one of the stopping of memory in traumatic amnesia. As in this latter case, the subject's interest comes to a halt half-way, as it were; it is as though the last impression before the uncanny and traumatic one is the one retained as a fetish. (*SE*, 21:155)

Halfway

We would have tracked back only halfway if we made only the one stopover at the uncanny. Freud's first public/published encounter with the uncanny double in fact took place over the symptomatizing body of the psychological casualty of World War I. Same time, same station as the essay "On 'the Uncanny,'" Freud's "Introduction to *Psychoanalysis and the War Neuroses*" characterizes the central conflict of war neurosis in terms of the internal doubling that pits one ego against the other one along this final frontier of defense. Fetishism and war neurosis are on one sliding scale of trauma internalization, but they also just miss each other on the scale of doubling. The hard-shell rapport fetishism got from war neurosis covers no direct hit or fit. It's the overlap between the two that peels away from and opens up a zone of treatability all the way down the borderline between the transference neuroses and the narcissistic neuroses. It's this border zone that fetishism's oscillation between neurosis and psychosis hovers over, out of range of the repeater trauma that brings down war neurotics. Fetishism—or gadget love, to cut it short—is user-friendly war internalization. But in the shadow of its flight there's the ongoing outbreak of traumatic or war neurosis. The oscillation Freud saw first inside fetishism drove both Simmel's reading of the World War I war neuroses as the "safety catches" that kept soldiers from falling psychotically ill and Adorno's recycling of Simmel's diagnosis to describe the larger psychotic structures brought to us by Nazi mass culture as giving the group members protection against going psychotic one by one (Adorno, "Bemerkungen," 439).

The U.S. compilation or reconstruction of Nazi reading lists that began in 1941 to fold out a map of mass psychology's rerouting across metapsychic airspace packed two references to fetishism (which were both backed up against war neurosis). But by implication, contingency, and absence, the vaster literature on mass psychology's polemo-techno-rerouting across the airwaves was also already (it goes without saying) on the fetish track. Hans Buchner's 1927 *Under the Spell of Film: The World Domination of Cinema* accounts for film's psychological power on the verge of entering its greatest force field. But in 1927, still strapped to the tracks of "Advertising and Fetishism" (one of the chapter titles), film remains under the spell of World War I (147–63). Film fetishism goes down and out as mass manifestations of a melancholia for which everyone's only available analogue is psychic traumatization during the war. That's why "Advertising and Fetishism" opens with the case of a Scottish war widow who falls for Rudolph Valentino and fights her way backstage to share groupie therapy. He convinces her with his "brotherly" bedside manner to stop leaning on her crushes; the recollection of their high-minded sublimation and near-miss total satisfaction becomes the light of her life. But when Valentino up and dies, she follows the downbeat, too. Her suicide is an example of "pathological fetishism" or "fetish idolatry" that stands for or follows many others in Valentino's wake. But Buchner's opening example folds into the otherwise interchangeable cases of pathological fandom the soldier-husband's frontline "sacrifice" (which, Buchner notes, impressed his widow far less than did the film hero's passing) (147). Buchner's bottom-line equation backing his take on film fetishism must be taken dead or alive: "For today's young girl the film actor has replaced the lieutenant" (150). But before Valentino took her down with him, their fetishistic relation had unstuck the war record from the groove or grave of her loss. The fetish may have a half-life built into it, but it's still the better half, the afterlife or double of a libidinal span of attention and invention that had already stopped dead in the tracks of lack.

Another fetish adorns the (by all German accounts) classic 1919 study "On the Psychology and Pathology of Pilots," in which Hermann von Schroetter considers those everyday-life aspects of pilot vulnerability and psychopathology that precondition the hardest-to-treat outbreaks of war neurosis down the ranks of the war effort. Pilots, who are under perpetual psychic stress brought on by the constant threat they're under completely on their own, with only the heady sense of omnipotence on their side (which sets them up for the downswing), turn to the superstitious relief that the decoration of their fighter planes gives them: "These personal symbols seem to possess the significance of a talisman or fetish not only for individual pilots but for entire squadrons too" (1:4).

Whereas techno-accidents are always at the tail end of "a failure of the pilot's psyche" (2:1), the most pathogenic strike against a pilot comes via the other. The one or two things that von Schroetter knows can "paralyze the psyche and the pilot's will power" are "impressions of the accidents of others, a comrade's death dive in burning plane, the horrifying view of someone being burned alive on the ground and so on" (1:2–3). Pilots, who are in the ever ready position with their inside views of loss or lack to go for the downer of war neuroticization, "fall somewhere between true heroes and hysterical women" (1:1). The pilot is traumatically self-aware that his "extremely inferior nerve apparatus" is not, on its own, up for flying (2:1). That's why the pilot must be trained relentlessly until the air-technical operations of flight proceed "automatically" (3:3). Radio abilities must also be kept in automatic readiness. To keep ahead of the inside-out range of

Erwin Spuler, from the series *Unsere Luftwaffe.* Reprinted from *Die Kunst im deutschen Reich* 4, nos. 8–9 (August–September 1940): 286.

neuroticization, the pilot must grow together with his machine in flight. The fetish logo on the plane's tail is the signature piece of this merger with the prosthesis that gets the pilot over getting stuck on loss.

It is in the uncanny place where intrapsychic theory and therapy joined the Second Coming of Germany's total war effort (and then served as model for the Allied inside view of warfare from 1941 onward, soldiers) that we get a fix on the trauma-fixated course of Freud's science. The restoration of this double account must, however, follow out the same logic of psychological warfare that got psychoanalysis—everywhere. In other words, the Allied following or understanding of what the Nazis were up to is the best footnote to put forward. But beyond that context of fixation there's the discursive one that to this day restricts use of psychoanalysis to the match made in sociology heaven. What's the big sociopolitical ideas? It's to their lip service that we're still expected to pray. That goes double for fetishism, which, on its own, covers the fly-by-night merger with the war machine, in which we copped or incorporated control of the airwaves. A post–World War II U.S. survey of Nazi aerospace therapy (prepared by the surgeon general, U.S. Air Force, and entitled *German Aviation Medicine*) is the first place to go to register the high points of the Nazi airman's merger with his machine. The hands-on or manual quotation is from Metz's "The Aptitude for Flying as Problem of Disposition."

> The plane—like any other prosthesis—becomes part of the tactile sensory organs in such a manner that sensory perceptions seem to be referred from the body directly to the corresponding parts of the aircraft. This is quite clearly the case in take-off, landing and banking. The incorporation of the flying processes into the tactile sensory system and into the tactile motor apparatus has been called by Metz (1938) "feel for flying" *(Fliegerisches Gefühl).* (1036)

Metz signals out Hans-Georg Gade as the author of the phrase "feel for flying." In Gade's dissertation the feeling is lifted right out of the psychotechnical lineup of predictors for selection or survival of the most efficient. According to Gade, the irrational element of "feeling"—like talent or a certain chemistry—cannot be ignored when it's up to top flight. It has to be a feeling for his machine (44). Thus his ministrations to the machine will not be deliberate but "affectively released, automatic movements" (44–45). His limbs extend out through the axes of machine flight, and this expansive feeling suffuses the whole body.

> He must be fused with his machine to such an extent that certain processes that are inside the machine and thus outside his body are felt by him fully. To these pilots the plane is no lifeless machine in which one sits but rather for them has a life with which their own life rhythm can be brought together in perfect harmony. (45)

If you have to think about steering while flying, Gade has to tell you, then you don't have the feel for flight. You may steer, but you can't fly. The same goes for truck driving. But when it comes to flying, Gade disagrees with a number of colleagues who, beginning in 1919, were putting eyesight up there on the psychotechnical checklist for determination of who shall fly. Gade says, It's the sense of balance, not vision, that flies. Not to be confused with a certain literal psychotechnical take, Metz reconstitutes the theoretically plain notion that's stowaway on such a great phrase from the inside out and then taxis his new "feeling for flying" to the intrapsychic clearing, between technology and the unconscious, for takeoff.

Following this opening back into the primary context (the one the Allies started covering in 1941), we find Metz's 1936 article "The Functional and Characterlogical Questions of Flying Aptitude." Here Metz connects the internality of flight to the race to compensate with in-flight prosthetic extensions or mergers for the traumatizing incommensurability between the pilot's sensorium and the plane's "autonomy." The pilot must get the internal "picture" he composes with the plane. It's the same picture that helps that part of himself that doesn't technologize or compute *out.*

> Flying means to move in the three dimensions of air space by means of the plane in such a way that corresponds to the conditions given by the air plane. . . . The pilot forms with his machine a unity. . . . The dead apparatus must merge with the living organism into a functional unity whereby the plane parts at the same time become external organs of the pilot. . . . The pilot . . . has become the center of the machine. The situation of the machine is his situation, both are identical and form a common "feeling picture." (154–55)

But the range of our sense organs, from vision power to the balancing acts of the vestibular organ, falls short. This "lack" or "gap" in the pilot's biological sensorium, in his so-called "orientation organism," cannot be removed or overcome through coordination with the other senses and their extensions. This is where Metz sees the necessary shift to the characterological register in any study of aptitude for flying. The half-life of active flying is brief, and the day is always coming soon when the pilot will have difficulties getting back into the machine precisely because "flying as such already has the effect of psychic trauma" (171).

> Flying itself is . . . a biological problem. And if the person senses that he is inadequately equipped sense-wise in biological matters, then this in turn has a lasting effect on the total personality. The person in the airplane exists always in psychic tension. (171)

The pilot must therefore "empathically" get into the autonomy of the machine's manner of movement. In "Preliminary Reflections on a Psychology of Truck Driving and Flying," R. H. Walther drives forward this narcissistic empowerment that flight conditions promote. That is why Walther is able to read the psyche of man *and machine* in the open book or sesame of the symptomatic movements of one apparatus. The pilot is the Nazi overman: which is to say, man as we've known him preflight is over and out. Training must keep this hypersensitive congruence with the machine's movements airborne all the way. To this end (and in order that the pilot can bring together, in one combo, the two psychological tendencies of art appreciation and soldierly discipline), "the use of the machine must in the truest sense of the word have crossed over into flesh and blood if he wants to free up all available energy for the flight" (21).

> The required exercise has the character of empathy and of entering into the spirit of the autonomy of the machine's manner of movement. This autonomy is determined by the element through which the machine moves and not by the means of propulsion. The autonomy of this manner of movement can convey to receptive natures unique and extraordinarily increased vital and aesthetic stimuli. (21)

W. Benary documents the World War I psychological tests designed to superintend the powers of discernment needed to recognize map icons on the ground from a pilot's-eye perspective. By 1935, as Metz sets forth in his guidelines, the capacity for orientation must be determined before selecting candidates for flying. Inside the plane in flight, the pilot—who must, on top of orientation, not only attend to the machine itself but also make photographs and maintain radio contact—cannot but leave out intervals that edit the flow of surveillance. On the outside, changeable conditions of visibility can introduce spatial lulls or gaps that make orientation intrinsically discontinuous, while the velocity of the plane (especially constrained by limited visibility) schedules the time allowed for the act of orientation to fall within a short attention span. In fact, adjustment of orientation largely functions independently of vision and waking consciousness:

> We have an organic sense, which automatically registers every change that movement makes in my alignment. It is an unconscious knowledge, which I can however make conscious at any time. (Benary, 306)

> The boundary where the sureness of this automatic registering fails is naturally different. The fact is though that I can greatly extend this boundary through practice. (307)

Only when one makes a physical turn (at least in the imagination) does the mental picture of surrounding space turn along. With eyes closed the consciousness of a changed alignment asserts itself unstoppably. On any absentminded stroll, registration of movement will fall behind; what falls short is not the organ but the relatedness to our surrounding space. But it's the organ that fails us when we move across earth by nonnatural means: disorientation is along even for the ride on trains. On planes, too, our organs aren't adequate to the changes in velocity, acceleration, and direction. Without access to any compensation for a lack of visibility, the urge to identify where one is going based on sensation of direction or inner alignment regularly leads offtrack, to getting lost. Where the psychology of, and aptitude for, flying come up in the Nazi German research, radio aptitude isn't far behind. (Already in 1919 Hermann von Schroetter was prescribing that radio abilities be kept in automatic readiness.) According to W. Dietsch, at the micro level, the transmission of military broadcasts, right down to their reception and transcription at the other end, must, to save time, be conceived "intrapersonally." But Dietsch also almost takes it interpersonally: those predisposed to radio work are not reactive types; the structures that hit them are at the same time processed internally. Persons structured in this way tend to disappear within the community or to withdraw into, and rely only on, themselves. "Their soldierhood culminates, just as the radio service demands, in pleasure to serve to the point of self sacrifice, in silent endurance, conscientious secrecy, in trustworthiness and thoroughness" (Dietsch, 145). They are natural born electricians who, like most soldiers, have difficulties asking why: that's why cinema is better suited for them than, say, the theater. Already in 1919 (in sync with the first intrapsychic takes on the pilot's apparatus in fight), Otto Lipmann addressed the psychic disposition required for radiotelegraphic performance. Right from the start, Lipmann makes clear that whether you consider the giving or taking of transmissions, it's a big mistake to assume that "interindividual" relations among the different aspects of radio operation can be extrapolated from what are in fact, one by one, independent or, in other words, "intraindividual" functions in their own right. By 1936, according to Karl Kreipe, the same ideological stress on the wholeness of objects and perceptions that helped put psychotherapy over the top in Nazi Germany was emitting static into the following or understanding of what makes a person available for radio recruiting. Because the radio operator must be able to concentrate on one process at a time, there remains one elementary function that carries out the essential achievement of radio: the ability to differentiate the acoustic-rhythmic gestalt. For Kreipe, the gestalt totalizes acoustic impressions, goes for their metric character, and does not therefore fall for "free rhythm." The ultimate compromise formation was, in a sense, for all the senses, "automatization," which allowed the whole process of radio transmission and reception to be conceived and retained part by part and then to unfold unconsciously and automatically and thus as a whole. This also summarizes Gotthilf Flik's "Psychic Processes during Broadcasting, in Particular Subjective Transformations."

The premier function of radio aptitude, Dietsch says, is "empathic submission." The rhythmic shape entering the ear is admitted through free submission, and "the rhythmic oscillation discharges itself into the oscillating movement of the psychic field of oscillation, which fills the carrier in his totality. For this reason it imparts itself unconsciously and directly, almost automatically, even to the peripheral structures; it connects itself in the hand with the symbol which in the course of training is linked to this oscillation, and the hand writes down the letter" (142).

Just as Walther, in his comparative study of truck driving and flying, analyzed the breakdown of communication with the apparatus for symptomatic values of everyday functioning, so Karl Mierke sizes up radio aptitude via analysis of broadcasters' slips. First Walther:

> Work on technical apparatuses has pointed up the advantage of offering the analytic psychological view a firm basis in the focus on the movements required for use of the apparatus. . . . We become conscious that movement possesses beyond its purposiveness a symptomatic value or expressive content which betrays something of the inner makeup of the personality. (14–15)

Through his study of radio control (in the wake of breaks with direct connection), Mierke discovered that with radio it's not so much aptitude or talent that counts, anyway, but a certain attitude of the will that promotes constant practice. There are those who qualify characterologically for radio service right away: they're "radio pious" *(funkfromm)* ("Versageranalyse," 299). And then there are those who must be disqualified right off: hysterics and those types who've got rhythm.

> Every too high-strung feeling for rhythm seduces transmitters to falsify or at least to use slang. It overburdens the clarity of the listener's perceptions. It becomes possible unconsciously to hear a pleasing rhythm in what is actually an arhythmic sign. (305)

However, with all these exclusions accounted for, for the rest, according to Mierke, training is the way to go. Another way to put it is that during the selection process acceptable candidates for training are those who appear able to overcome the identificatory, intellectual, or emotional "inhibitions" that are there. The microbarrier where natural inhibition is the other side of trained skill is the first, primal, or "identificatory" one. At this semantic limit, "fusion between the radio sign and meaning must be so unambiguous and secure that the sign counts not just as symbol of a letter or signal, but must rather, beyond that, be in fact identified with it" (307). While the complete absence of this ability can only be pathological, the capacity for making the connection can be heightened through training, all the way to automatization.

Claus Bergen, *Deutsche Wacht in der Nordsee* [German Watch on the North Sea]. Reprinted from *Die Kunst im deutschen Reich* 4, nos. 8–9 (August–September 1940): 230.

> But if the development of stronger identifications between sign and meaning can be "practiced," then it readily becomes clear that this process is concluded that much faster and surer the more the trained skill takes on the character of an automatic process. That is, this identification must proceed purely automatically and thereby seemingly unconsciously without the addition of the impulse of will or thought. (307)

The double goal of training programs should be, then, "simultaneous identification" and "automatization."

Ghost Appearances

The pilot, both video and audio portions, was all along being sent to the other front, the front of the assembly lines of cyborg production: his body and sensorium were the first in the military-psychological complex to be technologized and nonmachinically merged with the internalized apparatus. In his 1933 *Defense Psychology,* Nazi German military psychologist Max Simoneit put the pilot highest on the charts of the internal doubling and defense that Freud saw go down in 1918 in cases of war neurosis. According to Simoneit, self-observation is the crucial condition of all military preparedness and achievement; it is the capacity for switching on and switching over comparable to long-distance measuring through technological media. The self-observation, or objectivity requirement is to be enforced in particular when it comes to the selection of pilots. Especially firing while flying requires constant self-observation, which must tune out subjective and motile tendencies. Otherwise, in flight, you're constantly watching out for the subjective perceptual appearances and illusions that you must instantly delete on your inside-out monitors. That's why a disintegrative type is the one to look for, the type, you know the type, who can *sharply* distinguish the parts of his personality (38, 40–42).

To this day in haunting manuals, one of the largest number of sightings of ghostly visitations goes to the air force, which sends the doubles of self-observation on time travel missions of loss reversal (Blundell and Boar, 134–38, 143–46). The psychology of ghosts and gadget lovers belongs to the group in a state of catastrophe or war preparedness. But because in psychological warfare, as you know, you only know what the other thinks you know, the so-called psy warrior, like the fetishist, doesn't know when to stop winning. Lasswell therefore urged during the Cold War that psychological warfare must start out by setting limits to victory and thus set its purpose as the economization of the cost and body count of combat ("Political and Psychological Warfare," 22). Lasswell, remember, was the one who warned not to leave a soldier's gadget love unattended. In other words, in psychological warfare, if substitution (including substitution for victory without end) doesn't take place, loss takes its place. That's why the breakthroughs of media technologization come down so hard on the inside of psychological warfare (or group psychology). And that's also how they backfire. From U-boat to Stuka to V-2 rockets (and from psychological warfare to cybernetics), the series of inventions and sensorium busters brought to us by the German offense industry follows out the fetish beam of disavowal and splitting. The Nazis were the first in World War II to use air power big time. The air force, the motor of the Blitz, was even mediatized à la Wagner to give both audio and video portions of a show of total war that was meant to exceed its physical capacity for actual destruction and score instead within the register of psychological warfare (which, remember, the German military establishment considered, in follow-up reflection on the German defeat in World War I, the most decisive form of modern war) (Farago, 41).

Flying touches down in all the haunts of modern group psychology. It rewired preflight man, who is over and out, to tune in or turn into the new airman, the Nazi overman or air-yan. This change of subject comes complete with a change in perspective. According to Major Alexander de Seversky, in his 1942 work of caution to the Americans, entitled *Victory Through Air Power,* the German investment in air force had succeeded in reorganizing the dimensionality of war:

> In the past, too, there had been talk of "total war." But now it is being demonstrated for the first time. America is not being attacked piecemeal but *as a totality.* There is just one target: the whole country. A few farsighted aviation strategists had foreseen this type of third-dimensional warfare. (11)

What was still a timely warning on Seversky's part was a safer bet the following year in the Disney film version of *Victory through Air Power.* In 1943 we are treated to an eleven-minute animated outline of the concise history of air travel that leads to the development, down to the minute, of World War II planes. The destructive capacity of these flying machines is demonstrated by making an example of the bombardment of Cologne. We leave animation behind when Dr. Seversky and his book are introduced. Sitting at his desk, Seversky warns the viewers that neglecting one's own air power could affect the U.S. civilian population sometime soon. We are brought up to date with the state of war. Once upon a time there were many German victories. Now America is one big armament factory. But all that industry is then bottlenecked in the long way of ship transport. In contrast, the Axis powers are characterized as possessing shorter supply lines of support. What we see is a wheel pumping life support via many spokes to the outer rim. Arrows signaling Allied attack strike the wheel from all sides. But the wheel retains its shape and just keeps turning. Seversky suggests that we strike out against the center of the wheel with long-range missiles. In other words, rather than reinvent the wheel, it's time to destroy Germany. Before the film comes full circle in the animation representation of the American eagle fighting the Axis spider, we are shown a defense detail on the other plane: Allied bombers are protected by mobile machine guns. Their counterparts in the German Messerschmitt planes are fixed in place. On the plane of interplane conflict in the air, the Germans are in a fix.

By 1942 it was also already clear to Seversky that the Germans were on a losing streak with their one-sided and one-way staging of air power. The RAF was able to push back the Battle of Britain because its planes were designed to attack and defend against enemy planes in flight. Whereas each German plane packed one machine gun in the back as an afterthought or ornament, the RAF counterparts blazed one-on-one airborne conflict from many sides with as many guns. The lack of defense in an instrument of total offense brings down planes and pilots, but it's not the same downer for rockets. Out of the loss of planes utterly lacking defense, a loss that the sacrifice or self-sacrifice of pilots could not reverse, comes immediately the invention of the rocket: the Germans had all along been going for it without knowing it. Out of losses within the register of the automobilic technologies, a high-tech analog operation was raised: automatic pilot, computer engineering, one-way rocketry. That's why, according to the haunting manuals, the phantom aircraft from World War I, which were seen (in the early portion of World War II) to take part in air battles, diverted enemy fire toward their one-way mission. And that's why when ghost appearances of World War II planes have been sighted since the close of the war, they are regularly seen to be without any pilot (Caidin, 108). The ghost of a loss models the success of the follow-up fetish invention.

It's not so much that the fetishist does not see a lack, loss, or difference as that he writes it off as total loss against the substitute realization, which, as substitute for substitution, was what he all along was aiming for when he was losing the first time around. The fetishist triumphs, gets what he wants, and gets off via the misfire of a first attempt that packs in its blast the surprise of success after all on the same plane of realization. Fetishism's near misses skip the down or dead beat of invention to get to the only realizable aim. It's gadget love, and it's always getting into automatic functioning: the automatic implementation of mathematics in computers and of flight in rockets through the primal service of feedback.

Feedback is the lip service to which the German war efforts prayed. Follow-up to the production of Ersatz or simulated alternatives to missing supply items in Germany during World War I, feedback is associated not only with putting the flying machine on automatic pilot and keeping it internally (eternally) on track but also with running it on virtual empty. Rockets shoot up a need to get around the running out of reserves. In other words, what goes down with what Metz calls the "incorporation of the flying processes" is another void inside fetishism-in-flight, the one that registers either full or empty. It comes up with all the one-way clarity of paranoid attack in Herhudt von Rohden's 1938 series of articles on air power, in which he urges total air offensiveness against enemy fuel resources; annihilation of the inner and outer reserve supplies is what the air force is good for. It's the only way out of the World War I fixation of war fronts, which made that war one of supplies only. According to von Rohden, the premier targets of the offensive are the earthbound forces, their means of staying connected, in contact, and the system of their reserves. "The destruction of the 'heart' of the enemy corresponds to the essence of war, and is therefore the set goal of the air force too" (511). This brings up two aspects of air war that are connected in von Rohden's reflections, but only at their paranoid origin in the enemy's thoughts; von Rohden thus adopts a protective or projective position when it comes to thinking, one, air defense in flight and, two, reserve forces and supplies. When von Rohden declares tactical reserves to be a necessity, he points out that foreign nations have packed plenty of reserve plans into the organization of their war capacity to keep up the dueling strength of flying units. But even these reserves are already engaged, von Rohden counters, owing to the range of modern bombers. That's why reserves are finally less important than maintaining an economy of forces in the course of combat action. The strategy of cooperative offense (a view that's said to originate with foreigners) requires "alternation between strikes against the power sources of the enemy and against his air force, against his army and his navy" (516). Because of their negative reaction to static positional warfare (in other words, World War I), the foreigners have already moved to prepare for this shift into the new three-dimensionality of warfare (199). If air force was expended on one-on-one combat or dueling back in World War I, that's because the means weren't around for unified coordination of mixed weapons. Airborne showdowns are no longer part of the picture: now it's chain against chain.

> There will be great losses. They will not only impact materially and physically but they will also have a significant influence on the troops' moral resistance and willingness to fight. (631)

The disavowals punctuating this forecast of future wars make it too long-range by half. But it is a disavowal or split that gets a lot of press. Already in 1935 Wulf Siewert's reflections on air power, which accepted flight's paradoxical dependency on the earth, and thus opened onto the psychologization of the grounded group that must mobilize for air defense (508–16), there was also a surprising lack of dependency—on fuel reserves. For example, Siewert argued (without glancing at the gas gauge) that the oceans are no longer defensive spaces but have fallen away beneath the shadow of the airplane.

Air power, von Rohden argues, accelerates the metabolism of warfare and puts not only the usual energy sources but also the populace at large and even time on reserve. Owing to new developments in group psychology or psychological warfare, the air war effort now (in 1937) has a good view of the enemy psyche, to which it can give careful, close consideration when selecting targets. But these powers of psychological preselection are so crucial because speed, and that means supplies, must limit air power. In other words, the duration of a war can represent danger for air force (von Rohden, 349). To keep air war from going in one year and out the other, the emergency brake of the leader function must be pulled. After all, the "character of the operative air war" is "collective war" (348). And that means: "The basic conditions of technology, which make possible the conquest of space, must have entered every leader in flesh and blood" (352). Where the techno-leaders are, that's where the air defense community will be too. The techno-interiority of war must already be there when you and the führer look deep down inside yourselves:

> The thoughts that give direction to the construction of an air force which are the most important are whether and how the people and their Führer are able to think and act in a three dimensional space. (504)

The Heydays of Radarr

> The system devised by Lamarr and Antheil—known as frequency hopping—is now in extensive use in military communications. . . . So effective is the concept that it is now the principal antijamming device used by the U.S. government's $25 billion Milstar defense communications satellite system. . . . While her husband may have considered her merely decorative, Lamarr learned a bit about weapons design during her three-year marriage to arms manufacturer Fritz Mandl. An idea stuck with her. Naval attack ships frequently wasted multiple torpedoes on a single target when one might do. . . . One solution: radio-controlled torpedoes. The idea sounded good but was impractical because radios are so easily jammed. . . . When Hedy Lamarr met Antheil at Janet Gaynor's dinner party, she met exactly the right person to help develop her idea. Before coming to Hollywood, . . . Antheil had spent several years as an avant-garde composer. . . . Antheil understood instantly that synchronizing a series of split-second hops between radio frequencies would be no more difficult than synchronizing player pianos. As a matter of fact, the patent specifies the use of slotted paper rolls—similar to piano rolls—to synchronize the jumps in frequency in the transmitter and receiver. The number of frequencies proposed—88—matches precisely the number of keys on a piano.
>
> —FLEMING MEEKS, "HEDY LAMARR, HOLLYWOOD SEX GODDESS"

> When she died in her sleep, on January 19 in Altamonte Springs, Florida, at age 86, it had been 42 years since her last movie, "The Female Animal." But one of Lamarr's achievements couldn't be more contemporary: Brainstorming with an engineer at a party during World War II, she helped invent the "spread-spectrum" theory for controlling torpedoes by radio. The idea languished during the war, but today it's at the heart of cellular telephone and wireless Internet technology. Unable to attend a ceremony in 1997 honoring her for "blazing new trails on the electronic frontier," she told a reporter: "It's about time."
>
> —ED WEINER, "TRIBUTE: HEDY LAMARR"

The recesses of top secrecy have leaked a wartime undertaking shared by Hedy Lamarr and her musician friend: the invention and promotion of a special frequency hopper that would jam the radar detection capacity of any U-boat up to the moment of the torpedo's impact. In her memoirs, *Ecstasy and Me: My Life as a Woman,* Lamarr keeps the secret but narrates instead the birth of her first child, right in the middle of wartime, and how the birth pangs just wouldn't stop, like some phantom prolongation, like the symptom of nervous breakdown. Already her pregnancy had succeeded in "building a wall" between her and her husband (127). Now there were phantom pains that sent her into analysis in Boston (which was also the address of the famous "Rad Lab," where American scientists coordinated efforts with their British colleagues in the all-out struggle to win the "beam war" or the "wizard war" against the Nazi German all-seeing airborne offensive against the U.K.).

> But I suffered. So they recommended the best psychoanalyst for this kind of trauma. I flew to Boston for treatments. It became a shuttle trip. The doctor was marvelous. In time he cured me. Because of what happened with him, I will never decry psychiatry.... He made me forget the pain by forcing me to concentrate on other mysteries of my past.... The doctor and I talked sex interminably. The man who exposed himself to me when I was a school girl.... It was ugly, but I stopped once just to look. What probing it took to make me dredge up that extra fact! I felt so guilty about looking. I buried the guilt in my subconscious, too.
>
> A laundry man, finding no one home, tried twice to rape me when I was fourteen. More dredging... at last the memory: He succeeded... I hit him with a miniature ivory statue we had in the house and I hit where it would hurt most. The statue broke and I wouldn't tell my parents how it happened, so I was slapped. And I held this pain-shame memory against my mother!
>
> Thus I was discovering myself while playing marital comedies on the screen and marital tragedies in real life. (129–30)

And while she was working on other projects as well. The trick to radar is that it is the sheer acceleration of the media-range-of-the-sensorium contest: to turn on your radar set is to watch the advance of the enemy in the same time the enemy can be following your frequency to ex marks your spot, the spot you're in if the enemy is then finally faster to the draw. Thus radar must be jammed. Different frequencies must be tried out to be undetected for a while by the existing scanners. Or so-called spoofs divert radar attention to false military moves while the real and right moves are advancing under cover of jamming. These diversions were made by introducing reflecting bodies for the radar waves to bounce back from as though from squadrons of war machines, but in fact, and with the same effect, it all rebounded from big balloons or from showers of aluminum tinsel.

The Nazi German developments in radar technology lost momentum largely because the war effort was from the beginning conceived as Blitz. Hitler expected to win by focusing on marching forward along the edge the Germans held at that time in military technologies. But if the fast-forward didn't work, he'd be out of that time. There would be no going back for his forces. If you think that sounds suicidal, you got that right.

The RAF fought defensively, instead, relying on the Chain Home stations network that picked up rough radar readings that were then adjusted or "filtered" in special map-lined offices linked by phone to the interior. The defensive calculation sought to down more German planes in exchange for fewer RAF casualties. The Germans were ready with their shortwave sets to go win. Ready, Not!

By the time the German invasion was effectively halted during the Battle of Britain, American and British scientists and engineers were hopping ahead of the Germans, whose countermeasures from that point onward would lag behind Allied radar advances. Göring was apparently in time so impressed by the way the Allies were coming in for the radar skill that he swore that after the war he would buy a British radio.

The frequency hopper that Lamarr cosponsored is used today in our nuclear setting. In the course of her Boston analysis, she dredges up memories. Yes, she hops frequencies of repression to get at them and blast away their sub effects. But the technology of radar, in which the German-speaking world was way advanced still in the thirties, may have been a souvenir Lamarr brought to the states together with her jewels when she hopped, skipped, jumped out of her captive marriage to Central European arms magnate Fritz Mandl. They exchanged vows in Vienna on 10 August 1933. For the next two years, before her escape dressed up as the look-alike maid she had hired with this plan in mind, the young Austrian actress was Madame Mandl.

> As Madame Mandl, I presided at parties honoring all kinds of notables, from stage and screen stars to heads of state. There were fine men, and there were bounders. Posturing Adolf Hitler kissed my hand, and on another occasion pompous little Mussolini held my chair.
>
> Entertaining was Mandl's way of doing business. . . . In the big world, Europe was a cauldron of intrigue. War was in the air;

> Mandl was wheeling and dealing in his element. In the small world, *I* was the center of intrigues. (21)

Now we know much more about the intrigues, dear Hedy, in the small world after all of microwaves.

Another Allied Example

Gregory Bateson, who during World War II worked the internal or home fronts of psychological warfare on the Allied side of catching up with Nazi innovations, was invited to look back in 1966 and recall the big historical events that, in his review, had demonstrated the greatest determining force and staying power. It took just two to give us the worst and the best of times: the Treaty of Versailles and the introduction of cybernetics. The connection here is not just the personalized kind; it belongs to a stockpile of generic brands of gadget love that when reassembled one next to the other on a genealogical line puts through the direct connection between the two events. The Treaty of Versailles, which was already pulled over Germany by Allied propagandists when the Fourteen Points were billed as coming soon, led to the all-out psychologization of war. From the treatment plan for war neurosis to the psychological warfare plan of attack for afflicting psycho-trauma preemptively in the inside-out shootout of total war, we were brought to a state of war preparedness and readiness that Freud called group psychology.

> It's not only that World War II was the appropriate response of a nation which had been treated in this particular way; what is more important is the fact that the demoralization of that nation was expectable from this sort of treatment. From the demoralization of Germany, we, too, became demoralized. (*Steps*, 472)

On "the very edge of what later became cybernetics," Bateson still, in 1942, "lacked the concept of negative feedback"; only with the close of World War II did he attend "a conference on this then-mysterious matter," to which he owes the direction his work stayed with from this turning point on. Bateson's double-bind theory of schizophrenia's etiology led via a computing model of the processing of ideas as differential bits of information to the prospect of earth-to-schizo communication. The infinitely regressive deception that went down with the Versailles peace also looked forward through the decoding it required to a new order of encoding called cybernetics. The encoding of duplicity, once brought to consciousness through decoding encodes automatic (dys)functioning. That's how Alan Turing discovered digitalized computing—through the effort it took to catch up with the code of the Enigma, the Nazi message scrambler. The one-stop service of decoding creates a new invention out of the inoculative—double—bind we are in with the other when entering that new frontier bordering on psychosis (where the mobilizations of psychological warfare go down) in which the other knows only what we think he knows. In 1942 and 1943 Bateson (on the verge of discovering feedback) was one of the code busters enlisted on the Allied side of the invention of cybernetics to counter and contain the advances of Nazi psychological warfare. At the New York Academy of Sciences, Bateson gave a diagnosis of the Nazi propaganda film *Hitlerjunge Quex,* which he had specially glossed or inoculated for that screening with interpretations and diagrams through which he unpacked the artifact right down to its psychic battery where it was programmed and reproducible. The only leader American military psychology needed to follow belonged to this film.

> In America we tend to think of propaganda as consisting of a large number of separate utterances, pious sentiments or jokes, inserted into the more or less propagandically neutral matrix of communication. Publicity methods were developed on the basis of rather simple psychological theories of association and Watsonian conditioning and have been comparatively little influenced by *Gestalt* Psychology or psychoanalysis. The significant propaganda in the German films is, however, not of this sort. (Bateson, Section of Psychology, *Transactions,* 72–78)

In his essay "Morale and National Character," Bateson tested the borders of comparative national psychology, one of the psychodynamic mainstays of the German military establishment. Bateson was less concerned with retaliatory character assassinations of the Germans or with morale downers to be sent their way. Along those lines, Allied expertise was by and large way more invested in proofing the next peacetime against German hostilities. Bateson targets the German inability to be overtly submissive for future, postwar work: "We have the possibility of some threefold structure, within which both the allies and Germany would submit, not to each other, but to some abstract principle" (*Steps,* 105–6). But the Nazi advances in comparative national psychology showed Bateson the way ingroup experience of members of other groups (even or especially when they're all the Allies) will release prefab responses and interpretations that do not always meet midway in order, then, to go down safely and symmetrically but are often reinforced in the concrete. Thus in the course of analyzing the inoculative touch in which we must keep with the other (alien and allied alike) under conditions of total psychological warfare, Bateson repeats or rehearses his discovery of the double-bind structures of psychosis.

The mere application of computing (this is Bateson's example) cannot get us out of this double bind we've been in since 1918. But cybernetics as a science of language is all about all that's fair in love and war not being fair *about* love and war. Given its discursive edge, which comes down hard on the side of the rules and ethics of peace making, cybernetics does head off at the impasse a "maze of hallucinations": "But this much is sure, that there is also latent in cybernetics the means of . . . changing our philosophy of control and a means of seeing our own follies in wider perspective" (*Steps*, 477).

In his work on the larger structures of schizophrenia, Bateson was facing two outcomes of the primal, doubly bound communication of the peace to end all peace: the disintegrative destructiveness of the wars that followed (Bateson includes the Korean and Vietnam Wars) and the World War II theorization of the feedback all along vestigially inside every modern technological invention at least since steam power, but which, once brought to consciousness, led the way to the introduction of automatic mathematics. To borrow from the missing context, there where the danger was lying was also where the saving power grew. But inside this safety zone from hell, negative feedback (comparable, in more primal terms, to mania's alteration of, and alternation with, melancholia) erected the fetish invention of automatic flight and math.

Cold War U.S. military psychologists who specialized in the theory and therapy of war neurosis and in the conduct of psychological warfare (the larger inoculative context of absorption of, and preparedness for, the pathogenic war shock) found themselves in no time enlisting what they at least took to be cybernetics in the post–World War II war efforts that were late arrivals of the German loss of World War I. That left Bateson where the psy warriors (as they were called) wanted him, all alone on the upbeat. But we are at the same time brought back to Freud's inside view, given in 1933, of the primal psychic context or contest in which the leading powers, from the First World War to its nth power, have struggled to obtain remote control. Between post–World War I psychological warfare, or, in other words, the discovery of war neurosis and the cybernetic phase of conquest of space, there's the countdown of the automatic, which at the same time must inoculatively reabsorb—that is, control-release—the body count that threatens to shut down the metabolism or sensorium of escalation as grief stuck, stuck on the trauma, on the scratch in the war record, where one starts over, over and over again.

One Four Five Beachwood Drive

In the United States during the late 1930s and early 1940s, a clash happened only to recur between Karen Horney's (and Fromm's and Sullivan's) eclecticizations of Freud's science and the so-called orthodox or conservative position in psychoanalysis, which found itself in unlikely alliance with the "left-wing" agenda of such analysts as Otto Fenichel. By recurrence I refer to the whole series of conflicts making up what already in 1914 Freud admitted to be the history of the psychoanalytic movement. Just before the conflict underwent displacement in or to the United States, there had been the struggle back in Germany that peaked from 1933 to 1934 between Freud's in-group and sociologically identified analysts (Siegfried Bernfeld, Fenichel, Fromm, Wilhelm Reich, Simmel, and, at least in the eyes of their opponents, Horney, too). One outcome was the severing of official ties between international psychoanalysis and the corpus of Reich. This conflict internal to the psychoanalytic state bore some relation to external changes going down that same year when the rise of National Socialism brought about the eclecticization—and not the expulsion—of German psychoanalysis as one of a triad of psychodynamic approaches.

On 23 January 1941, number 73 of the *Rundbriefe* advertised the editorial address: Dr. Otto Fenichel, 145 So. Beachwood Dr., Los Angeles, California. It was a newsletter or "circular letter" (really a precursor of e-mail) that Fenichel had brought along with him into California exile and typed out in a new bilingual format (German and English). Three letters to the editor (on the same first page of the typescript) rally behind this form of organization—the *Rundbriefe*—and thus its perpetuation during this time of crisis in the history of psychoanalysis, as pressing now, the third letter writer admonishes, as in 1934, the year Fenichel at one point singled out as the crisis point. From the voice or vote of this reader, Fenichel—all ears or years—took down the reservation and confirmed it in subsequent issues as his own (*as if* it hadn't already been his own!). Reader number three refers to Fenichel's pronouncement in the preceding issue, on page 2 of number 72 of the *Rundbriefe,* that in 1934 the influence of fascism was threatening psychoanalysis from within to the crisis point of inside-out takeover. But is it really any different in 1941? The corridor war continues, the reader continues, here in America, now in 1941 the most important scene or stage *(Schauplatz)* of the psychoanalytic movement. "In my estimation, Horney, Rado, etc. represent together with the whole persecution of the lay membership a by far greater threat than those bourgeois elements, which were dangerous back then and certainly continue to be latently threatening, but are not currently pressing." The scene hadn't just relocated but, being on location, had been realigned. The old scene washed up on the coast, but in vestigial form, a leftover forum.

When the Marxist Freudians, still gathered around the Californian *Rundbriefe,* went into exile, so did their "reactionary" Freudian colleagues. Thus the European struggle continued. In subsequent issues, Roheim will be most frequently singled out. But in this issue, item 18, page 13, it's a certain "little" known analyst who is still putting some of the old static on the new lines:

> It was left to the former colleague from Berlin Ernst Levy ("little Levy") to be the first to represent here in America in the name of psychoanalysis the complete reaction. He published in the Menninger bulletin an article on accident and pension neuroses. Since Freud too claimed that we are responsible for our dreams, he reaches the conclusion that for accident consequences of a neurotic kind absolutely no compensation should be paid out.

So much for what's left over from the old Europe of conflicts in the analytic community. Letter to the editor number three, by contrast, was summarizing a new two-front corridor war that Fenichel found himself fighting in the United States up against two nonsuperimposable tendencies: one, the move on the part of American analytic psychiatrists to evacuate all nonmedical practitioners from psychoanalysis; two, the "progressive" moves made by Karen Horney and others against the "orthodox" establishment in favor of an eclecticization of psychoanalysis, one free to replace whole chunks of Freud with new improvements and still call itself psychoanalysis. Fenichel considered this progressive movement (which he associated also with Kardiner, Rado, and Fromm) reactionary, one, because it was a form of resistance to psychoanalysis that was far from creative; two, because he saw a fundamental Freudian theoretical inclusion of the social relation thus also elided. In issue number 80, item 1, dated 4 September 1941, Fenichel makes his "paradoxical" position explicit:

> Long before we came to America we had our criticisms of the turn of development taken by the American Psychoanalytic Association right from the outset of its foundation. We often spoke about how it would become necessary to organize opposition against this trend (though we also believed and believe that the time for this has not yet come). In our "oppositional" stance the argument that the "official" theses did not comprehend the true

> significance of societal factors played an important role.—And now we must experience how an oppositional organization has arisen against the American Psychoanalytic using precisely this argumentation, but in such a way, that Freud's discoveries are so completely abandoned, that there can be no doubt that with regard to this splitting we must fully and completely sympathize with the American Analytic, which on the whole understands Freud far better and tries to hold onto his science! It is a paradoxical situation, but this paradox has, as we noted once before, its full analogy in the great world of politics, where the most reactionary movements are also given to present themselves in the most revolutionary discourse of slogans.

Without comment, one might throw into the washup of innuendo and correctness that the issues of the Nazi German *Zentralblatt* for the reunified psychotherapies continued to track Horney's career, even registering her regular visits to the establishment of Nazi German psychotherapy, where she had a tried-and-true colleague in Schultz-Hencke. She left for the States in 1932. Some would credit her with politically astute and engaged foresight. I say she forfeited the benefits of hindsight by making her move early and thus to just another country in an international world. In the register of events reported in the *Zentralblatt*, Horney's *New Ways in Psychoanalysis*, even in her new language, was the topic of discussion at the Berlin Institute's meeting of 5 April 1940. But Fenichel's comment in newsletter number 90, dated 10 July 1942, that Horney's upbeat focus only on the "assuring part" of neurosis was other words for what Adler had called the unconscious arrangement (26), should be thrown into the static, noise, or snow between programs of renovation or compromise.

Fenichel made his name back on the former stage of international analysis as one of those who sought to make psychoanalysis compatible with Marxian sociology, and thus was already on the side of those who sought to update and eclecticize Freud's thought along these social or interpersonal lines. With Horney's proposals, he thus encountered the uncanny double of this own desires, which drove him to become strangely allied in the face of Horney's threat with the same "orthodox" establishment he was otherwise fighting on account of his own left-wing rereading of Freud, but most pressingly on behalf of lay analysts who were threatened with exclusion from the American reorganization of international psychoanalysis. The establishment of Horney's agenda as a separatist but equal school within psychoanalysis became his public enemy number one, not even second to the persecution of lay analysts. By issue number 83, item 10, Fenichel will pass as reviewing Zilboorg's 1941 paper "The Sense of Reality" in order to diagnose the pseudochallenge of Horney's so-called materialism as polemically "scientific" cover for a regressive return or redepositing of magic and animism inside analytic theory. This stray bit of projection shows Fenichel stuck on resistance to Freud's theory of haunting, one that was perhaps all along the rival accounting for the splitting off of portions of Freud's corpus away from "the underworld of psychoanalysis" (*SE,* 14:66). So there was a portion of Freud's thought that Fenichel may have death-wished to skip for the social relation. And then Fenichel was left with what woman wants at the social. In the language of the other *Schauplatz* of psychoanalysis, the terms of conflict—"lay" and "Horney"—were also running on the projective proposition and harassment of slang between the sexes. One Four Five Beachwood Drive, One Four Five Beachwood Drive.

Horney accepts the determining force behind every psychic occurrence, the unconscious, that emotional conflict predominates in human beings, that errors are the expression of hidden tendencies and that dreams are wish fulfillments, and that the relationship of the patient to the analyst is typical of all his interpersonal relationships. Fenichel gives us this acceptance list in newsletter number 89 and then continues: "But on the other hand she says: The theoretical superstructure, which is false, is to be stripped off, the correct observations, made by Freud, are, however, to be retained, and simply interpreted differently" (12). Fenichel doesn't get the distinction between Freud's observations and his theory. Another reader might not get Fenichel's use—or is it Horney's—of "superstructure." Fenichel gets it all right, because he identifies with his Freud under attack, the one open only to his sociorevisions. Horney's correction facility receives another listing: "What is it, precisely, that gives offense to Mrs. Horney and that must be changed so that psychoanalysis can attain its full flower? It is: the libido theory; the Oedipus complex; the concept of narcissism; the conceptions of the psychology of woman; the theory of the instincts; the theory that childhood is of special significance; the concept of transference; the concepts 'ego' and 'id'; the theory of anxiety, the concept 'super-ego'; the conception of the formation and significance of guilt feelings, the conception about masochism; and the conception of the mode of operation of psychoanalytic therapy. Anyone who knows psychoanalysis realizes that the things Mrs. Horney wants to do away with are the essence of psychoanalysis" (13). She might as well have rehearsed or repeated this strip show on the "analytic basis" of the Nazi German reunification of the psychodynamic therapies. But at the same time, Fenichel's curt dismissal notwithstanding, she is still under the influence, and she takes up her place within the post–World War I order of "greater psychoanalysis." One Four Five Beachwood Drive, One Four Five Beachwood Drive.

Another recurring figure in the coverage of analysis as seen from the Californian margin of the new center of psychoanalysis in exile is "the phenomenon Alexander," which deserves, Fenichel advises, "a thorough-going (sociological) examination in the context of the current analytic movement" (newsletter 73, item 15, pp. 8–9). Fenichel is grateful to Alexander's clarifications of key notions of psychosomatic medicine, of a specialization that served as the main medium of psychoanalytic influence in the old country, but about which there was still so much confusion in the States. But this same ability to introduce order into chaos backfires when Alexander proceeds too quickly, as when he manages to overlook in his so-called quantitative dream studies that one element in the manifest dream can mean its opposite in the latent dream thought. But Fenichel's antipathy is most stirred up by his compromise formations with regard to Horney. In "Psychoanalysis Revised" Alexander polemicizes against Horney, but only in order to admit, as compromise, that one extreme—namely, Freud's—deserves another, but that synthesis must now follow. The Horney extreme Alexander characterizes as too "dialectical" and too "materialist." Again Fenichel's own positioning doubles on contact within this American conflict, but without ever gaining representation: it is elided or upstaged through conspiracy theory. He could type it all out on the pages of his *Rundbriefe* and still have a lasting laugh.

> Alexander agrees with Horney that analytic theory requires complete revision. He is however prepared to excuse Freud's false theorizing: "One must realize that he did pioneer work in an almost virgin territory" (in which sentence the adverb "almost" pleases me most).

And just as with Horney's overcorrections, Freud's original suffered from its materialist conception of libido. (Fenichel could be grateful to Alexander for playing right into the court over which Fenichel would preside as claimant in the case for Freudian sociology—if only Alexander would single him out as the enemy. But, so goes the conspiracy, Alexander and Horney, the secret allies, stage a public controversy where, by absence and metonymy, Fenichel's Freud gets the silent treatment.) By 30 January 1942, issue number 85, Fenichel reports on Horney's New York success stories. In the meantime her revision of psychoanalysis has been further repackaged as "culturalism," and her following has succeeded in casting Freud in the role of rigid reactionary, fall guy to their free and progressive performance.

> A training candidate from Chicago who is just going to begin to work with patients, visited Los Angeles lately and joined two seminar sessions. He said afterwards that he was very impressed by our scientific sincerity but "I am amazed that you in California still are using such an old-fashioned terminology as Freud did in his time. Nobody in Chicago is using this terminology anymore. It only arouses resistance among physicians." (2–3)

But Fenichel's Freudian terminology is a translation in its own writing, one that slips in the beachhead and techno-setting of the total-war economies. Fenichel adds to his rundown of Freud on mass psychology:

> I only want to add that these insights into the regulations of "self-esteem" make the effectiveness of education in general understandable: educators have the power to influence children because the children are so much in need of their affection that they are ready to sacrifice other instinctual demands for its sake. The parents' attitude is: if you obey you get what you need; if you don't obey you do not get it; you will become or remain helpless and you will have to starve mentally.—This attitude might be called the promise of supplies under conditions.—The nature of the conditions and the way in which they were applied are later reflected in the super-ego. (3)

In California alone with Freud, Fenichel concludes the consensus in exile: those in authority misuse "the fact that once there was a nursing mother; because it is the memory of the pleasurable dependence of the infant on the mother which makes people psychically longing for outer supplies and ready to believe promises and to fulfill conditions. (I do not underestimate the fact that besides this there exists force.)" (3–4). At this point, the supplies displace the social position with regard to the parenthetical or encrypted position. The consensus continues: the same goes for religion, which reflects back a longing rereleased through disaster: "(The dead parents, or rather the dead social authorities, are the bridge between 'parents' and 'God')" (4). Religion is believable because something real, something real dead, gets projected "into an imaginative future" (4–5). Back in 1933, once upon a time, when Fenichel was on collegial terms and in agreement with Wilhelm Reich, Fromm, and Kardiner, there was a consensus in his own terms regarding the seductions of mass movement: "The illusion to be loved, supported by supplies of self-esteem and even exalted by the authority which actually first had deprived one of one's activity and then brought into a masochistic receptive attitude, is a means by which class-societies maintain themselves" (7). One Four Five Beachwood Drive. One Four Five Beachwood Drive.

Fenichel was not completely alone with his letters to the editor. He and Simmel, his friend and colleague, convened the "sociological evenings" in Los Angeles (which Max Horkheimer, for example, also attended). These two exiles of the 1933 left-wing consensus just didn't go for the before-and-after mistreatment of their relations with Freud's work. They wanted social studies. But they also knew they had to stand by their training, background, and transference. Whatever their disagreement may have been with Freud's science regarding the bottom line of human nature, they also recognized that the progressive consumer fascism seeking to improve psychoanalysis was the local real-time guise of the enemy. Issue number 89, dated 15 March 1942, opens as follows:

> Very often, the "psychoanalytic movement" seems to be a micro-cosmos which reflects the events of the macro-cosmos of the great world. Sometimes this reflection concerns even details. In micro-, as well as in macro-cosmos, we see reactionary movements starting with "left" ideologies, and being effective in such a way that a paradox coalition of conservative and revolutionary forces has to be the result.—Certainly the alliance between Soviet Russia and England is for many people difficult to take. An analogy may be valid in our little field of "psychoanalytic politics."—Nevertheless, I expect that you will agree with me that, in spite of some correct criticisms which are brought forward by the "advanced" people against Freud, there is no doubt that they are going to abandon psychoanalysis and Freud altogether. We, who are interested in the preservation of Freud's findings for a future better practical use in "sociology",—are forced to side in this matter unreservedly with "conservative forces" within the American Psychoanalytic Association.

Still the pages and pages Fenichel devoted to reviewing Fromm's *Escape from Freedom* read like a dead reckoning with his near-missing doubling. When a letter reaches the editor of the *Rundbriefe* interrogating Fenichel's claim of a fundamental social relation in Freud along intrapsychic lines, Fenichel publishes the letter, and then his upset response, in issue number 90. Fenichel: "Your criticisms, it seems to me, attack any psychoanalytic sociology; they attack at least the specific way in which we used to believe that psychoanalytic sociology had to be done" (21). He got that right! One Four Five Beachwood Drive, One Four Five Beachwood Drive.

The third news item on page 2 of issue number 73 concerns psychoanalysis in Nazi Germany. Bally writes from Zurich:

> By the way, I was in Berlin a few weeks ago and spoke with several of my old colleagues. One thing at least I found heartening, and which I could observe with my own eyes, was the way many had retained behind the facade of a unified institute their individual freedom together with an absolutely unambiguously Freudian perspective. I should also mention, however, that I came across counter examples, about which I would here rather remain silent.

On the next page, Fenichel fills in this silence via an American review of Harald Schultz-Hencke's latest book, *The Inhibited Man,* which he paraphrases:

> The chief characteristics of the book are the compilation from unnamed sources of a haphazard selection of factors, which are edited for pre-formed opinions. Many discoveries are credited with being correct, but are characterized only as generally known and the debt to Freud is unacknowledged throughout. The author refers to him only when he takes a distinctly different view (and that is very often the case) or when he reproaches him with confusing definitions or false conclusions. The author himself introduces several new concepts, among others the "captative" and "retentive" tendencies, from which he promises an enormous clarification of the data. He argues against childhood sexuality, however, but at the same time exploits countless deductions that Freud made precisely on the basis of his observations of this phenomenon.

In issue number 80, item 8, pages 19–23, Fenichel reviews the brochure *German Psychological Warfare: Survey and Bibliography.* It doesn't surprise him that the enemy had a better grasp of the significance of psychology, "but it is just the same amazing to see the range and systematic manner of this understanding." However, he immediately offers the comforting proviso that the psychology the Germans have mobilized is largely worthless. That may be true, but he also notices that the mobilization is so total that Freud has been included. Although the Nazi German colleagues are most impressive when it comes to psychological warfare, even here, Fenichel advises, they don't know what they are really doing, "since they do not acknowledge the unconscious." But it is their own unconscious that goes unacknowledged. The high beam is precisely on the other's unconscious. A paranoid system is designed not to understand itself. But its interventions in the other's unconscious can cause problems of one's own.

In issue number 85 (30 January 1942), Fenichel passes on to his readers some more details he has learned about the full extent of Nazi German mobilization of psychology:

> The need for psychologists made it necessary to create a new degree of "diploma psychologists" for people who do not intend to become doctors of psychology. "By decree of the Reichsminister fuer Erziehung a regulation for the degree of diploma psychologist was put in effect beginning April 1, 1941. The preparation for this degree requires six semesters followed by an examination in experimental psychology, applied psychology, educational psychology, cultural psychology, psychology of other countries, and medico-biological auxiliary sciences." (13)

The middle four psychologies were filled to some level of saturation by the influence that would go unnamed. One Four Five Beachwood Drive, One Four Five Beachwood Drive.

Another corridor war Fenichel regularly covers in the *Rundbriefe* is the one going down in London. In issue number 73, news item 5, pages 3–4, Fenichel quotes from a letter from Dorothy Burlingham, which begins as follows: "(The first, more personal part, is interrupted by an air raid.)...... Continued—It is quite impossible to sit undisturbed in the evenings for any length of time." Burlingham reports on the establishment together with Anna Freud of rest centers for the bombed-out families. She emphasizes how the life of psychoanalysis continues fundamentally undisturbed. Thus she closes: "Today I gave a lecture to teachers on the Relationship of the Child to the Mother in Wartime.... I am telling you all this for you to see how active life continues to be." The good news is that shell shock during this round of bombing is at a minimum. One American newspaper is cited as declaring that there were no cases of traumatic neurosis, none whatsoever, this time around in London. The same article quotes an interview with Glover, in which the British analyst explains this remarkable fact by the other fact that there is by now no safe countryside to which traumatic neurotics can hope to be evacuated. Fenichel's no-comment reporting announces with the ring of irony that Glover is in the "orthodox" corner of the ring. The other shocks that are currently spared the analysts in London, the Anna Freudians on their side, and their orthodox interpreters and guardians on the other (which for the moment is the same side), refer to

Melanie Klein's earlier evacuation to the countryside. Her return to London will be measured, even or especially in the Californian newsletter, several issues down the typescript and carbon-copy assembly line, on a Richter scale of shocks. In issue number 83 (27 November 1941), Fenichel cites from a letter reporting on analytic life in London: "Melanie Klein has just returned after a year, which she spent in the North and with her her wing returns too so that the meetings will get very annoying if not unbearable." Fenichel's commentary: "It is perhaps a comfort for us in America to be reminded from time to time that the London colleagues have at least as many worries with their Melanie as we have here with that Horney!" One Four Five Beachwood Drive, One Four Five Beachwood Drive.

Psychoanalysis in Paris is another regular newsletter item. Not as regular as London, or even as big as the news from Argentina. But it is a particularly ghostly item whenever it recurs. All the colleagues are in transit, all except Laforgue. Next to Hollywood, psychoanalysis was the other institution actively supporting with work permits admission of European intellectuals into U.S. exile. Loewenstein's whereabouts are of great concern. One of the founders of ego psychology, Loewenstein was Lacan's analyst. Lost again, in the negative transference. The period of Nazi occupation and analysis in transit is skipped by homeboy right to the postwar American consolidation of ego psychology from Paris. The only person thus protected is Laforgue, Lacan's supervisor in the war years. In the collected Californian *Rundbriefe*, the Paris reports tend to end the summary of latest efforts made by analysts to escape to the States with the refrain that only Laforgue seems to be flourishing in Nazi-occupied Paris. "One hears stories about Laforgue happily making his pacts with the Germans in Paris" (issue number 78, item 10, p. 17).

Coming full circle within his geopolitical coverage of analytic conflicts, Fenichel regularly returns to the American association's struggle to define itself with regard to psychiatry's controlling interest in psychoanalysis (which, by the way, is also, seen in reverse, the measure of analytic influence on wartime American psychiatry). Item 9, pages 5–6, reports on the Cincinnati meeting and the resulting proposal worked out there that each society have four categories of membership, two of which allow for a radically reduced participation of the lay analysts, and the other two, which are the only "membership" categories, remain reserved for those with analytic and medical training. Psychiatrists only may apply for membership. The American association, Fenichel comments, will thus no longer be that of psychoanalysts but one of analytic psychiatrists. One Four Five Beachwood Drive, One Four Five Beachwood Drive.

Item 17, page 13 is devoted to the latest H. S. Sullivan publications. These texts are difficult, highly intelligent and interesting and are thus "typical of American psychiatrists who are well-disposed to psychoanalysis." Fenichel, however, shows where Sullivan pulls up short of analysis. It is an observation focused on Sullivan's misunderstanding of psychosis (but one that also throws unwanted light on Fenichel's views of the social relation as grounded in Freud's thought).

> It is an extraordinary idea to represent the whole of psychiatry only as the history of "Interpersonal Relationships," since a significant portion of psychosis, after all, consists precisely in the loss of interpersonal relationships. This psychiatry that uses psychoanalysis without however fully accepting it, remains a strange phenomenon, and for all the good ideas which Sullivan has to offer (but which he unfortunately writes up without "secondary revision"), what predominates is the impression of resistance, and the sense that the man protects himself from recognition of the significance of the drives through the use he makes of Freud.

Psychosis and Freud's legacy provide a subtext or underworld in these issues with issues. Newsletter number 73, item 14 on page 8, covers the posthumous publication of Freud's "Splitting of the Ego in the Process of Defense." Fenichel rightly notes that Freud thus fortifies the notion of splitting (one that allows for a disavowal of reality without psychotic consequences) that he first introduced in his essay on fetishism. Fenichel prefers to lay the stress on the nonexclusivity of this one mechanism to psychosis. But Freud also thus began opening up the borderline zone inside psychosis to analytic understanding. The monolithic setting up of psychosis as boundary state and concept where the loss of all interpersonal relationality goes to get lost was no longer tenable in Freud's thinking by the end of World War I. When Fenichel starts translating, he catches this train of thought out into the no-man's-land of the opened-up terrain of psychosis: "What Freud has called 'fear of loss of love,' and which better would be called 'fear of losing necessary narcissistic supplies,' is often used to hide a deeper repressed castration anxiety" (number 86, p. 54). Or it's catching, and he just can't shake it. In number 96 (15 March 1943), Fenichel, in discussing Fritz Redl's thoughts on the importance of the witness in mass formation, supplies the "main 'service' which the 'witness' is able to render," but which "is not discussed by Redl in detail: It consists in the furnishing of 'narcissistic supplies,' which raise a threatened self esteem."

> We do not want to repeat in this place what we have stated so often, about persons of "oral character" who remain dependent on narcissistic supplies from objects; and everybody who has regressed in his way of handling his self-esteem, and is not fully regressed to "psychotic narcissism," will try to re-establish his self-esteem by such supplies.—We discussed the mass-psychological importance of these demands for narcissistic supplies, recently, in our criticism of Fromm's book. (18–19)

A supply train—like the *Rundbriefe,* which go around and come around—rescues us from psychotic shutdown.

Fenichel characterizes Alexander's position of compromise with a little help from his Freud and splitting as the splitting of heirs over the woman's body one sees and not sees:

> If one asked Alexander if he thought that sexuality plays a role in street phobia, he would answer: "yes." If you asked him why in the quoted passage he never brings it up, he would probably answer: "Because it is generally known." So has Alexander understood street phobia or does he believe what he wrote? It seems to me that here only Freud's new views on the "splitting of the ego" can help us out. Alexander has apparently understood psychoanalysis no better than the fetishist the anatomy of the female genitalia.

Issue number 73, which opens with the issue of the dating of the crisis of fascism within psychoanalysis, is dated after Freud's death, but also still at the time of his passing, that is, just in time for the mourning period that ambivalent commemorations would put at the end, as the end, of a reception. In item 16, pages 11–12, Fenichel reviews Helene Deutsch's and Theodor Reik's respective (but maybe not so respectful) tributes. The problem with the Deutsch piece is its two-timing: it situates her with Freud from the beginning while submitting evidence that she met him first in 1918. But she was with him from the onset of the second system, the one Fenichel cocommemorates by emphasizing all the splits that were being reunified in Nazi Germany and in California, including Freud's post–World War I discovery of splitting of the ego. Whereas Fenichel on Deutsch is more symptomatically complex in terms of both their receptions of Freud, Reik's essay "An Unknown Lecture of Freud's" seems a stroke of unambiguous opportunism. Fenichel gags on Reik's protestations of being only the executor of Freud's lost will, of words otherwise lost but that Reik had heard and can thus now play back at but one remove from the master's voice. But somehow the text of the playback makes it sound like Freud was citing Reik.

> I went to the trouble of comparing the new piece—"An Unknown Lecture of Freud's" with the prior piece: "A Case of Sudden Conviction" ["Ein Fall ploetzlicher Ueberzeugung"], and the result is: *the former is the unchanged verbatim translation of the latter.* Reik simply took his 1913 publication and translated it into English in 1940.... Wherever in 1913 "Freud" stood, now "I" stands, and where in 1913 "I" stood, "Reik" now stands.

But self-plagiarism or auto-cannibalism is also a tribute of sorts, out of sorts. Californian analysts, who at this time did not yet have their own society (they were governed from Topeka), but who at this same time, given the influx of instant colleagues in exile, were gaining the momentum to found a new society, became the test case of the open question of membership. In the subsequent issues, Fenichel documents his apprehensions. The analytic psychiatrists in California appear to be even more opposed to lay analysis, even more "orthodox," than what Fenichel and company had left behind on the other coasts, the East Coast and Europe (issue number 75, item 6, p. 5). Up north, in San Francisco, where the first analytic society in California would eventually be founded, a rehearsal conference for the analysts of California was convened under the title "Neurotic Acting Out." Fenichel plans to use this platform as the occasion to speak out against the so-called advances in psychoanalysis (issue number 80). By the next issue, Fenichel reports that the delegates at work on the constitution for the new Californian analytic society had been pressured to reverse the two points that Fenichel had worked so hard to guarantee, that nonmedical colleagues would be admitted as teaching staff, and that nonmedical analysts who were already members of the International Organization would have the right to full membership. Because of these uncertainties concerning the rights of the lay and the unlicensed, Fenichel and Simmel had withdrawn from the charter membership, in effect blocking the foundation of the society. Over their heads, and up north from them, the San Francisco Psychoanalytic Society was nevertheless founded. But in issue number 90, dated 10 July 1942, we learn of Simmel's betrayal. Simmel had agreed to represent the San Francisco Society at the Boston meeting in the hope of being able to steer the Californian Society toward the sociology setting down south. But when he was told that the admission of lay analysts, which he had been able to write into the Californian Society's constitution, was in terms of the

American Analytic unconstitutional, he backed down and admitted the official marginalization of lay analysts into California. Through compromise, his colleagues assured Fenichel, they could first found the society and then reform it from within. Fenichel: "The progressive suppression of the non-physician analysts in California is going on since I am in this country; it is a symptom of the development of the progressive degradation of psychoanalysis into a psychiatric method, and is carried out with extremely unfair methods. These resemble fascistic methods—and any Munich has to be avoided" (10). Simmel "has always been an appeaser"; "the analogy with great politics is striking" (12). And then there was only one. One Four Five Beachwood Drive, One Four Five Beachwood Drive.

The publication of Horney's *Self-Analysis* brought back a question that had been raised, already by 1942, several times, and indeed, exemplarily, by Freud himself. Fenichel gives us a typo slip for his readership to see through. He types: "Freud himself is the best example of the fact that—to a certain degree—this impossible." Then he crosses out the "im" and writes "is" above. Horney both knows and does not recognize, as though it were a question of degree, the analytic consensus that the possibilities of self-analysis are necessarily limited for the two reasons Fenichel counts down. First there's resistance. While a strong personality might overcome resistances without being pushed by another person, "the overcoming of resistances becomes entirely impossible if the resistance consists of a 'blind spot,' in just not seeing what one does not like to see. If the analyst is another person, he can demonstrate to the patient his blindness. In self-analysis, the blind spots remain untouched" (29). The second reason that self-analysis remains limited is that there is no transferential relationship to work with, whether in the context of overcoming resistances, or as model for studying a patient's behavior patterns. In sum, "specific analytic assistance—handling of 'blind spots' and 'transference interpretation'—is entirely lacking in self-analysis" (30). When Fenichel rejects Horney's attribution of pessimism to Freud regarding the outcome of analytic therapy (on the basis of his theory of the death drive), he overshoots himself in the aside where he wonders, since he himself hasn't bought into the highly dubious death instinct, why she brings it up at all (30). Then Fenichel argues that Horney's presentation of the case of an analysis partly conducted within the analytic couple, partly conducted on the patient's own, in which morbid dependency was the presenting problem, ends right where the interest of the analyst should begin. For Horney, the woman's dependency hides her contempt for people. Fenichel, in contrast, would expect a fixation in early development. Because of where she starts and stops, Fenichel concludes that the unconscious she refers to is not at all the one discovered by Freud. But then the unconscious Fenichel adapted to social studies also doesn't rise to Freudian consciousness.

Fenichel draws on supply lines to set the limits of narcissism and of total warfare at once. Horney mobilizes in *Self-Analysis* the total air war as indisputable fact of life, as proof that limitations can be overcome, those of self-analysis too. In *Self-Analysis,* in other words still in 1942, Horney continued to cite her two colleagues who happened by then to be affiliated with the Göring Institute in Berlin: Fritz Künkel and Schultz-Hencke. Before there was National Socialism, the former was just another Adlerian, and the latter an innovative eclecticizer, which is how Horney saw herself, beyond oppositional politics.

Can there be self-analysis after Freud? Is possible or impossible? And yet Horney isn't all wrong. How could there not be, always and already, self-analysis after Freud? In addition to Freud's own mythic and makeshift self-analysis, complete with all the props borrowed from the other, there is another "underworld" notion of self-analysis stowaway in Freud's borderline explorations of psychosis. A certain self-analytic breakthrough is on the inside track of Freud's notion of endopsychic perception. If delusional systems can, as in the case of Daniel Paul Schreber, give us inside views of the functioning of the psychic apparatus, then the blindness in psychosis often offers inside views. In psychotic development there is a speed race on between the auto-analytic breakthrough and psychotic shutdown. If or when it all shuts down, then we have psycho fade-out, cessation of life. But there can also be the emergency projection of a new world and word order to replace the lost habitat of the psycho's libido. This new order is built up, in short order, out of endopsychic perceptions. Already in his essay on Leonardo Da Vinci, Freud addressed the race but in other terms, in the terms of sublimation versus repression. But repression always wins out in the end. The death drive can thus be seen to emerge here on the sidelines of Freud's thoughts on a certain auto-analytic momentum racing against mega-repression, melancholic undeath, and psychotic shutdown.

In her 1942 self-help study, Horney insists on the upbeat that self-analysis, especially occasional self-analysis assisted or framed by a stop-and-go proper analysis, is possible. It had been her way. She interrupted her analysis with Karl Abraham because she foresaw the father transference not as part of treatment but as the foreign body of an illness that was not yet her own. She also moves to dismiss the impasse blind resistance introduces into self-analysis. According to Horney in *Self-Analysis,* there are two main frames of resistance: blind spots and one-sided emphasis. The latter is exemplified by Freudian analysis, which in its one-sidedness is foreshadowed by Rousseau's *Confessions,* where one-sided openness about sexual matters blinds us to the problems that in fact afflict him, problems that are, as in all cases of neurosis, the wrongheaded or, again, one-sided beliefs one holds about oneself. But on the other side, Horney is equally upbeat about the prospect of outing of blind spots. "Blind spots will often clear up in time if the work is carried on" (245). But time—at least "the art of timing and meting out interpretations" (126)—isn't a factor in self-analysis. By definition, the analytic or transferential relationship is missing, doubly missing. For Horney, the analyst is the helpful adjunct to the cooperative effort of observation, really self-observation (135). But if the two are just on a fact-finding mission, then one can do it, too. No wonder she's so optimistic. "It seems to me that the wish for developing one's energies belongs among those strivings that defy further analysis" (22)—indeed, they defy the father of analysis. Freud just didn't believe in "a wish for self development," a resistance on his part that Horney links and limits to a finite network of beliefs, like the notion of the death drive, that were Freud's own and that don't belong intrinsically to psychoanalysis. Out, out blind spot.

In her history of the "mothers of psychoanalysis," Janet Sayers describes Horney's disappointments over the reception of *Self-Analysis.* What is more or too much, the case of dependency on father figures presented in the book had in fact been an amalgam comprised in equal measure of Horney's own autobiography. Whatever her "materialism" amounted to on Fenichel's sliding scale of Marxo-Freudianism, she tried to make a special (ideal) case for mothering rather than just take the usual, another ride around the complex. This counts as a self-analytic discovery to the extent that it is blind-side-lined by—*what* resistance? But the sidelines demarcating the immediate receiving area of her very own "self-analysis," in private as in published life, started closing in on her counterconcept of mothering.

> Some dismissed Horney's resulting book as simple-minded cultural determinism. Most ignored it. Perhaps this contributed to the cooling of her relationship with Fromm. Certainly his recently published *Fear of Freedom* was much more widely acclaimed, and she seemed to feel bereft and in search of someone else close. Her bitterness at his abandonment of her—she even called him Freud by mistake—made it difficult to bear his continued presence in the AAP. Nor could she bear his popularity with students. . . . The crunch came, however, with her Institute's January 1943 refusal of a student request that Fromm teach clinical as well as theoretical issues. The Institute also revoked his teaching

> privileges, ostensibly because his lack of medical training made him unacceptable to the New York Medical College with which the AAP was then seeking affiliation. In April 1943 he resigned. . . . Torn between Fromm and her mother, and much to the latter's embitterment, Marianne also increasingly withdrew from the AAP. The rivalries her mother provoked there, she said, were much the same as those she provoked between her and Brigitte. (133)

Alone with his *Rundbriefe* in California in 1942, it was Otto Fenichel—impossible, is possible—who was as close to being in self-analysis as had any analyst to that date since Freud.

Cyber-Lacan

> During a lecture at the Neuropsychiatric Society of Vienna, in 1955, Lacan claimed to have from Jung's own mouth a curious item of information. Approaching the American continent in 1909, Freud was alleged to have said to his disciple: "They don't know that we're bringing them the plague." . . . The French thus attribute to Freud a sentence transmitted by Lacan without perceiving that Freud never uttered it nor did Jung confirm it. Thus progressed the rumors that give rise to legends and end up becoming history itself.
>
> —ELIZABETH ROUDINESCO, *JACQUES LACAN AND CO.: A HISTORY OF PSYCHOANALYSIS IN FRANCE, 1925–1985*

The turns Lacan gives cybernetics and psychoanalysis around their common "axis" in "language" highlight all the "empty places" that science's clock power left unfulfilled. Contrary to the PR job, the exact sciences did not overcome the ritualized rapport of animistic man with the staying power of "the real." Lacan lists cybernetics and psychoanalysis as co-occupants of one era of thought experiment. His calculation of their history can't stop short with the start date of Norbert Wiener's invention of the word or name, however, but must go behind that scene to meet the competition between clock science, on the long hand, and—on the short hand—a science of empty places. The first science to run on empty placeholders was Pascal's 1654 invention of the arithmetic triangle, which Lacan counts down as already "the first machine" ("Psychoanalysis and Cybernetics," 299).

There are three coordinates to Lacan's maps of cybernetics as overextended, coextensively with psychoanalysis, beyond or way past the time alotted for specific terminologies and technologies. First there's that calculation of chance Pascal started rolling (and Freud picked up with the *fort/da* game) that takes a chance with binary order to "search for the laws of presence and absence" (300). Next are the games of chance. Not by chance, the calculation of the evens and odds for winning was the prize for which the application of Pascal's triangle, just another gamble, was originally commissioned. Finally there's game theory, which, according to Lacan's setting of the range, can at once play monopoly capitalism and march as to war.

A door that opens only to shut and shuts just for the opening serves Lacan as the pretechnological origin or essence of the "apparatus" of electronic circuitry. The face-off or balancing acts between transference and countertransference cannot be separated out as the before (open door) and after (door closed) but must swing together, in our interface, as both charged communication and, at the same time, empty place. That the door isn't open or shut but open and then shut, and then opened and then shut, describes the relay of "feedback." "In this way what is called an oscillation is produced" (302). Yes, the door is and gives symbolic order, swinging open now on the real, now on the imaginary. Through it, there it goes, "man's passing, through the cross it sketches, intersecting access and closure, can always be recognized" (302.) Following cybernetic adjustments in miniature scale, made to techno-internal order, man's passing in and out at the door also frames the opening and closing of circuits and sets up its cross where password exchanges guarantee recognition. "The one thing which cybernetics clearly highlights is the radical difference between the symbolic and the imaginary orders" (306). Lacan nails to the cross sketched above the mistakes of Gestalt and object-relations brands of analysis. Gestalt, which takes from nature and therefore has nothing to give the symbolic, runs on an "inertia in the imaginary" that it cannot check or gauge, and which amounts to a far-reaching "discord in the discourse of the subject." Another captive audience with the imaginary sensurround is granted so-called object relations.

> Is this imaginary homogeneous with the symbolic? No. And it would be a perversion of the meaning of psychoanalysis to reduce it to an emphasis on these imaginary themes, to the coaptation of the subject by an elective, privileged, prevailing object, which gives the modulus of what is called, in what has now become a fashionable term, the object relation. (306)

Feedback, oscillation, and perversion follow, while filling in for, the bouncing object of loss.

Lacan's relation of his objections thus resonates within another empty place, the one set aside in Lacan's theorizing for melancholia. It dis-appears to be a mistake or thought disorder that hangs over the imaginary excess and access of the mourning show that must fill in for the rupture in the symbolic, that which the departing object opens wide. In the essay on cybernetics, Lacan appears, by implication or exclusion, to assign the repression of mourning to the subject that's not the machine. The machine's manically short retention span at the same time models, only in absolute reversal, the total hold of melancholia, which comes down, not to our machines, but to us in time, the time held over and out on us by the suspension of repression.

> With a machine, whatever doesn't come on time simply falls by the wayside and makes no claims on anything. This is not true for Man, the scansion is alive, and whatever doesn't come on time remains in suspense. That is what is involved in repression. (307–8)

It's like, when you can't stand the suspense any longer, and you wonder: What was Lacan up to between 1936 and 1950?

French Dressing

When Elizabeth Roudinesco sweeps the Nazi era of French psychoanalysis with her searchlight, she finds only one collaborator doubly hiding out in his "blind ambivalence" (156): René Laforgue, founding father of French analysis. All the histories of the period hit on Laforgue as the one soft spot that French analysis had for collaboration with the Nazi occupation or cathexis. But one man's "ambivalence" is, to another power, along for the drive that's bigger than life. Why restrict attention to a bunch of certified analysts when assessing for the influence of psychoanalysis or its collaborationist prospects? Matthias Göring didn't. Laforgue took the mis-lead, perhaps, when he faked a list of supporters for Göring's interest, which duped the list in front of him of the membership of his own analytic group: "It included nearly all SPP therapists—from Lagache to Lacan, and including Schlumberger and Juliette Boutonier—who were neither Jewish nor exiled nor foreigners" (158). According to Roudinesco's final tally, charges of collaborationist activities of French psychoanalysis can barely stand up under scrutiny and be counted. By 1942, there had been two meetings between Laforgue and Göring, and another meeting between Professor Claude, a few French physicians, and two "pitiful" functionaries of the Reich (159). But: tally Heil! Roudinesco's view seems restricted to a downsizing of evidence that's really as big as all it took to found the Göring institute.

Chasseguet-Smirgel wonders in time for the Hamburg Congress how French analysts could be so indifferent to the "Jewish problem and the event of the Second World War" ("Time's White Hair," 433). The splitting in the part of those who back then looked away gets doubled and carried over, in theory and therapy, all the way into the ongoing work with patients: "Why should we be so amazed and helpless at certain 'borderline cases,' when the history of this century has shown us how easily the superego can be swept aside, reason destroyed and thought placed in the service of the dehumanization of others? Is all this really of no interest to an analyst?" (434). It's this duplicity, the one Laforgue fills in for, scapegoat style, that Chasseguet-Smirgel sees still shadowing the French at the time of the Hamburg Congress: "After all, we French are children of Vichy, pursued henceforth by our shadows, split and double, like the faces on playing cards, half pro de Gaulle and half pro Pétain, half for the Resistance and half for collaboration, half risking our lives to conceal the Jews and half betraying them to the Gestapo" (434).

As in all the other historical records that groove on this period, Roudinesco's calling to account does not leave out Lacan, at once as openly Freudian analyst who didn't permit the occupation to interrupt his practice and Laforgue's assistant, the sidekick who knocked about the better part of the mentor's ambivalence. In 1940 Georges Parcheminey, one of Lacan's colleagues in outright Freudianism, gave the inaugural lecture to the newly reopened, new and improved psychoanalytic section of the Sainte-Anne Hospital. He "offered ringing praise of his master Sigmund Freud. The result was the exit of the German officers present from the auditorium" (Roudinesco, 152). But before sliding all the way into basic identification with such *Casablanca*-style shows of resistance, Lacan was way more remarkable, by all his own accounts, for the neutrality and hovering attention with which he took to current events.

The Games

The Olympic Games had already broken their 1916 date with Berlin. Even after the war, Germany first had to wait out a chance at the international competition and communion. But then the 1936 games were given, as restitution, a Berlin address, c/o the Weimar Republic. The showcasing of an end to World War I thus fell right into the rap or rep of Hitler's Germany. Berlin's postreunification bid for the millennial games (which sported plans for value-free incorporation of the existing facilities within a network of new stations of the crossing and passion) lost out to Sydney's offer, Demeter style, to depart—a reason for the seasons—for the "land down under." In the seventies, Berlin was passed over for Munich, another fly-by-night screen for a kinder but more Gentile projection of associations that owed the slip they gave us to Disney's lube job. But where there's projection, there can be shooting, too: the Israeli track team ran right into it. What couldn't be given back to postwar Berlin, *the* pre-1933 uncontested capital or champion of psychoanalysis and psychodynamic therapies, was finally permitted at another safe displacement in Hamburg, another make-believe haunt swinging with resistance to the rise National Socialism got out of all the other Germans.

As recollected in "The Direction of the Treatment and the Principles of Its Power," Lacan gave himself a station break from the 1936 Marienbad conference, the day after his address on the mirror stage, to go to the Berlin games. It was a real guilt round-trip. He effortlessly writes off Ernst Kris's objections to his Berlin tour of the "spirit of the times" to the respectability that limits a certain Krissy understanding of transference and acting out ("The Direction of the Treatment," 239). The case presentation that gets no respect from Lacan treats a patient, taken over from Melitta Schmideberg, whose pressing problem is that he can't bring his research to publication on account of the compulsion to plagiarize everywhere in evidence throughout his work. Schmideberg was sticking to the original rip-off complex established early on in infancy as the sponsor of the finale of a series of delinquent acts. But Kris decides to check up on the current references backing the plagiarism self-charge. When all he discovers is academic business as usual, he proceeds to the interpretation: "In short, having assured himself that his patient is not a plagiarist when he thinks he is, he sets out to show him that he wants to be one in order to prevent himself from really being one" (238). But the patient doesn't take to the interpretation and flashes back on a running encounter commentary that he's been pulling off on the

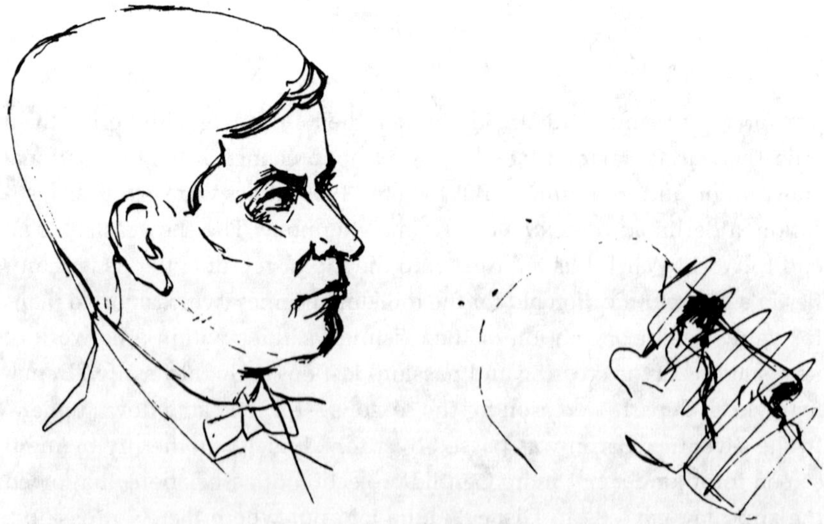

Sketch by Irma Last of Jacques Lacan participating in the Fourteenth International Psychoanalytic Congress in Marienbad, 2–8 August 1936. The original sketch is in the private collection of Ernst Federn, who inherited it from his father, Paul Federn. Reproduced from the appendix containing all the Last sketches of the congress participants in Tomas Plänkers and Ernst Federn, *Vertreibung und Rückkehr: Interviews zur Geschichte Ernst Federns und der Psychoanalyse.* Reproduced by permission of Ernst Federn.

analysis. The patient is trying, through his *"acting out"* (239), to get a corrective value any way he can when, as he tells Kris for the first time in the afterglow of the interpretation, he admits that he wanders the local streets after every session looking for his fave fare—cold brains. These are not the brains of the organization of obsessional neurosis Kris has joined to his patient's material. "Contrary to what you believe, it is not his defence against the idea of stealing that makes him believe that he steals. It's his having an idea of his own that never occurs to him, or hardly even crosses his mind" (239). But in his intervention and reinterpretation, Lacan in fact plays back those endopsychic perceptions Freud was picking up in Rat Man's obsessional thinking that the other knew his thoughts without his knowing it. Lacan's reading of the Rat Man case comes down to the thought of a connection that he prefers to pass on, leaving it all up to the other's knowledge of his evil thoughts that he won't recognize: "Were I to add that I do not think that the analysis is entirely unconnected with the tragic conclusion of his history by death on the field of battle, what an opportunity for evil thinking I would be offering to those who wish to think evil!" (237). What's not entirely disconnected here is the direct line to the war neurosis front, the primal scene of a greater psychoanalysis, a scene that Lacan, who prefers to go native or anti-American, splits and not sees in order to attack only the neodevelopments of post–World War II Americanization.

Then there is one seemingly extraneous fold around Lacan's correction of Kris and Co., if only because folded in along the seam of one of Lacan's own cases. But it's a disagreement that slides onto the other center stage of Lacan's dismissal of a controlling interest taken in group psychology or psychological warfare. On one continuum with all the other American mistakes, right next to Kris, is a knee-jerkoff overreliance on repressed homosexuality in transference interpretations. The dream the patient heard told by his mistress, which double-features her hermaphroditic endowment with the oscillation between gender and genital identifications, cures his case of impotence. Referring this case to one of the popular fables washing up on all the shores of Freud's successful American trip, Lacan plays the analytic dupe: "I guessed from the demand that my patient had addressed to his mistress that he had been trying for a long time to get me to confirm his repressed homosexuality" (267). Lacan reads past the specifics of one man's orientation to everyman's graduation ceremony. The dream brings back the maternal phallus, the primal refusal of castration. Kris's and Schmideberg's patient, in Lacan's rereading, does not so much *not* steal as he ends up in effect stealing nothing (239).

What comes across in the long stretch of Lacan's essay is almost a topography of psychoanalytic history in the twenties and thirties and then, looking back, in the fifties, the one that skips Nazi psychoanalysis in the beat the Americans are seen to police, the upbeat of adaptation through an eclectic mix of psychodynamic therapies with or within U.S. psychiatry. But the consolidation of ego assets externalized as American is only the late arrival (and victorious rival) of that more primal and less consciously deliberated-on era of Nazi accommodations for a greater psychoanalytic setting that was changed, back then already, to the channel of improved efficiency, functioning, bonding.

Thus when Lacan takes on the American streamlining of analysis in "The Direction of the Treatment and the Principles of Its Power," he straddles the almost two-decade span of his united states of amnesia between the basic conception, research, or first airing of his findings in the thirties and, in the fifties, the final work of revision and publication. In other words or worlds, for the fifties, Lacan sets up all the pinhead goals of American neoanalysis—autonomous ego, happiness, security, team spirit—for one strike (231). But underneath the blanket order of these charges there reemerges, not without psychohistorical connection to the era Lacan always leaves out, long-distant references in theory to melancholia. It's always in the course of duking it out with the dupes of analysis that he trips up and over the melancholic consequences of the other's mis-takes on analytic theory.

Object relations is top of a line that slides immediately into implied or excluded zones of material loss. The pattern and patter of American psychology or self-help for success holds on to the related, objectional attempt to balance as "economic" activity the oppostion between life and death drives (243). On "the other side of the coin" (presumably referring to the currency of selling psychoanalysis cheap) is the focus on what precisely "eludes the transference, namely, the axis taken from the object relation." While granting the focus on this relation a noble origin in the work of Karl Abraham (and thus in, just take a look, a melancholic collection of parting objects), Lacan attributes to this legacy (which includes Melanie Klein and Schmideberg) the workings of what an imaginary. The "notion of intersubjective introjection," for example, merely reflects the establishment that produced it inside the dual relation (246). The tensions that attracted the object-relationists in the first place, like the span of attention awarded this force field in the same place, comes down to a security drive Lacan diagnoses within Anglo-American analysis:

> It has nothing to do with any counter-transference on the part of this or that individual; it is a question of the consequences of the dual relation, if the therapist does not overcome it, and how can he overcome it if he sees it as the ideal of his action?...
>
> But that one should confuse the physical necessity, the patient's presence at the appointment, with the analytic relation, is a mistake that will mislead the novice for a long time to come. (235)

The security drive covers the analyst with its tall blanket order whenever he treats the transference as the object or objective of consolidation and then, once interpretation can be made, as the model to which all else can be reduced. Thus all systems are going for the "working through" that grants the analyst open season to do whatever it takes to strengthen the patient's ego. The move that Lacan keeps current in the fifties (but in fact dates back to World War II) from the duo to the group makes for little surprise and even less difference. In a move that Wilfred Bion could have followed, Lacan folds the interest in group psychology and the psychotherapy of that name or concern back onto what comes out in the groups of training analysands that get formed, by no default of their own, around their common trainer. But if there's no transferential relation to the analyst to be found in these groupings, the mutual identification that one expects to find in its place consists only of the sharing of traits or tics in common with all that is inadequate in the training analyst's own work (275).

Just like a melancholic, Lacan resists group-level interventions. He proposes instead taking "desire" literally. But what's in the word in Freud: there's the wish, the *Wunsch,* that can be seen as the opening of the psychoanalytic account of the unconscious in *The Interpretation of Dreams.* But the wish that Lacan would reread as desire, as the languistic desire that must be taken literally to the level of the signifier, has more diversity in Freud's usage, at least in the realm of objects and objectives. The direct line of theorizing for Freud makes a wish in the first place always the death wish. But Lacan is pushing for a ghost-free sense of feedback via his psycho-semiology of desire: "The channel of desire flows, and the subject must have the advantage of a cross-over to catch his own feedback" (259).

At another crowded crossover of transferences, on the way back from the Hamburg Congress, Chasseguet-Smirgel looks up from her psychohistorical view of the doubling and double crossing inside every French analyst of the identificatory legacy of the "Jewish science" to let go a reactivity that nevertheless proves, in a scratch-and-sniff mode, somehow fitting: "As some of us know, certain psychoanalysts said after the French split that they were leaving the Jewish society (ours) to join the Christian one (Lacan's)" (Chasseguet-Smirgel, "Time's White Hair," 433).

In 1936 Lacan turned to and tuned in the New Testament technology of TV in what had formerly been the projective realm of the phantom, double, automaton. In Lacan's electronic and languistic restaging, these psy fi figures are *the* ungraduated holdovers from the mirror stage whose hold over us is psychotic sublime. By 1936, then, these cinematic or Old Testament techno-embodiments of the death wish were rerunning on live or life's transmission (on death drive). This doubling on contact fits right in and takes over where the omni-reduction of analysis to the in-session transference opens wide: "In my handling of the transference . . . my freedom is alienated by the duplication to which my person is subjected in it, and everyone knows that it is there that the secret of analysis is to be sought" ("The Direction of the Treatment," 228). Lacan flips past the transference or countertransference, the identification or projection, to the double-or-nothing alienation of the alien on TV. When in his text *Télévision* Lacan locks in his interest in the discursive event of TV, he shoots up to the first moon landing. But he only touches the tip of these real-izations of psy fi fantasy that landed from those first stirrings of Nazi rockets and anti-Nazi decoders and were transmitted back to earth, live, via the medium before which Nazi Germans had first stood at total attention.

The Berlin Olympic Games doubled as the first media event of this order to be televised live. Lacan's rapport with the techno-future computes in a thirties setting. Outside that context, in a split-off mode, his techno-rapport is retrograde. Thus at the Paris World Congress of Psychiatry in 1950 Lacan reproached American neo-Freudians with a cautionary science fiction of their own making: the reduction of man to a mechanical animal, one that just might, in some brave new future, manifest anew the desire to make love (Roudinesco, 176). One contemporary's approval of Lacan's "new integration of Freudianism in France" (155) puts out there the integrationist agenda that Lacan prescribed for Freudian analysis with a French mix of structuralism into edited-for-*Télévision* receptions of German philosophy.

Trippy

The 1936 disagreement between the two transference travelers Kris and Lacan runs down the divide of the two approaches to World War II, which together, in their split-leveling, tune it in as media event. In Kris's reading, the danger zone of propaganda refers to the new psycho-discursive state of propaganda beside itself, at once self-reflexive and dys-metafunctional, one that muddles the boundary between pro and anti: "The anti-propaganda movement has become propaganda itself" ("The 'Danger,'" 20). Kris plots, as though developmentally, a difference between World War I propaganda and the psychological warfare that takes over where propaganda let us off at the new fronts and dimensions of World War II. The Germans realized too late, the first time around, that they needed to study American advertising to grasp their disadvantage in their own propaganda. By World War II, the deceptive propriety of propagandistic manipulations had switched, in a word, from copyright to "copy writing," "to the repetition and variation of slogans, the hammering in of a formula" (27). Where patent or parent can't get in an edgewise word to interrupt repetitions of repetition, or mutual identification, group psychology now makes the scene.

That's why we're too far gone into the new era of unpropaganda or psychological warfare to protect ourselves, inoculatively, by raising the anti in fear. There's nothing to fear but fear of propaganda itself:

> There seems no reason to believe that at any time—with the exception of the consumer movement and in relation to advertising—the fear of suggestibility and of propaganda has worked as an inoculation. I am, on the contrary, inclined to believe that this fear paralyzes active response against the pressure of propaganda. (21)

If the world wars have introduced propaganda to researcher and consumer alike, then a certain degree of suggestibility and dependence can be taken at the same time in the study of psychoanalysis. "This dependence is constituted by libidinal and analytic attitudes; they correspond to two main wishes in the child's life: the wish for love and the wish for protection, both once attached to the parental figures. These wishes never die and under specific conditions they may later awake in full strength again; they are the motor powers of transference" (6–7). Propaganda both invites gadget-loving attention to details of psychic manipulation and functioning and withdraws the attention, also by invitation, back inside the unstoppable coextensivity of propagandistic and psychic apparatuses. Only with the establishment of a social imperative of "integration of the personality of the adolescent" can a limit be set (42), viewable from both sides now, to the media manipulation of what "might be called the 'transference situation'" (31).

The bottom line of the transferences pulls up short before the same-sex bonding in groups. "The 'Danger' of Propaganda" takes the homoerotic group dynamic right to the change of heart through which war keeps on bringing up the rear. Writing during a "period of remission of Luftwaffe attacks on Britain" (29), Kris reflects on the psy war enemy's capacity for instilling and installing in us the desire to be dominated. "It is related to the sexualization of the desire for guidance and is, with the male, the expression of a passive homosexual attitude. This is the most widely spread and at the same time the most dangerous condition of increased suggestibility" (14).

The part of Lacan's understanding that, by the fifties, is cybernetics compatible (in the thirties all the parts were on total TV, the only mirror stage in town, from Marienbad to Berlin) plays the war game of electronic languistics. In Don Gordon's account of the emergency and emergence of "electronic warfare" out of the transferential spirit or decoder of World War II, he performs the two-timing that split-levels, in principle, the fifties version of Lacan's power address, by putting his cathected object of study behind us:

> The advent of modern electromagnetic systems is so complex that there will most likely never again be the opportunity for opposing forces, fighting on a modern battlefield, to read the secret messages of the other to the extent that this was done during WWII by both sides. (2)

What's also behind us, men, according to the plainest text around, the letter of Gordon's study, are all the transferential feelers and periscopes put out by a couple of insights into losing still to be gained along the reproduction battle lines between the sexes.

> As any wife learns, it is easy to predict and control habitual and routine behavior of a single opposing mind. Rather than be required to predict the operational behavior of hundreds of U-boat commanders operating as circumstances dictated, the British OIC had to contend chiefly only with the single mind of the U.d.B. control center. The Germans insisted on centralized control to increase efficiency; what they accomplished was the efficient destruction of their U-boat fleet. (22)

The so-called U-boat war, the one that Gordon would introduce as sub for opposition or couplification between two sexes, was a first time in military history for the campaign to get the name of a technological weapon. It had finally been brought to consciousness that Gadget had gone to war. What had been Germany's greatest techno-victory could be contained only through a form of language, the successful cryptanalysis by 1943 of Nazi communication systems. "One thing is now clear after forty years. The Allies were not winning the battle until cryptology and radar were used as a multiplier of combat power to defeat the U-boat as a strategic weapon. If we do not learn that lesson now we may not again win the battle at sea, on land, or in the air" (64).

The closing chapter that follows this warning shout, "Can the United States Win the Next War," is preoccupied with the "lethality of electronic warfare" as first demonstrated in the 1973 Mideast war. In the course he has us take in the history of war's intelligence and mediatization, Gordon summarizes murky prospects: "When barrage jamming is combined and coordinated with direction finding and massive suppressive fires against friendly command and communication centers, the effect can be devastating. The enemy calls this radio electronic combat or REC. Unless the U.S. Army trains to fight on a dirty electronic battlefield, it can lose to REC" (72). According to this wreckommendation, the field of future battles lies beyond cryptanalysis, within the after-math of intelligence, outside any reservations held for intelligent life in the survivor zone, the I of the war storm. Future war will be more totally disseminated by the new organ or dimension that psychological warfare, group psychology, media war have already spawned.

> The ability to manipulate the opposing force by controlling the electromagnetic spectrum has the potential to provide the winning side with an even greater advantage than provided by "code breaking" during WWII. . . . If there is a next war, a modern battlefield will include not only the customary three dimensions of depth, width, and airspace of previous wars, but an added dimension as well. The fourth dimension, the electromagnetic spectrum, is a mostly invisible medium which will saturate the entire battlefield upon which the use of all electromagnetic devices will depend. (2)

But this pre–Gulf War prospect seems too intelligent by half, by the better half of libidinization. Trauma's staying power, its station identification, has not stopped sponsoring TV viewing of the automatic reruns of former war phantasms.

On Turing

What also comes out of the clearance sale of World War II military secrets is a longer-term modern legacy that was along for the Polish emergency transmission of the original decoding machine for makeover by Alan Turing. Even or especially at the level and leveling of conceptualization, the crack of the code folded out from a couple of gendered transferences. The Polish analysts started out surveying the entire "traffic" of Enigma messages for the patterns of untranslatability given in repetitions:

> Sometimes it would happen that first and fourth letters would actually be the same—or the second and the fifth, or the third and the sixth. This phenomenon was, for no apparent reason, called a "female." . . . More precisely a core-position would be said to have a "female" letter, if that letter's encipherment happened to be the same three steps later. . . . The analysts could easily locate all the observed females in the traffic of the day. . . . This information yielded a pattern of "females." (Hodges, 173–74)

Over the read body of female patterns, the decrypting accelerated out from under the perforated sheets of test scoring all the way into the machine.

> This was not the only method they devised. The perforated sheet system required the location of about ten females in traffic. A second system required only three, but it used not only the mere existence of a female, but the particular letter that appeared as female in the cipher-text. . . . But it was impossible to catalogue in advance all the female letters of 6 × 17576 positions, and then perform a search, even by staggering sheets. There were far too many possible cases. Instead, they took a radical new step. They would search through the properties of the rotor positions afresh each time, doing no advance cataloguing. But this would not be a human search. It would be done by a machine. By November 1938 they had actually built such machines—six in fact, one for each possible rotor order. They produced a loud ticking sound, and were accordingly called the *Bombes*. The *Bombes* exploited the electrical circuitry of the Enigma machine, by using an electrical method of recognising when a "matching" had been found. The very fact that the Enigma *was* a machine, made mechanical cryptanalysis a possibility. (174–75)

German belief in the unbeatability of their network of thirty thousand Enigmas was legend—the kind that let the Allies read the map. The German code machine was, then, already cracking for the 1939 invasion of Poland. Polish intelligence, which at the time was top of the line, only had resources, however, to build the six *Bombes* required for the first decoding encounters (tick, tick, tick) with Enigma's latent text. But once the Germans put another wheel to their wheels, the Enigma started spinning its manifest text to higher powers. Now that sixty *Bombes* were required to translate the German messages, the Poles didn't have the technology but still had the intelligence to pass their prototype of the *Bombes* to the British for safe keeping up with the war effort. The Polish legacy served as first model and inspiration for Turing's progressive crackdown on German secrecy, which by 1943 was complete. Without the protection or projection of an Enigma, the German command system was a quick read in one open book. Communications were so centralized that one message across the vast airways of a symptomatic overreliance by the Germans on radio (symptomatic, for starters, because way in excess of any necessity) gave the Allies the dotted lines along which to cut their losses with every German maneuver.

Through the "Probable Word" method, the British analysts, led by Turing, spiritualized or paternalized, to borrow the idiom of *Moses and Monotheism,* the sensual female patterns for the now millions of connections per unit to be translated. The new method was helped out by another proper-name effect that shadowed the Enigma with another giveaway reliance on sensation: no letter in the German text could be enciphered into itself. Whereas the Polish prototype was based on a simple form of recognition (between the interpersonal columns of sexual difference), Turing's new machine required "circuits for the simulation of 'implications' flowing from a plugboard hypothesis, and means for recognising not a simple matching, but the appearance of a contradiction" (181). But even this machine or method, which moved one baby step away from the *Bombes,* still depended absolutely "upon finding closed loops in the 'crib'" (182). One of Turing's colleagues added the so-called diagonal board, which meant that the decrypt team "no longer needed to look for loops, and so could make do with fewer and shorter 'cribs'" (183). Now out of the loop requirements, they could raid the crib for rich combinations with no more limit than the Enigma had to observe. In 1940 the first Luftwaffe messages to be deciphered in a timely fashion included mostly practice transmissions reciting nursery rhymes (186). But it marked the beginning of a lull in the war, one that would soon turn it around and start it flashing before Nazi eyes with the end in sight.

By 1954 Turing's legacy, the universal machine, held the delegated place at the end of the war work that produced the Colossus and, for the audio portion of encryptment, the Delilah. Turing had for several years been forced to submit to hormone treatments to curb his homosexuality, which came out when his deviance crossed the path of a delinquent and brought them both before the law. The treatments created female patterns, notably breasts, within the traffic of his bodily existence. After the physical treatments were stopped, Turing opted for treatment by a Jungian analyst. Now the regression seemed to register all the phases, in flashback and reverse, of the mounting of a psychologization, mediatization, and not-seeing of the war to which Turing's universal machine was heir. The heir was conditioned by its service as decoder of what the Nazi Enigma had first encoded and, protected by the Nazi mode of not seeing, grew up into full computing capacity.

In the 1980s, printers ticked so loudly in the workplace that they had to be soundproofed with large plexiglass covers that added another sense of encryptment to the legacy. What preceded the hiding and preservation we associate, ever since Disney's film, with Snow White's coffin was another gag of sui-cite. In 1954 Turing put himself to sleep, sleep, by taking a bite out of the poisoned Apple.

REOPENER

Air Head

> Picture men in daily routine flights, constant prolonged patrols, or even watchers in far off, lonely islands. It is reasonable to suppose that anxiety and fatigue will be apparent in these situations, as there is never an opportunity to discharge the stored up emotional tension.
>
> —FRANCIS BRACELAND AND HOWARD ROME, "ANXIETY AND FATIGUE"

> Every Youth a Flyer!
>
> —1938 HITLER YOUTH SLOGAN

The extent of Freud's entry into the military, psychological, and military-psychological establishments worldwide can be tracked through the outer reaches of its reception, which, after a delay, scored on the Allied side the kind of recognition associated with surprise attack. Take, for example, a U.S. report on the neuropsychiatric casualties of the Tunisian campaign in World War II that shows both the intake of Freud's World War I intervention and the diversification that had gone into the war neurosis portfolio by 1943. It's also symptomatic of a take by surprise that the direct connection to Freud everywhere in evidence in this first, classified documentation ends only a couple of years later in hang-up. The postwar book version of this account, Roy Grinker and John Spiegel's 1945 *Men under Stress,* which turns the airman into the unknown soldier of total warfare, no longer sharply outlines his psychoanalytic profile, a blur in focus, however, which could also be taken to prove that the connection is there, following the digestive course of all genuine influence. But certainly Freud "was there" when the authors of the 1943 report found that the gadget love binding pilot to plane had, in the special case of air power, relocated the site of war traumatization. The ego-libidinal rapport with the flying machine is where the trauma goes.

> The central unifying force through the Air Corps is the intangible and yet powerful devotion to aircraft felt in different degrees by all its members.... Planes receive an almost libidinal investment of interest. They are loved for their beauty, their performance, and their strength. They are loved because this beauty and strength and skill in performance are the results of the combined efforts of the men who service and fly the planes with the men who make them. The mechanic, the engineer, the radioman,

> the prop man, the navigator, the bombardier, and the pilot all take an intense interest in their plane. It becomes an extension of their own egos, so that they are affected by things that happen to the plane as if they had happened to themselves. They react to the various types of aircraft as they would to individuals they meet, forming loves, hatreds, and jealousies out of all proportion to the realities of the situation. Indeed, under such circumstances the aircraft become anthropomorphized, and take on individual human characteristics.... This continual preoccupation with the sight, the sound, and the fate of aircraft and their aircrews is the psychological background upon which the symptoms of the neuroses of war develop within the members of the Air Forces. (99–102)

What the authors refer to as their "'unnatural experiments'" (299) with war-sick airmen, from the ground or grounded personnel all the way up to those taking flight, opened up an analysis of the ego in all the phases of its dis-pair and re-pair. The 1943 U.S. view of ego libido with no place to go thus soon ran up against psychosis, going into a tailspin somewhere over the trauma of loss so central to war's production of the narcissistic neuroses. Together with the "severer psychoses," depressions "resulting from ambivalent identification with a dead comrade" often proved intractable (147). They could be distinguished from the war neuroses "by the absence of anxiety in relation to the specific traumatic situation" (94). The war psychotic often suffers from the impression that they're all spies, all of them, or he breaks through enemy lines single-handedly and irresponsibly stakes the outcome of the war on his manic courage. If in the big picture of operations, prevention had to be promoted and not the transference, not the cure, that's also because the psychotic anxiety-free disposition was in excess of what in fact was a very good wartime attitude. The psycho soldier has lost his group and has turned its group psychology into an individual concern. He thus embodies the limit concept of the internal defense policy taken out against war neurosis. The inoculative administration of psychosis inside neurosis gets us to that in-between zone of oscillation where group psychology *is* psychological warfare (and *is* total war). "Psychological warfare against the enemy we know is necessary; but psychological warfare for our soldiers is even more pressing. It is one of the greatest prophylactic measures against neuroses" (138).

But *we* saw it first with the Nazis: two years earlier, the 1941 survey and bibliography *German Psychological Warfare* documented the special consideration given the psychology of air war by the Nazis. The selection cri-

Eduard V. Handel-Mazzetti, *Ruhmreiches Ende* [A Glorious End]. A commentary follows: "The destroyers 'Hans Lüdemann,' 'Wolfgang Zenker,' and 'Bernd v. Arnim' in the Rombakenfjord near Narvik scuttled following glorious combat on April 13, 1940." Reproduced from *Die Kunst im deutschen Reich* 5, no. 5 (May 1941): 136.

teria for their aviators admitted them at the front of the line of permanent present tense or tension: "The Germans consider the prime requisite of a military aviator to be his ability to adapt himself completely to his machine and to regard the individual components of a plane as he does those of his own body" (Farago, 21). From the Air Ministry to the central psychotherapy institute (the one that packed a major psychoanalysis section), a standard of intrapsychic theory and therapy was advanced in the Third Reich that in 1941 was the focus of the Allied all-points effort to keep up with the Nazis.

Into Africa

> The first messenger of the new era of gigantic conflict appears above this desolate place. It is the source of the singing sounds, brightly rattling and sonorously roaring, a monstrous mixture of rage, power, will to combat, pressing forward.
>
> A german airplaine *[Flieger]* . . .
>
> Roulers lay spread wide open under the flight of the bird. Its eyes recognized clearly how dense crowds of people pressed together in the streets looking up at the solitary alien that announced a new era with loud song.
>
> —WERNER BEUMELBURG, *YPERN 1914*

In 1939 Elly Beinhorn-Rosemeyer published the memoir of her "28,000 kilometer flight to Africa," *Berlin–Kapstadt–Berlin,* in a special subseries of the German Soldier Press (Deutsche Soldatenbücherei) devoted to "adventures of pilots." She also filmed her spectacular flying tours, as in the movie she made in 1939 documenting her flight to India, "30,000 Kilometers Solo Flight over Persia, Siam, and India." A 1940 flyer advertises her appearance at the screening of her short film at the Atrium in the Kaiserallee, Berlin, on 14 January. In print and behind the lectern, she was in the souvenirs-of-her-flights business again by 1952 at the latest, the publication year of her autobiography *I Fly around the World.* In contrast to her German colleague Hanna Reitsch—or to any number of women pilots on the other side of world war—young motherhood limited Beinhorn's war efforts to courier work in the opening Blitz years. Her 1950s recollection dates her desire to fly back to 1928, specifically to her attendance of a lecture by pilot Hermann Köhl on his flight across the Atlantic. The hall was packed! Her life now had a direction (11), indeed a beginning and an end.

In 1930 she was one of twenty-one women pilots in Germany (37). "Not in my entire life will I forget the moment I first had Africa under me" (50). After one emergency landing in the desert, she is a bit apprehensive about the leprous look of the open wounds on the limbs of the natives. "In spite of all that—it is wonderful, to fall from the sky like that, right where no white woman has ever been before" (60). Then she is the first German (or German woman) to enter Timbuktu (62). In turn she can well imagine that many Africans had never before seen an airplane. But one farmer doesn't even look up from his work, even after another emergency landing, repair work, and takeoff: "He was right. He harrowed his field, and I flew around in the air. We had nothing to do with one another" (65). On 4 December 1931 she takes off on her next big flying adventure, this time around the world. Always solo: "I don't know, but maybe I just lack the organ that releases fear in normal females (I of course consider myself the most normal woman in the world)" (85). But to fly in two-plane formation with an other: that was her dream (90).

For the solo round-the-world trip, she finds room for "a traveling gramophone and a good supply of records" (69). Later on, in order to install a sixth fuel tank for her flight from Australia to South America, she had to give up her "beloved" gramophone along with several suitcases, everything, in short, that had been piled up next to her on the passenger seat. But once the beloved has been given up, all the rest can soon follow. To fly over the Andes, she needed an oxygen tank: by then she's down to one tiny suitcase (82). When crossing the Himalayan mountain-scape, she looks down onto what looks just like "an alien planet" (78).

While on this world tour, she had been surprised when a fellow German contacted her in India: why, it's her good friend Hela! The Indian beau who was a foreign and very decorative engineering student back when Beinhorn last saw the two of them in Germany was now Hela's husband. But when love between cultures on German soil moves to foreign turf, it just goes to hell (72–75). A subsequent trip reunites her with her British and American flying boyfriends (her "daddies" [111]) in South America, where the international cosmopolitan group visits the territories of "the still living race-pure descendants of the Mayas" (101).

By 1933, the date of her second trip to Africa, Beinhorn flies a small one-seater plane, an experimental design built by Heinkel just for this flight, this time all around the "dark continent" (94). Beinhorn was off to see the former German colonies in Africa—but only among two or three equally good reasons for her to go back. The trip lasts only a few pages. She shoots leopards, takes photos, and films. But all that's history by 1952: "Fire as a consequence of bombing annihilated all these trophies collected over many years and excursions" (95). And she closes the brief chapter on this second trip with the story of the burden imposed on her flight by British insistence back then that a woman could not fly across African territories under British jurisdiction without a chaperone male pilot flying alongside. Her gentlemen bungle it, get in her way: she outflies them. She is woman, watch her fly. She belongs to the new order. The Brits with their old-fashioned chauvinism will be left behind. It doesn't cross her mind—or rather she crosses it out in the reader's mind—that the British might have considered her a spy or at least a propagandist sent to close the ranks of potential African supporters of the new Reich.

In the 1939 memoir of her trip all around Africa as emissary from the new Germany, Beinhorn recaptures her enthusiasm, just how she looked forward to visiting all the former colonies. "I am so proud to be transmitting to them greetings from the homeland and from our new Minister of Flight Hermann Göring" (7). And these greetings will be welcome because they're upbeat: "We Germans have become secure in ourselves again under the new regime and trust that now everything is going upwards with us. Our countrymen in Africa in particular need to feel the fresh wind coming down to them from their homeland" (8). It's springtime for Hitler and Germany.

But when she takes off and sets her sights for the south, her own thoughts of her home have gone the way of all exhaust (16–17). When she can't see anything, she has "abandonment" issues: "This endless nothingness causes the strangest thoughts to cross my mind. Is it in any way important whether I now fly here or make an emergency landing or plummet into the whiteness?" But she dismisses this foolishness once she catches sight of train tracks. "Odd, how an increase in visibility of a few hundred meters completely transforms a person. All indifference is gone" (24).

Filming isn't always from the air. It's safari time, but not really: "Hunting safari would be an exaggeration, since this time we only hunted with the camera, although we always had a gun along, ready to shoot" (55). On this safari shoot Beinhorn was advised "to take a 'white hunter' along, because it would bring me so close to the wildlife that I could quite comfortably take portrait pictures of the individual species." Proximity is everything however you shoot your game (56). She experiences this technologization of her range of vision: "It remains a mystery to me how the eye can in time learn to adjust itself so well to the demands that are made of it. . . . We in fact came so close to the giraffes that . . . I could get either just the head or just the leg in the picture" (60). When the camera team breaks for lunch, the giraffes keep coming up to see what's going on "just like curious teenagers" (61).

But stalking with the animals is time-out from the total mission of this flying tour: reestablishing contact with the Germans still residing in the lost colonies. "The idea to focus my Africa trip entirely on visits to our former colonies and with the foreign-Germans *(Auslandsdeutschen)* came to me when in February the new government declared black-white-red the official German flag" (63). Now Germany had something black on white that could be read all over by all the scattered countrymen who needed to rally to the writing on the wall. "The entire German populace *(Volk)* had closed ranks internally and was attempting by honest efforts to regain its former significance in Europe. With an airplane in particular one has with relatively minor expenditures huge possibilities for propaganda. I cannot imagine another means whereby one can rally so many people under similar conditions, especially in Africa and above all—that's just the way it is—when a solo-flying girl sits at the controls" (64). Beinhorn is moved and impressed by the "hot love" binding her countrymen down here to their homeland, "even though they are after all with all their interests anchored in East Africa" (66). Some news and much of the spirit of Germany's national *Erhebung*—a rising up that borders on tumescence and arousal—had already sparked down in Africa. Because these outsiders had to rely on the foreign press and thus had a broader view of politics they saw clearly "that first on the basis of a cleansing and concentration of the people in the Reich could a revitalization toward the outside become possible" (66). "Even a gramophone record with the Horst-Wessel-Song was available down here, and there was hardly one young German who did not already know the text by heart" (67). At one of her stopovers, the usual effect of her visit is doubled by prior absence: this was their first encounter with "a German machine" (72). The visit with these isolated gold miners is her first film op on this mission-controlled focus of her tour.

She is losing control of her plane in flight, and checks "automatically" the cabin door in case she has to jump, but the opening is blocked. "Everything that immediately followed took just seconds. I am well aware that in my entire life I have not often been in such a serious situation, and somehow it is not at all I myself who acts, but rather something inside me does for me whatever is necessary" (93). What is inside her, however, is still female. When she takes out her pocket mirror, the thought crosses her mind that she doubts her male colleagues would be as well equipped. She reconnoiters with her side and rearview mirroring and discovers that the baggage compartment has opened up and was trapping her inside the cabin with the steady flow of items falling off the plane: in Africa every item thus lost was attached to a piece of her "heart": "for everything here in Africa is irreplaceable" (95). But she stabilizes her flight over what looks just like a "vast cemetery" (97), which later she is informed is in fact a completely abandoned area. "That's just the way I imagine it to be on the moon" (98). Southwest Africa does not show the unhappy signs of assimilation to the British takeover that Beinhorn had witnessed in East Africa. These Germans living in Southwest Africa, many of whom are second-generation south-of-the-equator citizens, have not undergone any loss in generation: they are still "of the same blood and the same race" (103). German flags wave from the rooftops as Beinhorn flies a couple of rounds just above the city, and the Deutschland song welcomes her upon landing. However, especially in the southern region, drought conditions give little hope for the future. For her next safari, she does a camera and gun combo. She shoots a leopard: "I have seldom in my life had such an uncanny feeling as then, when complying with my fellow traveler's wish I carried the still warm wild animal on my back and posed for photographs" (109). She also has opportunities in the Southwest to take documentary footage of sheep breeding on a German farm and of the local scout organization, which, just in time for her visit, had already converted to the "Hitler Youth" movement (110). The girl members honor the visiting pilot by founding an "Elly-Beinhorn-Group"—her own fan club in the Nazi girl scouts (112)! "Rarely has it been so difficult for me to fly away on to what lies next as in the Southwest" (113).

Marga von Etzdorf, another new girl in the German pilot series, crosses Beinhorn's path one last time during this Africa tour. Beinhorn receives the news of von Etzdorf's fatal crash during her Australia flight. They had missed each other in Bangkok while Beinhorn was completing her round-the-world flight. Von Etzdorf had been held up by the war conditions in Manchuria. But upon her own return to Germany after completing the total round trip, Beinhorn was greeted by von Etzdorf. They met again before Beinhorn left for Africa. "Now suddenly this telegram! It came from a private source and was given in code" (116). In Windhuk all the German flags were lowered to half-mast. "For out here, where for years now Germans have been struggling for recognition, one knows what it means when a young girl flies out alone to visit all nations of the world, in order to woo friends for her fatherland" (116). Crash!

Another story that crosses her path. A South West African Airways flight entrusted with the emergency transport to the nearest hospital of a patient suffering from some local fever crashed, destroying the machine but leaving the passengers unharmed. "The sick man, whom all had really already given up on, was restored to health through the shock. Could be that this type of therapy would prove effective in other cases too. But no one can expect an airline to crash one of its machines each time a sick passenger's life could thus be saved" (120). On long stretches of flight along the African coast, Beinhorn's "subconscious" registers how far away other planes are in case of an emergency (123).

Does she take it all back, or is she by now really getting into it? "The belief, however, that such a flight—to the extent that one can use it at all for propaganda purposes—could prove significant for the later destiny of a colony, seems to me highly exaggerated. On the contrary, this visit was often, as happened quite consciously in Southwest Africa, an occasion for confirming anew the bond of international comradeship" (128). They confiscated her cameras in Cameroon for the duration of her visit.

In the capital city of Togo, where there's only one German family still in residence, Beinhorn meets the many other Togo-Germans, native Africans who still speak German. "But just the same it gave me pleasure to observe the ties of affection still binding the natives to our former administration" (134).

Another aside that belongs to the inside: Beinhorn witnesses and learns the story of the madwoman from Austria who was abandoned by her husband on the Gold Coast when their business went bad. Soon it went to worse, and she was found in a native village, improperly attired, confused, but claiming to be an Austrian princess. The local authorities tried to have her transferred to an Austrian asylum, but the war intervened. And then the postwar version of Austria was not interested in the transfer. The English asylums wouldn't admit the foreigner. "In the meantime over twenty years have passed, and one can see the woman every hour pressing her face to the bars on the window in the delusion that she, Princess of Austria, is waiting for the heir to the throne to pick her up. But every car drives on by" (138).

On the way back, "Casablanca, Oran, Algiers, Tunis pass by me like on the screen in the movie theater" (148). But when she lands in Casablanca, all her suitcases and trunks are thoroughly searched. "Then all my cameras and films and my small revolver were confiscated and then a rigorous search of the machine was undertaken" (148). They charge her with smuggling cigarettes. As soon as she takes off, she makes sure to outfly the French planes that start out accompanying her. She's glad to enter the airspace of fascist Italy. She has a private meeting with fellow pilot Mussolini, who, she notes with amazement, takes time out to greet her in the middle of his own African campaign, in which Italian pilots were performing stunts that the world had never before seen (154–55). Beinhorn's closing line: "Till we meet again, dear Africa!" There's an Aryan African world out there, an Aryan African world.

1945: There's Still a Place for Psychoanalysis

In his contribution to a textbook collection of essays by experts on the various medical therapies taught and conducted at the Berlin university clinics, M. de Crinis gives us the "Therapy of Psychic Illnesses." This sixteenth edition, published in 1945, is still pretty much the same as the thirteenth edition, in 1942, into which major changes were introduced on account of combat experiences. When it comes to psychosis and psychopathy, treatment is not so much of the diseases as treatment of the afflicted patient (423). De Crinis cannot overemphasize the seriousness of symptoms of psychic illnesses; they are often life-threatening and should be treated with serious professionalism (424). For the treatment of depressives, psychopaths, and other specialized cases, de Crinis basically counsels empathy and a focus on the total personality not just on discrete symptoms. He accepts hypnosis only if the patient appears to be suggestible in the first place. "The same suggestive effect as hypnosis can be achieved through the influence of unpleasant situations. Admission into the hospital for agitated mental patients and treatment with the faradic brush can be therapeutically very successful" (425).

> That psychoanalysis has the therapeutic value that its supporters and practitioners claim for it can not be proved. It cannot be denied that the preoccupation with the patient required by this therapy can exert a beneficial influence in many cases. Through psychoanalytic assistance the patient can become clear on his own psychic misalignments. A thorough discussion under psychiatric auspices achieves the same effect. Not only pointless but indeed damaging, especially with youths, are the often embarrassing analytic interpretations which refer to sexuality. (425)

Rudolf Hengstenberg, *Durchbruch durch die burgundische Pforte* [Breakthrough at the Gates of Burgundy]. Reproduced from *Die Kunst im deutschen Reich* 5, no. 5 (May 1941): 139.

1945 Allied-Style

> Yet in civilian life during treatments patients experience sensations similar to air sickness, as symptoms of overwhelming anxiety liberated by the psychic probing.
>
> —R. R. GRINKER AND J. P. SPIEGEL, *WAR NEUROSES IN NORTH AFRICA: THE TUNISIAN CAMPAIGN*

In the August 1945 issue of the *Bulletin of the U.S. Army Medical Department*, an extract from an article by Charles Miller on "delayed combat reactions in Air Force personnel" appeared under the title "Psychotherapy with Pentothal Narcosis." The news flash concerns the efficacy of the drug treatment, and the article is not impressed, if the treatment stops short of synthesis and integration. What's more, abreaction under the influence right away gives the therapy a false focus fixated on some recently past event in the patient's military career, often to the exclusion of a fuller exploration of earlier pasts, but always without a view to the current situation, which includes both the social context right now for the soldier in the war zone but also, inevitably if implicitly, the therapeutic setting or relationship itself.

> The patient may find it much easier to talk about his combat experiences than about the current situation of stress, even though it may be relatively trivial. The psychiatrist may fall into this trap and a sort of *folie-a-deux* may be set up, in which physician and patient become lost in the past and center their attention on nonexistent or minimal combat reactions, thus missing the present frustrating situation, which must be dealt with before recovery can occur. (U.S. Army, "Psychotherapy," 133)

But before airtime can be given the transference, there's the gut-level response to being in the machine. William Console's "Psychiatric Reactions to Aerial Combat and their Sequelae" describes the creation of an apparatus so in excess of its war function that "the killing of other human beings is only incidental" (901), or in other words: "With all this mechanization, aerial combat approaches complete depersonalization" (900). Console continues to diagnose the flying situation in terms or degrees of psychopathology:

> But consider the markedly introverted and even schizoid quality of his work. He operates a complex machine alone. He withdraws from worldly things in a real physical sense—something you can appreciate by sitting in the sky at 20,000 feet, high above

> clouds, surrounded by a vast nothingness. And you can intensify this by taking a night hop and surrounding yourself with an endless black void. (901)

After giving us the old "how-to," the author touches down on earth, to our level, and consoles us with our relative safety (the relative in fact being "mother"): "Those of you who have been under artillery fire or aerial bombardment know what it means to give mother earth a lascivious caress—the pilot is denied even that dubious comfort" (901). But when he in any way breaks down, he reenters "civilian life lubricated by the absence of guilt" (902). The least complaint will take him out of the pilot's seat and relocate him within the air-ground network, and the adhesive symptom labels circulating out there as general knowledge stick on contact: "He developed somatic complaints referable to his ears and sinuses, probably because of his knowledge of their peculiar vulnerability at high altitudes" (902). At the same time it is this "knowledge of aviation" that keeps him, even when he's let go from flying, forever wired to the war effort. He gets assigned to "less hazardous pursuits," like teaching. But his more general label knowledge as consumer will give the pilot, soon to be teacher, a more common sense of disturbance: "He had gastro-intestinal complaints because he was an American and had read the ads" (902).

James Halstead, in his digest of the gastro district of disorders for the November 1949 special issue of the *Bulletin of the U.S. Army Medical Department,* concurs: "Fashions in neurotic symptomatology change with the times, and the stomach was a favored center during World War II" (U.S. Army, "Combat Psychiatry," 163). William Menninger points out that the human body spreads its wings across contact with the outside on two planes: "Next to the skin, the gastrointestinal system has more contact with the external world than any other part of the personality" (Menninger, "Psychosomatic Medicine," 547). Here's another mouthful: "Many terms indicate a very definite relation between personality traits and various parts of the gastrointestinal tract" (548). Menninger has in mind such terms and phrases as "sucker," "sinking your teeth into something," "stomach something," "a belly full," and "biting off more than you can chew." Leslie Farber and Leonard Micon take it from there: "Unconsciously the wish to be 'taken care of' might be expressed by a wish to be fed" (346). The gastric neurotic is cornered by all that war has to offer *plus* the bogeyman bringing up the rear:

> With these persons particularly, the conclusion was inescapable that even though the foe had been vanquished realistically, there still remained the phantom from childhood who could never be

Rudolf Hengstenberg, *Die Ersten in Dijon* [The First Ones in Dijon]. Reproduced from *Die Kunst im deutschen Reich* 5, no. 5 (May 1941): 138.

> outdone. The outcome of the battle for these people seemed never to be either victory or defeat, but always dyspepsia. (356)

But if the hospital stay is always maternal care for these patients, then psychoanalysis (which the authors are using here as code word for psychotherapy today) is equally counterindicated, since it would represent another return to a subservient relationship. Plus there's no time for analysis (or therapy) in the service. And even if available, how many do you think would seek it out? And yet after this buildup of resistance, the authors poop out. Why seek something that isn't hiding? If "the ideal treatment would be one which aimed at effecting some change in the ego of the gastric neurotic," then psychoanalysis, we have already been positioned term by term inside it, is the only option. But the analyst must first adapt to the new situation! (Indeed, in the closing sentence, we learn that modern society would also have to change first.)

> With a well-trained psychoanalyst, who does not have too much trouble with his own ambitions, he might be able slowly to reexperience the helplessness which he was forced to abandon prematurely, and in the process achieve real rather than artificial independence. (361)

TAKING APART

Air Defense Mechanisms

> In conclusion the question can be raised whether the technologization of the armed forces as already determined by the war of the future does not also introduce new standards of training with regard to the basic psychic structure of the soldier.
>
> —VIKTOR LUCKE, "SOME QUESTIONS REGARDING THE PSYCHOLOGY OF MILITARY TRAINING"

Walter Ludwig hears the call for the development of military psychology in "the unique psychic structure that every weapon possesses" (129). Psychic capacity for empathy gets us together with our comrades and all of us into machines. What's required is a "reproduced self-observation" as a teleguide within our techno-relations (136).

> A feeling of unity with others develops, a kind of collective ego, before which the individual ego-feeling pulls completely away. I encountered a particularly clear instance of this phenomenon in a flying unit, in which the comradeship was remarkably cohesive and strong.... It was the case here that when individual comrades flew against the enemy, the sense of unity among all the rest was clearly apparent. It asserted itself visibly among those on the ground watching an air fight.... Everyone identified with "his" pilot. (148–49)

Along the intrapsychic lines binding gadget lover to his machine, the further consequences that Nazi research worked double time to follow belong to geopolitical conspiracy theories ranging from the remapping of terrain in the shadow of flight to the psychic rearrangements made by air defense on all sides of World War II. In "Geopolitical Effects of Air Travel" Eberhard Billeb investigates the peacetime reorganizations of entire countries already under way in anticipation of the total war that air power was guaranteed to bring. Air travel takes off from streets that are turned into runways to be touched down on, and keep in touch via flight trajectories that are now the "axis" or "air cross" holding together each world empire. Just as firearms transformed the role of the infantry, and the fleet was reorganized around the submarine, so the entire country from coast to most remote outpost in the interior has been dismantled by air force. Intersections or concentrations of people hitting the streets are no longer desirable constructions. The immediate geopolitical effect of air force, then, is freedom from streets (but not from weather conditions), an expansion of the range of the visual sense not just upward but depthwise too, and thus, in sum, a deconcentration of human activity formerly organized in nodal points and down streets. The shift to a state of preparedness for takeoff on isolated runways, an internal state that is already in 1937 making its connections via the vast "visual medium" of air travel, was initiated too soon (as far as the progress of its technology goes) during the First World War. More so than the introduction of submarine warfare, it was air power that had been Germany's only compensation for England's naval superiority. In "Airplane and Earth Space" Siewert also recognizes that there is a "compact fusion between the peacetime and wartime assignments of the airplane . . . as exists with no other means of transportation in the same strong measure" (509).

But whereas flight liberates us from the centrality of street networks, the landing on and takeoff from runways makes the link to earth space an absolute requirement: "It is almost grotesque that the dependency on earth in fact rose rather than decreased with the further development of flight" (509). The legal and insurance networks of risk containment and violence control were also expanding and diversifying geowide on contact with advances in media communication and transport. But the World War I results, which were in, represented way less freedom from earthbound limitations than the prospects originally along for the fantasy. In his "War Rights and Neutrality Rights" Josef L. Kunz explores the new issue of "air war right" *(Luftkriegsrecht)*, which is one category of wartime law among many others, including "radio right." "Air war right" was first settled by analogy (like the one between ships and air ships) with the right obtaining on the high seas or, with even greater limitations, with the one covering land war. It soon became clear that the legal situation would have to reflect the independence or autonomy of air war, which was not just an auxiliary service to land and sea operations. The highpoint of this right by analogy was the guiding notion of "air freedom," which was challenged right off by the views of "air sovereignty," which then triumphed during World War I. It was the not so neutral notion of neutrality that gave rise to an all-time high in the conception of borders and property rights. Only airspace over neutral nations could count as neutral territory. But neutrals also have the right to regulate or interdict traffic across their airspace. Another direct connection—CRASH!—between mechanical flight and the earth is guaranteed by the psychogenesis of plane wrecks, a growing concern as their incidence continued to be proportionally constant even as the apparatus was becoming technically more and more perfect. As velocities increased, security risks were also on the rise. As in Münnich's "Man as Cause of Accident in Plane Wrecks," rigorous standards of psychological preselection, training, and supervision could no longer be uncalled for.

But the "almost grotesque" intimacy with the earth at the same time leaves Siewert upbeat but defensive on the ground side of air war.

> The element of surprise, which played such a decisive role in the last war, today doesn't count. The effect of material destruction was back then surpassed by the panic-like moral effect on the population.... All that has changed now. The air defense weapons have been greatly improved in the last years and their efficacy has grown manifold compared to before. The feeling of security has risen on this relative scale. In addition, with ongoing educational work and the spread of the sport of flying, one can no longer speak of ignorance of the dangers of flight. (515)

But the leftover (that is, technologically superseded) concentrations of civilian population are still in line for war shock. "A great danger of panic and breakdown exists in particular for the big city masses, for gatherings of people in general, even more so when they are internationally mixed" (515). The unmixed Japanese don't break under this psychological air pressure. "Given their over-exposure to earthquakes, typhoons, fires, the Japanese are best protected morally against air attack" (515). It looks like the Nazis weren't into Aryans only. They respected other pure races (Riefenstahl's postwar African photo excursions were not even the displacements Susan Sontag thought she was knocking out of the way). In each "air defense community," as the Nazis came to rename their own group psychology, there had to be one race at a time. This worldwide multiculturalism of pure identities in their separate places was the breeding assignment of the geopolitical network of air defense on every home front.

In his 1937 "Reflections on Air War," von Rohden indeed lays the blame on the home front for any war effort that falls short of total fulfillment.

> These armed forces can fulfill their tasks if there is a committed population...closing ranks behind them, one that uses any means of power within reach, without regard for individual groups. (213)

Amplified by "technical war media of heretofore unknown efficiency and efficacy," the totally popular military effort will "conduct war without limits regarding time and space and with greatest intensity." The rise of air force has launched this new dimensionality of conflict. Central Europe's sense of limited space (and time) required that a supplemental theater of war be opened up through the conquest of airspace: "The theater of war for the air force is the world" (200). It's the only way to get around the complete surprise of enemy attack and those border-patrolling fortifications that can shut down advances along the fixed fronts of protracted war.

War's arrested development gets symptomatized by the captive audience as "depressions which often lead to betrayal of the fatherland and to pronounced pacifism" (212). Down to earth (and in group-psychological or psychological-warfare format) air war builds a group that must defend against the downswing of war traumatization from the depressions of World War I to their psychotic breakthrough the second time around. "Because the populace's diverse sectors are all equally afflicted by the same renunciations and the same dangers under air attack, the mass psychosis that can develop cannot but undermine national defense" (212).

Nazi psychology and psychotherapy were under orders to mobilize the last resources of group psychology following Hermann Göring's 1937 directive that psychological preparations alone were the only effective defense against all-out air attack. In "On the Psychic Conditions of Air Defense" Hans-Heinrich Grunwaldt sides with Göring's diagnosis: no matter what the size of the air fleet, active air defense can never preserve the Germans from the monstrous consequences of air war. That's why so-called passive air defense takes over where its active partner leaves off. In "The Fight against the Panic Problem in Civilian Air Defense," Fischer recommended cathexis of leadership as the most libido-efficient way of delivering the mass psyche from its panic affliction. The leader personality, which is "immune" to "psychic infection" (21), is the essence of the new "air defense community." By turning up the volume on the human voice (with special thanks to current technologies), the panicky, staticky noise of large masses of people is blown away. It's called turning up the speaker full blast.

P. Kecskemeti and N. Leites's wartime study *Some Psychological Hypotheses on Nazi Germany* cashes in on one note of the benefits the Nazis were able to collect from the air war against Germany: a certain "equality-in-deprivation" reset the balance across Germany. The authors stress Nazi propaganda's capitalization on this "social" resource of gratification but leave out the therapeutic advantages of equalization the Third Reich was extolling over and beyond social opportunities afforded by air raids (46).

At the Berlin insitute, J. H. Schultz was in charge of research on maintenance of general mental health during air raids (the research agenda cosigned by both Görings). According to his 1940 "Psychic Reactions to Blackout," only psychotherapeutic intervention could both eliminate the "distortion neuroses" that had emerged under blackout conditions and prophylactically reinvest for a therapeutic purpose the collective darkness of group shelter that goes down during enemy air attack. Air raids thus afforded the ultimate communal or even primal conditions for the city dweller to get in touch with his inner self in harmony with natural phenomena. Schultz was following Göring's lead when he thus developed the notion of the "air-raid shelter community," which was now the place where a truly therapeutic environment for everyone's bonding-happiness with and within the community could emerge—from the grounding of children on up.

Bomber Room

Case No. 7

When the nine-year-old boy, son of an ordinary bureaucrat, is sent to the first session, the purpose is to ascertain, with the assistance of the sceno-test, the nature of his inner life and how he arrived at his particular symptom of singing in his sleep.... Finally the boy builds an air raid shelter with the roof-top cannon aimed at the dolls representing father and mother. In front of the air raid shelter he builds a prisoner of war camp in which, the boy alleges, English and French prisoners are interred. The air raid shelter is without windows or door. The little patient comments that no one is allowed into the shelter, neither the prisoners nor the other people.... In response to the question: Does the bird sing something to the father?—the boy says it's singing him the song "We will make your life bitter." He uses here the aggressive form of the revised text which ran originally: "We won't let our life be made bitter." In this way the unconscious aggressive attitude is very clearly expressed. It's even more evident when the boy inserts the further text: "And when Churchill burns in his nightshirt." ... Not only the warlike rendition of the song ... but also the further construction of the scene show that the boy has decided against his cold mother and for the heroic-warlike attitude. He grows hard, not only against himself, but also against others. That's why he builds an air raid shelter without an entrance and in which no one can seek refuge. There are thus safe places in life but no one is permitted access to them. Since all persons are experienced as enemies, everyone really should die.

—GERDHILD VON STAABS, "THE SCENO-TEST"

When, on their way home, her mother pointed at something in the sky and said: "Look, Joan, there's an airplane on fire," she answered: "No, Mummy, that's no plane, that's a rocket." When the crash followed, she began to run, calling: "Quick, Mummy, or we'll be killed." When subsequently she heard people in the street discuss the rocket, she said proudly: "See, I said it was a rocket."

—ANNA FREUD AND DOROTHY BURLINGHAM, "INFANTS WITHOUT FAMILIES: REPORTS ON THE HAMPSTEAD NURSERIES (1929–1945)"

In 1940 Fritz Mohr reported receiving a letter from a former patient who wondered if there was a psychotherapeutic way for her breast-feeding ability to be restored to her, which the horror of witnessing children die in a north German city under English air attack had shut down. Could a purely physical disturbance be accessible to psychic intervention, she asked herself. Willpower alone will not get the milk to flow again, Mohr responded: but the image of its flowing can influence the body. Lie down two or three times per day, relax, and imagine that the milk is flowing. But beware that given the way the unconscious is always out to assert itself and get its way, small differences you may be having with your husband or your family can provoke resistance in you which, taken together with the special shock effects of the bombing, can amplify the direct hit. She promptly wrote back to assure Mohr that the milk secretion was again in full production even while air attacks were under way night and day. This is the kind of folk work psychotherapy is good for, as Mohr concludes in his "Letter to a Mother Who Became Incapable of Nursing through Air Attack."

Already for the first world air war, Karl Abraham closed his 1919 contribution "Psychoanalysis and the War Neuroses" with the report of a twelve-year-old boy's phobia regarding air attack, which Abraham had successfully treated in just a few weeks. The cure took and held even after the boy returned home and even when the threat of air attack was back, whereupon he bore up under air war pressure as would any other healthy individual. For Abraham this is *the* test case for the staying power of the analytic intervention, one that should accord Freud's science, Abraham concludes, first place in the treatment of war neurosis.

In World War II the institutionalization of children evacuated from the urban target range of enemy bombers (where their mothers continued to work) provided the laboratory conditions for a quick study of psychic development in real time. Therapists were in attendance because it was assumed that the children could already have been damaged psychically by the air war they experienced pre-evacuation (but then it turned out that the separation from both parents was the hardest blow of their war experience). Real-time travel through childhood development had been an Adlerian exclusive during the twenties (you also saw psychodynamic group therapy first with Adler). Work with children at the Berlin psychotherapy institute during World War II, which was still modeled after Adlerian prophylaxis in schools, also admitted, in certain cases, a new improvement: the theory and therapy of "depth psychology" (code word for greater psychoanalysis). It was at the Berlin institute that the sceno-test (a test that would be kept up as postwar standard) was developed for treating disturbed children and for studying human development at large. Thus the test permits therapists to make prophylactic diagnoses that help parents prepare for the development of neurotic disturbances that could be coming soon under the right conditions. The sceno-focus not only is on the structural background of neurotic symptoms (which the test does unpack) but also is fixed on the unconscious life of healthy children and youths. The test consists of an extended family of dolls and barnyard animals, which the little patient rearranges into primal scenes. A couple of dolls gather graveside, others huddle together in tight places, and one doll (see epigraph) isn't allowed to enter what looks like a shelter without any access. But when all the dolls of the family scene hit the deck or drop dead just as the cow enters stage right, the therapist must come up for air war and translate "cow," which means "bomb." This little patient, whose presenting symptom was a severe case of stuttering, is suffering in the first place from the trauma of his parents' divorce, which destabilized his relations with mother.

> The depth-psychological treatment... leads gradually to reconciliation with the destinal experience of his early childhood and to building up of contact with the environment—and also with his mother—and, in addition to that, the boy finally builds a kindergarten, in which he allegedly experienced "the happiest time" of his life.... This kindergarten, together with an apartment he builds next, which has the same groundplan as the kindergarten and which is "very cozy," is not destroyed by bombs. The treatment is interrupted when the boy is evacuated to the country for several months. The improvement of his stuttering is maintained despite the new environment. (Staabs, "The Sceno-Test," 38)

Freudian hands-on work with early developers was initiated on the other side of the world air war by Anna Freud, who studied the children who were evacuated from cities during the Battle of Britain and kept out of range right through the V-1 and V-2 attacks. To mount her analytic on-location study of childhood development, she first had to unearth her charges from the rubble of bombed-out sites as documented in "Infants without Families: Reports on the Hampstead Nurseries (1939–1945)" and then, separate the incidence of traumatic neurosis from the constant features of development that would stay the same in peacetime. The fact of life of all-out destruction of cities under air attack "led many people to expect that children would receive traumatic shocks from air raids and would develop ab-

Reproduced here (in the same order) are the complete illustrations from the appendix of illustrations in the special issue (6th supplement) of *Zentralblatt für Psychotherapie:* Gerdhild von Staabs, "Der Sceno-Test: Beitrag zur Erfassung unbewusster Problematik bei Kindern und Jugendlichen," 1943. First illustration: Dolls and a sampling of the materials.

Second illustration: Father on the school bench.

normal reactions very similar to the traumatic or war neuroses of soldiers in the last war" (160). But "it is a common misunderstanding of the child's nature which leads people to suppose that children will be saddened by the sight of destruction and aggression" (161).

Early education and socialization have all along been focused on changing (by around age four or five) the child's natural attitude toward the aggressive and destructive impulses inside himself.

> The real danger is not that the child, caught up all innocently in the whirlpool of the war, will be shocked into illness. The danger lies in the fact that the destruction raging in the outer world may meet the very real aggressiveness which rages in the inside of the child. . . . It must be very difficult for them to accomplish this task of fighting their own death wishes when, at the same time, people are killed and hurt every day around them. Children have to be safeguarded against the primitive horrors of the war, not because horrors and atrocities are so strange to them, but because we want them at this decisive stage of their development to overcome and estrange themselves from the primitive and atrocious wishes of their own infantile nature. (163)

That's why in the lexicon of the evacuated children, "bombing" is often used indiscriminately for all types of destruction of unwanted objects, and "war" signifies in the first place the period of time of their separation from their parents (159).

> Jeffrey (3 years, 8 months) asked to have a house drawn for him. As soon as it was finished, he scribbled over it wildly, covering it all up in black. When asked why he did this, he said: "The airplane has spoiled it all to bits, no, the big bad wolf has done it." The "airplane," like "the warning," like "Hitler," or "the bad wolf," are now equally convenient symbols for everything that is considered evil. (428)

Anna Freud explores the internal trajectories of "air-raid anxiety" from this child's-eye view. Because the child is working double time to contain his own aggressivity when he's also in an external war zone, real bombs release "real outbreaks of anxiety" when they are dropped during these early stages of the development of an inner conscience or superego (166). But that's why the bombs you want to see explode "are simply a new symbol for old fears" (168). "We shall know that peace has returned when nothing is left for the children to be afraid of except their own former ghosts and bogeymen" (169). The shock troops of conflict are not an outside threat, not even at this early age or stage, but mobilize their pathogenic force within zones of development where the intrapsychic reception already responds to all the interpersonals.

Third illustration: Child in the forest.

Fourth illustration: Two-story house.

First off, separation from both parents already marks the spot of traumatization the evacuated children are in. With the father's absence, third-party identifications, like the ones with the aggressor or, for pity's sake, with the victim, could be observed. Both case scenarios are the legacy of one fact of life: "the ability to defend oneself develops later than the ability to attack" (570). While still with their mothers, the children were exposed not so much to the air raids themselves as to the reactions of their mothers. "The primitive emotional tie between mother and baby, which in some respects still makes one being out of two, is the basis for the development of this type of air raid anxiety in children" (169). But if "protected and fortified by her mother's lack of fear and excitement," another child in the same holding pattern "will not develop air raid anxiety" (170).

Little Richard

> When told that the German airman might have been taken prisoner, he protested: "He is not an air-man, he is a Ger-man."
>
> —ANNA FREUD AND DOROTHY BURLINGHAM, "INFANTS WITHOUT FAMILIES: REPORTS ON THE HAMPSTEAD NURSERIES (1929–1945)"

While Anna Freud was creating under air war pressure a different child analysis that left the analysis of adults intact, Melanie Klein was changing the whole analytic frame from treatment of child patients on up. At the time of her analysis of the ten-year-old Richard, Klein, who, like her little patient, had left London for the country to keep out of range of the bombing, was lying low to prepare for another war, the one between Freudian émigrés and her brand of analysts. It was during the two-front war she faced beginning in 1940 that Klein pushed her transformation through, her total emphasis on the transference as the open book of the patient's internal metabolization of objects.

For the wartime, Melanie Klein readjusted her brand of analysis to short-term format and intensified—and thus invented—what would be her distinctive intervention: saturation interpreting of the transference, in particular the anxiety along for the insight in session. The patient's internal world is reduced, for easy followability, to the rebound of good and bad objects. "Richard's progress was bound up with improvement in his relation to his good object," at once mother and analyst (Klein, 465). With the first improvements in little Richard's object relations, "more scope for sublimations" became available (268). The boy's paranoid tendencies are thus decathected and recontextualized in their beginnings, which lie in psy fi. Second session:

> He said he remembered something else he often worried about, but added that it was very different from the things he had talked about yesterday, altogether far away. He feared there might be a collision between the sun and the earth and the sun might burn up the earth; Jupiter and the other planets would be pulverized; and the earth, the one planet with living people on it, was so important and precious. (23–24)

Before she can turn on the narcissism of the interpretation of their relationship in session, the analyst must face head-on the budding delusional order of the world by regrounding it in the home, which is where the uncanny is.

> Mrs. K. interpreted that the "precious earth" was Mummy, the living people her children, whom he wanted as allies and friends; hence his references . . . to the planets. The sun and earth in collision stood for something happening between his parents. "Far away" meant near by, in the parents' bedroom. The pulverized planets stood for himself (Jupiter), and Mummy's other children, if they came between the parents. After speaking about the collision, he had again referred to Hitler destroying Europe and the world. (24)

That's why little Richard starts out identifying (with) the analyst as the enemy, which the cross interpretations of the transference reveal to the boy to be his own internal state of emergency:

> The German aeroplane into which Richard had secretly gone represented Mrs. K., who was suspect and disloyal because she interpreted to him his sexual desires towards her and Mummy. Since Mummy slept in the same room with Daddy, and Richard had to sleep by himself, Richard felt her to be bad and even a spy and allied with Daddy against him. Then he wished that Mrs. K. and Mummy should be destroyed—the lightning that struck the aeroplane—and he hated and distrusted himself very much for wishing it. (269)

Klein comments on a particular session with little Richard in terms of her taking on both anxiety and defense: "Richard was aware of his fear that the tramp would kidnap and harm his mother. He was not conscious of the fact that this fear was a derivative of the anxieties relating to the parents' sexual intercourse. When I interpreted that specific anxiety content, I also stressed that it was too painful for him to think of his father as a bad man, and that therefore he had turned his fear and suspicion against the tramp and Hitler. This implies analyzing a defense as well" (27). Klein thus demonstrates her departure from Anna Freud's hard line on treatment of children in which "the analysis of anxiety should be left for a later stage and the defenses (either against anxiety or against instinctual urges) should primarily be analyzed" (27). "It is characteristic of my technique and my whole approach that analyzing anxiety when it is most acute, either manifest or latent, has the effect of alleviating it" (40 n. 1). With anxiety relief comes an increase in the most essential ingredient of the cure: the positive transference. But first she teaches the patient how much he hates her, I mean loves her, I mean hates her. Anxiety must be produced in session before relief is on the way of the transference.

Fifth illustration: Lying-down house.

By the successful end of the analysis-Blitz, little Richard's improvement can be measured in the same terms as those of global diplomacy or war: his newfound ability to win the peace. Early on during her short-term work with Richard, Klein interprets for a more positive transference in a safety or neutrality zone alongside the negative one that both readily admit is all fired up inside and around him:

> He thought Hitler was probably gloating in his room.... Brave little Switzerland had dared to shoot down planes, German or British, which flew over her territory. Mrs. K interpreted that the... little countries, such as Switzerland, also represented himself.... Mrs. K referred to yesterday's material about his attacking the tramp and suggested that when he was in bed at night, he not only feared that Daddy would hurt Mummy, but sometimes he might also think that his parents were enjoying themselves.... If he wished to hurt them because he was jealous, he would feel very guilty. (23–25)

"Another sign of the increasing predominance of the life instinct, and with it of the capacity for love, was that he no longer felt impelled to turn away from destroyed objects but could experience compassion for them. I have referred to the fact that Richard, who so strongly hated the enemies threatening Britain's existence at that time, became capable of feeling sympathy for the destroyed enemy" (466).

Klein's first success in tugging at his identifications with the war zone right where they were cornered and covered in the home by murder or merger until there was more stretch or bounce to his object relations was over the *Vampire,* a destroyer from the Land Down Under.

> Richard replied that he had previously called the destroyer which he had left with Mrs. K. *Vampire.*
>
> *Mrs. K.* interpreted.
>
> Richard then replied that *Vampire* was the name of a real destroyer. (187)

> *Mrs. K.* interpreted that the British navy, representing the whole family, had died. The *Vampire* stood for Richard. (287)

> In the end *Vampire* (Richard) was sunk, but the other destroyer went on firing at the British fleet until they were all sunk and remained the only survivor. (408)

Little Richard was a gadget lover of the war who followed its news releases with maps, toys, and his own drawings. As Klein admits in an aside that takes us into the inside of the case: "He had mentioned, by the way, that he read three newspapers every day and listened to all the news on the wireless" (24). His presenting problem—fear of bombing—is just a sentence above the news he followed closely and the interest he took in the changes in the war situation: "This preoccupation came up again and again during the course of his analysis" (16). Richard exhibited symptoms comparable to those of traumatic or war neurotics in which the opposed sides of world conflict kept switching allegiances. When Richard drew his war pictures, the swastika would turn into the Union Jack and back again: But if he bombed Mummy or Mrs. K. with his scribbling and "big job" to get at the "bad Daddy Hitler penis" inside them, then the good objects, which were innocently standing by, would also be hit. Besides, when he put on Hitler faces, gave the Heil salute, and started goose-stepping around Klein's office, it looked like he would not be able to be evacuated from the bombing. Klein compacted the analysis down to the microlevel of transference interpretation, which she escalated to help draw the line of separation between the good and bad objects rebounding inside and around him. After four months of saturation interpreting and total transfer of all the externals and stray interpersonals to a strict keeping of transference accounts, Richard began to internalize the "good Mummy-Mrs. K-object" that Klein had force-fed him, and as a sign that through this piecemeal internal reorganization he would win the peace following termination of his stay with Klein in the

Sixth illustration: Park with two decked tables.

war zone of psychoanalysis, he started regretting the damage done in RAF raids on Berlin and Munich. Even though or especially because the analysis was so radically modified for the air war, Klein saw her case study of Richard as the first "all-round picture" of her technique (11).

Emergency Island

> Mentally the patients complained of the usual symptoms of the acute anxiety state: sleeplessness, terrifying bad dreams, a feeling of inner unrest, and a tendency to be startled at the least noise but particularly at the sound of an aeroplane going overhead or any sound resembling it.
>
> —FREDERICK DILLON, "NEUROSES AMONG COMBATANT TROOPS IN THE GREAT WAR"

> Differences are shown in the striking regressions that often follow being oneself, or seeing others, blown up, and in the temporary disturbance to the sense of reality caused by the bizarre effects of high explosive. The most fantastic dreams are suddenly realized, as though by magic, in actual life; and the mind regresses to primitive mechanisms appropriate to the time of life when such fantasies seemed real. . . . Or projection mechanisms may come into play, the man believing that every plane is coming specially to punish him.
>
> —GILBERT DEBENHAM, DENIS HILL, WILLIAM SARGANT, AND ELIOT SLATER, "TREATMENT OF WAR NEUROSIS"

For the British side effect of war, Louis Minski counts down the factors leading to shell shock in the wounded. The escape mechanism view won't hold for those who have the wounds to prove it. Constitutional predisposition is most important. Number three is a direct strike in the object relation, the transferential frame on Emergency Island for processing what's new in traumatization:

> A personal worry is often the final precipitating factor. For example, one patient who was wounded by a flying bomb in Belgium was perfectly all right until he realized that his family was in a part of this country exposed to flying-bomb attacks. He then became anxious and apprehensive. (445)

Air war broke out of the Oedipus complex of in-house research with one's own children at home alone. Schreber, Freud, Klein, Spielrein, and Piaget were among the many scientists whose research with human subjects often never left home. Powell's *Peeping Tom,* in which the serial killer protagonist photographs and kills the women who stand for the stepmother standing in for the mother whose death left him alone with a scientist father forever recording his own son's visible reactions of fear—and grief—under the uniform lab conditions of traumatic home life, gives the psychotic-mediatic rundown of this history of surveillance-survival research.

Although I take Powell's *Peeping Tom* as the inside view of, and mascot for, the busy intersection of the genealogies I am unpacking, there turns out to be a World War II specificity to the film's inception binding psychoanalysis to the making and breaking of codes. Leo Marks, who wrote the screenplay, came up with the idea for *Peeping Tom* while working in the offices and briefing rooms of the Code Department. His double interest (since childhood) in cryptography and psychoanalysis led him to contemplate the psychic conditions for an "indecipherable," a coded message from a spy on location behind the enemy front that, because it cannot be decoded at the British end, leads to the request for an often fatal act of retransmission. Two transmissions of the same message in a row, and the enemy knows where you live.

Whenever he was in charge, Marks delayed retransmission while he and his team of four hundred girls worked round the clock to break through to the message. In decoding an encoded message that's not up to code, it is not surprising that you would make recourse to the unconscious. One example standing in for countless others, but this particular one hailing from the Nazi German side of code cracking: "The solutions took a heavy toll of nervous energy. 'You must concentrate almost in a nervous trance when working on a code,' Miss Friedrichs recalled. 'It is not often done by conscious effort.' The solution often seems to crop up from the subconscious" (Kahn, 439).

Marks took the unconscious to the briefing room. At the same wartime, he wrote a report entitled "Cyphers, Signals, and Sex," in which he interrogated the unconscious motives behind mistakes made even by the most reliable coders or behind the failure to bury parachutes when the lives of agents dropping in behind enemy lines depended on the disposal service. Because of the dangers of capture and torture that they faced, and the risk of the enemy obtaining code and security check that was in this face, Marks tried to evaluate and communicate with the agents unconscious to unconscious. "Now, all I had to do during those exercises was to watch them, unobtrusively; to 'photograph' them when they were coding. . . . I became convinced that all cryptographers are basically voyeurs. And in my case, I was staring at these agents. I wanted to remember them—in case they sent an indecipherable message back—watching them, probing them, trying to *belong* to them. And so the idea of a voyeur was born. . . . So Peeping Tom wanted to photograph the impossible, the way I wanted to create the impossible—unbreakable codes" (Rodley, xiv). This last analogy seems in turn indecipherable. The clear text suggests that Marks and Mark Lewis (Peeping Tom) both sought through unconscious connection (within a melancholic retention span in Mark's case) to project a certain transparency onto figures who would precisely never slide into the unsafety zone of indecipherability. For Marks, it was all about getting around or across (trans) the parent with a legacy to bestow.

Marks's father owned a famous rare book shop where little Leo spent the first part of every Saturday learning the value of books. As a reward, he spent the second part of the day with his mother at the movies. When his father one morning showed him a first edition of Poe's *The Gold Bug,* Leo was just a few heartbeats away from getting the code bug. "I began reading *The Gold Bug,* and it was about codes—the first time I'd ever heard about codes. And when I looked at the back of the book, I found that Marks and Co. had put the cost of the book in code, which they did at the back of all their books. And as Dad had told me it cost £6.50, I was able to work out their code. I then decided that one day I wanted to understand codes and write a horror story, like Edgar Allan Poe" (x). He would reject the delegated run of his father's bookshop and accept the codes on the backs of the books. He needed to keep his relationship safe. What fascinated him so about codes was "the fact that so much depended on their being safe" (xi). Freud came right in and set a spell: "An interest in Freud was almost instinctive, in an only child destined to run a book shop, hooked on codes." The interest in Freud was instinctive in the father's heir who would turn down the inheritance given with his name. The price code, the bookstore's undercover means of maintaining the profit margin, was his way around the conflict. "The greatest code of all was the unconscious, and Freud appeared to have deciphered it" (xii).

Marks embraced the peep show in cinema (with his mother sitting next to him), cryptography, and psychoanalysis, but precisely as impossible desire for self-relation (Mark Lewis's ultimate fear photo was of himself, by himself). Thus the relationship to the father is underscored, even in its absence, as the opposite of impossible, namely, as necessary. What wasn't possible back then under wartime pressure was able to emerge in some other place and time in *Peeping Tom.* But just when you thought it was getting personal, Marks makes a determination that remains cryptic: "There was not time to explore, deal with, or acknowledge the unconscious resistance in a Resistance Movement agent" (xv).

Seventh illustration: Boy rushes to catch the train.

Eighth illustration: Three graves.

According to the many how-to histories compiled by and for the Anglo-American military psychological establishment, rediscoveries of energy and languistic contamination (or, respectively, of psychotic and neurotic transference) in the course of treating symptomatizing soldiers during World War II could even be made latently or inadvertently. More direct hits of discovery concern group or adolescent psychology. So-called shelter life tested new grounds for therapeutic intervention and support: "The feeling of being together seemed to enable people to withstand the conditions of intensive air raiding better than if they remained relatively isolated in small groups in their own homes" (96). But what groups release must also be recontained within the family system. R. D. Gillespie gets around the contradiction by treating the wartime access to adolescent populations as a separate issue: "The war may be a blessing in disguise to such children, whose problems may have to be dealt with at an earlier date than would otherwise have been the case" (159). Not every blessing must come in disguise. But the wound of evacuation, the origin of the science of adolescent psychology, which is neither addressed nor dressed up, becomes the opening up of the borderline in groups and in teens. In this concluding context, Gillespie singles out "security in family relationships" as "one of the most important factors for insurance against" the disturbances encountered both in the population of teen evacuees and down the military ranks (230). What the family provides at this juncture is a limit to sexual thoughts in groups—recreational or replicational sex—imposed by the thought, language, or energy controls of its reproducing and reducing plans for the future:

> A realistic type of education can contribute toward the rapprochement between the ideas of sex and the ideas about reproduction in the mind of the individual at an early age. At present in the adolescent these ideas are often so intellectually disconnected that they are about as distant emotionally as they were in the case of people so primitive that they did not even guess that a connection existed. (235)

Because her turn to acting out in theory and therapy acts out the relationship to her mother, Melanie Klein, which was peeping hot and hostile, Melitta Schmideberg really gets in to the act of wartime discovery or study of delinquency. On the margin or setting horizon of her 1948 *Children in Need,* Schmideberg finds that loss in generation gets handed down from the war's neuroticization of a father to his daughter and all her children:

> The main cause of her illness lay in the fact that her father, after being torpedoed in the last war, had developed a severe neurosis

> and had never received adequate treatment for it. Unless my patient receives treatment, her illness, may, in its turn, mar her marriage and make her children unhappy. (16)

The inheritance or orphanage of the war has left behind 500,000 neglected children:

> They are most likely to become neurotics, criminals, or, in general, unsatisfactory individuals, who are potentially as dangerous to the nation as 500,000 Nazi agents. (17)

But the war also introduced benefits. The air pressures of evacuation led to the establishment of special hostels for difficult children:

> We all know that the future of the nation depends on the welfare of the children. It was an unparalleled achievement that during the war we succeeded in maintaining and improving their health. Similar efforts and sacrifices are needed to achieve a higher level of mental health of the nation. The family should be helped before the child becomes maladjusted. (18)

Under the new air war conditions of subject or object access, psychoanalysis in Britain refocused its intrapsychic theory and therapy on a new brand of "object relations." These relations occupied or cathected, at least in their origin as theory, condemned sites of the first developments into which regression evacuated you when the shock of trauma took you all the way back, back down the line of segregation between (and that means inside) the good and bad identifications or objects of earliest childhood. It was the symptom of separation anxiety, the bouncing ball to follow when it came to the traumatic or war neuroses not only of evacuated children but also of soldiers, that first dropped the shadow of its trajectory across intrapsychic space, a war zone Freud had reserved for ego libido, but which the founders of the British object-relations school of psychoanalysis reorganized up and down the line of object rebound. The economic theory of libido was new and improved as the wartime school (or war economy) of relations with good and bad objects moving in place across one line of internal or projected segregation.

The matchmaking of libido that must score good or bad accelerates the violence or identification already under way on the way to the object. In other words, war may be the measure of excess in relations, but that means it's also a norm. That's why D. W. Winnicott admitted certain standards of object diplomacy not only for the objectives of war. In "Berlin Walls," the "line and the segregation of benign and persecutory elements" that Winnicott

Ninth illustration: Confessional.

finds inside "inner psychic reality" at large allow, before marching orders to war are all that's left to be given, for the projection or export of what's good along the track of idealization and of what's bad down the "disposal of dangerous or waste products." Whether in war or in the piece by piece negotiations of peacetime, the "individual with no line down the middle in the diagram of the person" does not exist except, perhaps, during the full half-life that the emergency relief organization of a "scapegoat mecha-

Tenth illustration: Church interior.

nism" or "a real or an imagined or a provoked or a delusional persecution" affords us.

The settings brought to us by air war imposed new therapeutic standards of broader applicability even inside analytic understanding. For object-relations analysts D. W. Winnicott, W. Ronald D. Fairbairn, and Wilfred R. Bion, the wartime stress was on the new distinction between rehabilitation and therapy with which they formed a compromise on the way to colonizing psychosis, perversion, and group psychology for psychoanalytic management. In his review of Fairbairn's work, Winnicott agrees that wartime conditions introduced management and occupation procedures that should be followed first before deep work can begin in cases of acute regression. The therapeutic dimension of management comes up again in his review of Anna Freud's reflections on her time done down at the Hampstead War Nurseries, in which Winnicott seconds her notion that the prospect of air attack had in fact mobilized in the staff and their charges the group resources of self-healing.

During the war, Winnicott specialized in the treatment of children and adolescents evacuated to the countryside, where they began giving grief to the locals. As documented in his 1947 "Residential Management as Treatment for Difficult Children: The Evolution of a Wartime Hostels Scheme," the authorities on location had already awarded the children individual psychological treatment while relocating them to facilities where they could stay in the meantime out of trouble. When Winnicott's team introduced at these facilities "residential management," it turned out that this intervention "in itself constituted a therapy" (89). The institution of child care in England, Winnicott reflects, was thus founded only under these emergency conditions (92).

The problem children of the air war either had no satisfactory home of their own or had already experienced the breakup or the danger of breakup of their home life. That's why a "primary home experience" is what is needed to lay down a foundation of mental health and thus a working relation to external reality. The creation of a therapeutic home or internal front at the hostels could install an inside-out blender and stabilizer for the child's destructive and reparative urges. But that's also what makes the maintenance of such an ambivalence-proof holding pattern so difficult: as they begin to get hope these children first increase their level of being difficult. But it's just a test that the therapist in attendance is hard-pressed to pass: "The experience subsequent to this state forms the essence of hostel therapeutics" (97). Winnicott's basic insight into the hostile auto-therapeutics of delinquent children and adolescents, who remain stuck on the series of before and after pictures to which the shudder or shutter of early deprivation (or, at the psychotic end, privation) reduced their lives of acting out, was thus set on wartime access. Beginning in these zones of evacuation where the fit of juvenile delinquency with group-therapeutic management was first recognized, Winnicott continued to see through the adolescent generation of hostility as the repeater attempt to get back at the present and get back to a past prior to the trauma of deprivation or loss, which is thus the acting-out teen's disowned but perpetual present tense and tension.

Under the conditions of total air war, open therapy was the password that introduced analysis into new frontiers of psychopathological and institutional resistance. And this brand-new access to patient populations or object relations brought about a shift inside psychoanalysis away from the allegorical split between theoretical shorthand and the transference toward total therapeutic functionalism that, even in theory, stays with the material relationality of the analytic setting. This mobilization of the therapeutic setting (of world war) hit the rock bottom line of the neurotic outbreak of internal war and worked regression close to the borderline, along which group protection takes over where negative transferences leave off. Problem children, juvenile delinquents, and incapacitated soldiers were all in the same kind of misrelation to a lost object that, as the symptom-building trauma center of group psychology, calls for a brand of therapy designed for group-level intervention. Group therapy was seen to open, isolate, and protect access ways for treatment even all the way down those one-way tracks of severe regression. Air pressure released the peer pressures of socialization, maintenance, and reeducation with which the group experience automatically comes complete, and which opened and kept open the transferential lines of communication otherwise psychotically foreclosed in one-on-one relations, including the Big One of individual therapy or psychoanalysis.

As documented in his 1943 "Intra-group Tensions in Therapy: Their Study as the Task of the Group," when Bion took charge of the training wing of a military psychiatric hospital during the war, he soon determined that if, in the treatment of the individual, neurosis is displayed as a problem of the individual, then in the treatment of groups it must be displayed as a group problem. Although the men were already in units and thus, he concluded, already in therapeutic formation, the greater discipline of the war effort, organized around a common danger and a common aim, was just what the doctor ordered.

> The common danger in the training wing was the existence of neurosis as a disability of the community. I was now back at my starting-point—the need, in the treatment of a group, for displaying neurosis as a problem of the group. But, thanks to my excursion into the problem of discipline, I had come back with two additions. Neurosis needs to be displayed as a danger to the group: and its display must somehow be made the common aim of the group. (678)

Group psychologization, Bion came to realize, was as much an intrapsychic fact of modern life as industrialization or technologization. Bion designed group therapy to catch and treat group-psychological symptoms (or symptoms of group psychologization) where they breed. Bion thus subsumes couplification (of sex, repression, and transference) as coming under group experience where it represents the "pairing assumption" of one-on-one relations, which alternates with the other two, "fight or flight" and "dependency." Indeed, psychoanalysis, when it has a single mind to promote and track the transference alone, is elaborating its own symptom of overidentification with only one out of three assumption groups.

> Freud was handicapped by having to deduce group situations from his study of the transference.... Indeed, it is in the group situation that we can most easily find the source of both the

Eleventh illustration: A fox comes around the corner of the house.

Twelfth illustration: Snowman on a pedestal. (In German, “pedestal” can also mean “toilet,” in slang.)

> prominence of sexual elements in psychoanalysis and the suspicions and accusations of the opponents of Freud that psychoanalysis was "sexual." (Bion, "Experiences IV," 226)

All symptoms are group symptoms, which "arise precisely from the nature of the group itself" (296). The emotional experiences patients introduce into group therapy as their own symptoms "are really derived from their being at one with other members of the emotionally reinforced group, and their conflict both with themselves and the group" (Bion, "Experiences V," 4). Group development is the goal of being in groups, but it's also the focus of greatest resistance (even the usual worries about the time, about when to begin, express resistance to this goal of development).

Bion's system not only puts the psychoanalytic couple in its place but also, through absorption and expansion of the transference, interrogates medical science's segregation of somatic from psychosomatic disorders. The group matrix extends to a phase of symptom formation "where physical and mental are undifferentiated" (9). From his treatment of soldiers who were no longer able to be at ease, Bion first picked up the application for monitoring all aspects of what he sets in our type-face as "dis-ease." By getting with his system, one can thus exercise vigilance precisely where personality changes prior to the appearance of tubercular lesions, for example, traditionally led "to suggestion that the patient was malingering" (10). The Bionic system is modeled ultimately on the evidence of war neurosis: the symptoms of shell shock, which pop up and linger or malinger in zones of nondifferentiation between the physical and psychical, turn on receptions of real trauma (or disease) that were all along staying tuned to primal time programming. The intrapsychic dimension is back where you least expect to find it: in the psychology of groups, which Bion first encountered when he tracked the ultimate location of shell shock's absorption of disturbance, and then continued to follow out throughout an era he saw as characterized by a new double body of knowledge: the "mechanics" involved in flying airplanes and in managing groups.

Bloody Freud

> In her paper, "Mourning and Its Relation to Manic-Depressive States," Mrs. Klein says: "In mourning as well as in infantile development, inner security comes about not by a straightforward movement but in waves." Her use of metaphor here for the mysterious unseen movement of the libido is surely a "live" one.
>
> —ELLA FREEMAN SHARPE, "FROM *KING LEAR* TO *THE TEMPEST*"

Lewis Yealland specialized in treating long-standing functional speech disorders during World War I. The patients that were sent to him as the last resort were already considered chronic cases; they were, moreover, veterans by that time of all the psychological interventions mobilized for the war, from "hypnotism, psychoanalysis" to outright "electricity." "It must be remembered, however, that faradism employed without suggestion and persistence in otherwise intractable cases will fail to produce recovery" (3). Yealland's suggestion is to exhort his patients superegoically in one-on-one group-psychological treatment, punctuating crowd appeals to the heroic ego over the cowardly one with a jab of faradic current to the numb body parts of speech.

> He became quite excited and said, "Doctor, doctor, I am champion," to which I replied, "You are a hero." He then said, "Why did they not send me to you nine months ago?" With a view to impressing on him the certainty of the cure being permanent, I answered him by saying, "Such a condition as yours could not have been cured nine months ago. You have had time to rest, your general condition had localized itself in your voice, which could not have been treated so quickly had you come here earlier."
>
> This hitherto intractable case received four hours' continuous treatment. (15)

It's psychological warfare, but based, let's face it, on transference, identification, and the intrapsychic model of conflict between the ego and its double.

In 1939 Frederick Dillon gave a completely up to the standard reception of World War I neuroses based on the laboratory findings of an inside job: "The war neuroses could actually be observed in their development" (64). In treating the neurotics at the special center, an "adaptation standard" was upheld that was the external measure of the ongoing inoculation going down against the overwhelming conflicts to which a soldier must return, turning it back on, on the inside:

> This did not imply the abolition of conflict in his mind, for that was impossible, but the building up of a state of controlled adjustment to active war conditions which, in itself, at basis, was actually a state of conflict. . . . This power of adaptation will probably be put to a greater test in the next war, and if it is realized in official circles that there is a breaking-point for every individual, arrangements may be made to give more frequent relief from the continued strain that such adjustment implies. The fact that civilians will be involved will make the whole question a much larger and more complex one. (66)

Writing up at the close of World War II all the contributions British psychiatry was now able to make "as the result of its opportunities in wartime" (11), J. R. Rees looks forward to a time when war neurosis would not be such a widespread threat, since hand-to-hand combat will have been completely replaced by "aerial torpedoes" (113); but as he writes, he still checks in with the present spread of total or media war:

> Appropriately, as I write this my room shakes, for a ton of explosives in one of our "flying bombs" has gone off nearby. We cannot forget that the civilian population is in the war. Just as the civilian has had many similar adjustments to make, so the soldier finds his anxieties increased by the very fact that his family at home has to suffer these difficulties and stresses—this apart from and in addition to his own inner separation anxiety. (16)

The dotted or broken line of separation anxiety (the object-relations school exclusive) was, Rees too admits, the only news on war neurosis that World War II theory and therapy had come up with in Britain. Although the military did not apply itself following World War I to yesterday's new knowledge about war neurosis (including prophylaxis, remedy, and production), the medical profession, and through it the country as a whole, had benefited "from that mass experience of neurosis" (30). For example: "In Great Britain child psychiatry grew out of this quickened interest in the neuroses after the last war" (31). In turn, "growing interest in the sociological and psychological aspects" of psychiatric work is owed to children's psychiatric clinics (32). At the same time, mental illnesses were coming to be "regarded not merely as individual matters but rather as an expression of group maladjustment" (32). The service remains the place for the most thoroughgoing investigation of these "sociological and psychological aspects of the group" (52).

Military psychology, Rees reports, took an at once psychoanalytic and evolutionary turn over the new issue of selection (which emerged as a way to keep down the incidence of war neurosis by selecting out those so inclined). To this end, British army intelligence testing was first modeled after the tests already in place for defective children (57). Whereas Rees sees U.S. military psychology as having been in the lead in time for World War I, in the meantime "Germany borrowed much of [the U.S.] . . . last war work and built on it the psychological department with its elaborate selection techniques, out of which grew the still wider department of psychological warfare" (34). A certain British officer instrumental in setting up special selection boards "had, before the war, the distinction of being the only serving British officer who had seen the German army officer selection work in progress. On his return to this country he had pressed the authorities to start some similar work in the British army, but the suggestion was turned down and he was told, 'X you're the bloody Freud of the British Army'" (67). But that was one bad air day. By the time all of Europe was coming up for airwaves and copping the high of total war, even the British military, like the Freudian German one, was shooting up with "battle inoculations" that fortified soldiers and civilians alike against the mediatic side effects of the war. These were the inoculations, in sum, of greater psychoanalysis.

> War is an affair of morale and all weapons have, or should have, a morale-destroying effect: the dive bomber, the tank, the mortar, and, indeed, most weapons affect morale more than they take life. In training we want to debunk the noise and frightfulness of these weapons so far as it is safe and wise to do that. (81)

Bion the Pleasure Principle

From World War I onward, Freud turned to the pathogenic intersections of the couple and the group. But as Bion realized right away, group psychology is not on its own only a symptom of disturbances within the formation of the couple but is, instead, the modern habitat within which we find ourselves acting and interacting symptomatically or, better yet, relatively free of symptoms.

Another way to put it is that psychoanalysis stays with our inner other world and pushes us to the borderline where regression meets ego strength. But beginning in the 1920s, Freud came to realize that it is our group formations that are already taking a walk on the borderline. It is at this group level that interventions must be made into the otherwise uncontainable, unmanageable emotional turbulence of the twentieth century's encounter with the other. The problem children and juvenile delinquents who were under therapeutic supervision at the centers and homes to which they were evacuated out from under the air war proved to be in the same kind of misrelation to a lost object, in the same mode of separation anxiety, as were the unhappy troopers of war neurosis (the sole subject population in the World War I research lab). A new brand or outreach of psychoanalytic therapy was called for, one tuned to the group frequency of running commentary or interference. Air pressure released the peer pressurizations of reeducation, maintenance, and socialization with which the group experience automatically comes complete. Group therapy, the object-relations analysts discovered on Emergency Island, could open and keep open the transferential lines of communication even or especially within the psychotic foreclosure of the one on one, including the Big One of individual therapy or psychoanalysis.

Bion's recontextualization helped Freud out: sexualization or repression of the one on one (both in fact and in theory) must be subsumed by group experience as one of three basic assumptions: this guilty assumption Bion calls "pairing," which, he says, alternates with the other two, "fight or flight" and "dependency." With the basic assumption of dependency in the ascendant, members of a group believe "that if they were not led by a madman, then they ought to be" (Bion, "Experiences VI," 399). In other words, the psychotic or genius on whom this group depends is also a dependent. "Perhaps it is an unconscious recognition that the baby, if only we had not become accustomed to associating its behavior with its physical development, is really insane" (399).

The basic assumption group of pairing, which is where transference, psychoanalysis, and sexual elements belong, responds with anxiety to the prospect of group and individual ending up "subservient to the unborn genius" (Bion, "Experiences VII," 227). The two groups Freud recognized, army and church, cover only the other two basic assumptions. Pairing, the native habitat of psychoanalysis, was another self- or group portrait that was not admitted into the first analytic reflections on group psychology. In its single-minded promotion of the transference, psychoanalysis is but a side effect or symptom of overidentification with only one out of three assumption groups. That groups are automatically out to preserve themselves is the insight or instinct that keeps group experience flipping (out) through these three major networks. Bion describes it as "a convenient hypothesis for explaining why the group, which shows itself intolerant of activities that are not forms of fight or flight, will, nevertheless, tolerate the formation of pairs. Reproduction is recognized as equal with fight or flight in the preservation of a group" (Bion, "Experiences III," 15). But that's also why Bion must rework psychoanalytic theory around the expanding emotional field of these basic assumption groups. It is not, for example, a case simply of "group transference" when the group starts working the network of changes in position or assumption: "It becomes possible to use these changes, to the benefit of one's clinical observation, in much the same kind of way as scientists in other fields are able to use changes of wavelength to obtain different photographic appearances of the object they wish to study" (21).

Since its first broadcasts across the heir waves, psychoanalysis has been submitted over and again to streamlining translation into the terms and time frames of mass modernism (in the fifties and sixties in America, new improvements by Eric Berne, Albert Ellis, and Fritz Perls were late arrivals of Nazi German and British efforts to control or remetabolize the transference). Beginning with Melanie Klein, we can observe an escalation of transference interpretations that aim to access energy reserves through literal translations or object relations. With Bion, object relations are replaced by group relations. Thus a group member who "finds himself persecuted by internal objects" has in fact left himself open to "the emotional movements of the group of which he is a member" (Bion, "Experiences IV," 302), which he registers as internal persecution by *the* bad object—the group (Bion, "Experiences VI," 395).

Bion's new "test field" owes everything to its relocation with respect to the transference. And just as the transference is not limited to the analytic session where it becomes demonstrable, so being-in-groups is not a

Thirteenth illustration: Sister buried.

Fourteenth illustration: House and family with many children. (In German, "Haus mit kinderreicher Familie.")

condition produced by the formation of the therapeutic group or even of the masses at large:

> It is necessary for an analysand to come to a psychoanalyst in order that the transference relationship should be rendered demonstrable. In the same way it is important that the group should come together so that the characteristics of the group and the individual in it should be demonstrable. (Bion, "Experiences VII," 224)

The Father's Daughter

The Ego and the Mechanisms of Defense, the study that was Anna Freud's metabolization of the double time (air war and heir war) of World War II, occupies "the ego as the seat of observation" (title of chapter 1). She sets up in her father's footnotes an ego psychology that flexes a complexity (through the working of identification) comparable to what object-relations analysis had to offer. Ego psychology is not, for example, about the ego being in control. "The various measures of defense are not entirely the work of the ego. Insofar as the instinctual processes themselves are modified, use is made of the peculiar properties of instinct. . . . We may conjecture that a defense is proof against attack, only if it is built upon this twofold basis—on the one hand the ego and, on the other, the essential nature of instinctual processes" (192). The ego's sphere of influence is at best a balancing act "between the id, the superego and the forces of the outside world" (193).

Without ever mentioning Melanie Klein by name, Freud does, however, cover the differences between ego psychology and object relations with the twist-off comment that dismisses the import of the disagreement in the face of an obscure concern that no one had as yet successfully illuminated. "According to the theory of the English school of analysis, introjection and projection, which in our view should be assigned to the period after the ego has been differentiated from the outside world, are the very processes by which the structure of the ego is developed and but for which differentiation would never have taken place. These differences of opinion bring home to us the fact that the chronology of psychic processes is still one of the most obscure fields of analytical theory" (57). In the original setting of its introduction, Anna Freud's notion of "identification with the aggressor" (which has ever since been on relocation in interpretations of social or interpersonal relations and events) is on its competitive edge with the English school's new notion of projective identification. Together with the "altruistic defense" (whereby someone fights for the rights of another because in his own case he had to forgo these same rights), identification with the aggressor supplements the transference relations without, however, canceling the analyst's countertransferential responsibilities.

Identification with the aggressor (or with the aggression), which is fundamental to superego development, is a "particular combination of introjection and projection" that "can be regarded as normal only so long as the ego employs it in his conflict with authority, i.e. in its efforts to deal with anxiety-objects. It is a defensive process which ceases to be innocuous and becomes pathological when it is carried over into the love-life" (129). Where the love life is, there transference complications will be too. But first a slice of love life: "When a husband displaces onto his wife his own impulses to be unfaithful and then reproaches her passionately with unfaithfulness, he is really introjecting her reproaches and projecting part of his own id. His intention, however, is to protect himself not against aggression from without but against the shattering of his positive libidinal fixation to her by disturbing forces from within" (130). The result is a husband's obsessional fixation on his wife in the form of projected jealousy. Paranoid delusions result when, in defense against homosexual impulses, reversal gets added to the mechanisms in jealous love. In sum, "the ego's choice of a billet for its own unconscious impulses is determined by the material at hand" (130). But while in theory, as illustrated earlier, "analysis of the process of 'identification with the aggressor' assists us to differentiate the various modes in which the specific defense mechanisms are employed," "in practice, it enables us to distinguish in the transference anxiety-attacks from outbursts of aggression" (130–31).

Anna Freud's strategy in this book is to eclecticize and reunify as offshoots of her father's science (as all in the family) the divisions into left and right wings that split psychoanalysis going into World War II. References to Wilhelm Reich and R. Laforgue are diplomatic ties in the race to fortify analysis in the asides largely occupied by Sigmund Freud (or, as his daughter refers to him, "Freud").

Laforgue's career in Nazi Europe remains up in the air of je ne sais quoi. But the rumor milling about during the war had him playing happy mediator between French analysis and Nazi German psychotherapy. Anna Freud drops the footnote to Laforgue's notion of scotomization (with the neutral call to compare their notions, which can refer to influence or could imply that the reader should heed her second opinion) from the psychotic end of her revalorization of denial: "In psychotic delusions, for instance, a piece of wood may represent love-objects which the patient longs for or has lost, just as children use similar things to protect them" (97). When her father schlepped Laforgue through his 1927 essay on fetishism, scotomization, a mechanism of "not seeing," comes up only to be knocked down in the new frontier zone Freud was opening up through dissociation, the borderline where what you see is what you get *and* forget, double *and* nothing. "It turned out that the two young men had no more 'scotomized' their father's death than a fetishist does the castration of women. It was only one current in their mental life that had not recognized their father's death;

there was another current which took full account of that fact" (*SE,* 21:156). But Freud's intervention with regard to scotomization is overdetermined. It is not that dissociation enjoys a better fit with fetishism than Laforgue's notion, which comes to us from the context of psychosis research. Dissociation also requires a retrofitting of the analytic encounter with psychosis at large. In the footnote to his first reference to scotomization, Freud argues that by his very use of Laforgue's term in his text, he has misused it: "It is clear... that 'scotomization' is a term which derives from descriptions of dementia praecox, which does not arise from a carrying-over of psychoanalytic concepts to the psychoses and which has no application to developmental processes or to the formation of neuroses" (*SE,* 21:153 n. 2). In other words: do not use this term. While kept largely between the lines, Laforgue's dismissal from psychoanslysis seems, just the same, as finally reckoned as Reich's exile in 1933 proved to be. Anna Freud brings up the "armor-plating of character (*Charakterpanzerung,* as Reich calls it)" in the course of reviewing Reich's "remarks on 'the consistent analysis of resistance'" in an article published two years after his expulsion from international psychoanalysis (35). The notion of character armor may owe to the father's daughter its confused status as part of the original legacy (to this day) in the receiving area of Freud's science.

Whereas her father called repression the oldest piece of psychoanalysis, Anna Freud makes a case for considering defense as "the earliest representation of the dynamic standpoint in psychoanalytic theory" (45). True, repression was introduced to replace the term "defense." But their undetermined relationship led just the same to Freud's return in 1926 to the old concept of defense as general designation, while keeping repression specific to one type of defense, like projection or identification. OK, but let's keep in mind that she would also have us believe that with his id concept, her father "replaced" the so-called system unconscious.

The defense defense allows Freud to theorize an ego psychology that borders on and supersedes object relations while maintaining relations with drive theory. What is recognizable in California today as "OR" (one of the accepted theoretical perspectives candidates for a license in Marriage Family Therapy may choose for their oral examination) dropped drive down inside generation gaps a long time ago. But what became true of her followers was not yet unequivocally true of Klein, whose theory was still death driven. However, for example in "Some Psychological Considerations: A Comment," Klein in 1942 reads the example of the enemy along lines of personalized relation that do not designate a drive. In analyzing the enemy, moreover, the relation to what is Nazi in name also includes, between the lines, dismissal of a (received) notion, like "identification with the aggressor," that functions pathologically as the one-sided externalization of relationality.

> An instance of distortion, or rather reversal, of the primary pattern which at once presents itself to the mind is the Nazi attitude. Here the aggressor and aggression have become loved and admired objects, and the attacked objects have turned into evil and must therefore be exterminated. The explanation of such a reversal can be found in the early unconscious relation towards the first persons attacked or injured in phantasy. The object then turns into a potential persecutor, because retaliation by the same means by which it had been harmed is feared. The injured person is, however, also identical with the loved person, who should be protected and restored. Excessive early fears tend to increase the conception of the injured object as an enemy, and if this is the outcome, hatred will prevail in its struggle against love; moreover, the remaining love may be distributed in the particular ways which lead to the depravation of the superego. (322)

There is something to be said (in a word) for the staying power of drive or *Trieb,* running on identification and group psychology, and the word on the minds of practitioners in the outer reaches of greater psychoanalysis (like Klaus Conrad on the Russian front), which is really the same word, which gets spun around a metathesis when doing prefix duty, namely *Treib-*, as in *Treibstoff,* which means "fuel." In addition to all the externalities of lack that *Treibstoff* or *"Triebstoff"* must overcome in total conflict, it also refers to the fuel lines (instinct with repetition) of melancholic identification, where loss gets acknowledged, I mean unacknowledged (same difference). The object relation in the fuel-driven psychonomy is always at a loss and thus cuts its loss with identification.

Anna Freud depolemicizes her entry into the field by blaming it all on "theoretical discussions," which are necessary but "tedious and detailed," as she just demonstrated "in the last chapter" (30). She continues to disarm us as she plods along. But by the end, she has taken us by surprise. She fills in (for her father) psychoanalysis's missing entry on teen psychology. Her previous elaborations of differences among defense, repression, and denial carry conviction in the closing sentences handed down on adolescence. In the company of her analytic women colleagues, including less well known Brits but also Helene Deutsch, Freud builds bridges between infancy and adolescence.

> In contrast to academic psychology, psychoanalysis has hitherto shown remarkably little inclination to concentrate on the psychological problems of puberty, although in other connections it has very often taken contradictions in the psychic life as a starting-point for its investigations. If we except a few works in which the foundation for a study of puberty has been laid, we may say that analytical writers have rather neglected that period and devoted more attention to other stages of development. The reason is obvious. Psychoanalysis does not share the view that the sexual life of human beings begins at puberty. . . . It is in the early infantile sexual period and not at puberty that the crucial steps in development are taken, the important pre-genital phases of sexual organization are passed through, the different component instincts are developed and brought into action and normality or abnormality of the individual, his capacity or incapacity for love, are determined. (151)

But to this end infancy must be understood in the terms of "endopsychical conflict," the internal psychic forum for the external world founded "in the shape of objective anxiety," "a kind of 'fore-pain'" that is the superego's "precursor" (and curser) (155). The sexplosion of puberty strikes up its crescendo between the fault lines of this early conflict. Typical by-products include "the asceticism and the intellectuality of adolescence" (167).

Self-isolation is not the only trend to be settled. If asceticism can already be seen as the measure of the sexual force that is with the teen, then what immeasurable pleasure must be attributed to sexual acting out in adolescence?

> Many new attachments take the place of the repressed fixations to the love-objects of childhood. . . . While they last, these love-relations are passionate and exclusive, but they are of short duration. Persons are selected as objects and abandoned without consideration for their feelings, and others are chosen in their place. The abandoned objects are quickly and completely forgotten, but the form of the relation to them is preserved down to the minutest detail and is generally reproduced, with an exactness which almost suggests obsession, in the relation to the new object.
>
> Besides this striking faithlessness to the love-object we note another peculiarity of the object-relations at puberty. The adolescent does not aim so much at possessing himself of the object in the ordinary physical sense of the term as at assimilating himself as much as possible to the person who at the moment occupies the central place in his affection. (183–84)

In this respect, teens (like melancholy babies) "resemble a type of patient, described by Helene Deutsch as being on the borderline between neurosis and psychosis.

Following World War II, Anna Freud's science focuses on adolescent or group psychology along the borderline it shares with psychosis. This is what is meant by ego psychology. This teen psychology takes out its life insurance policy with death drive, thereby driving object relations back home, where they occupy the backseat to ego identifications in group format. What we encounter in all these traits of adolescence is the "antagonism to instinct" that Anna Freud views as the bottom line of the psyche. With the return of infantile sexualization, all the teen's family members are suddenly provocatively addressed. At that point antagonism to instinct is the only defense available. "The suspicion and asceticism of the ego are primarily directed against the subject's fixation to all the love-objects of his childhood. . . . From this time on, he will live with the members of his family as though with strangers" (182). Once he hits this bottom line, the teen walks the borderline inside psychosis:

> The rupture of former relations, antagonism to the instincts and asceticism all have the effect of delibidinizing the external world. The adolescent is in danger of withdrawing his object-libido from those around him and concentrating it upon himself; just as he has regressed within the ego, so he may regress in his libidinal life from object-love to narcissism. He escapes this danger by convulsive efforts to make contact once more with external objects, even if it can only be by way of his narcissism, that is, through a series of identifications. According to this view, the passionate object-relations of adolescence represent attempts at recovery—another respect in which they resemble the state of psychotic patients whose disease is about to take one of its periodic turns for the worse. (187–88)

But can we really still consider these acts of teen passion as "object relations"? "These passionate and evanescent love-fixations are not object-relations at all. . . . They are identifications of the most primitive kind, such as we meet with in our study of early infantile development, before any object-love exists. Thus the fickleness characteristic of puberty does not indicate any inner change in the love or convictions of the individual but rather a loss of personality in consequence of a change in identification" (185–86). In other words, the introduction of adolescence into psychoanalytic theory restores ambivalence to its primal scene in a drive setting beyond or before object relations:

Long ago the analytical study of the neuroses suggested that there is in human nature a disposition to repudiate certain instincts, in particular the sexual instincts, indiscriminately and independently of individual experience. This disposition appears to be a phylogenetic inheritance, a kind of deposit accumulated from acts of repression practiced by many generations and merely continued, not initiated, by individuals. To describe this dual attitude of mankind towards the sexual life—constitutional aversion coupled with passionate desire—Bleuler coined the term *ambivalence.*

During the calmer periods of life, the ego's primary antagonism to instinct—its dread of the strength of the instincts, as we have called it—is not much more than a theoretical concept. We conjecture that it is invariably the basis of instinctual anxiety, but for the observer it tends to be obscured by the much more conspicuous and obtrusive phenomena arising from objective anxiety or anxiety of conscience and resulting from shocks to which the individual has been exposed.

Probably the increase in the quantity of instinct at puberty and other periods in life when there is a sudden accession of instinctual energy accentuates this primary antagonism to such a degree that it becomes a specific and active defense-mechanism. If this is so, the asceticism of puberty must be interpreted not as a series of repressive activities, qualitatively conditioned, but simply as a manifestation of the innate hostility between the ego and the instincts, which is indiscriminate, primary and primitive. (171–72)

Breaking Up and Making Up

> "Good" and "Bad" are the flags under which nationalisms and ideologies march, gaining recruits through a contagious belief in a good object. "Good" and "Bad" are the magical words of propaganda by which mass psychology is manipulated. . . .
>
> It seems paradoxical that psychoanalysis which aims at making individuals capable of resistance to mass psychology is driven to use phrases that are its mouthpieces.
>
> It should not be beyond the power of a scientific society to find terms less appealing to the unconscious superego. The difficulty perhaps is that "satisfying," "frustrating," while adequate in meaning are inadequate in conveying the feeling of absolution. . . .
>
> If we cannot find more discriminating epithets may it not be because of the incantation power through sheer repetition of "The Good Object," "The Bad Object" and proof enough of the common unconscious belief in white and black magic?
>
> —ELLA FREEMAN SHARPE, "A NOTE ON 'THE MAGIC OF NAMES'"

Even though by 1946 the British Society, following Anna Freud's lead, was reorganizing itself around the split ends of the "controversy," the changes that the air war had introduced into both Anna Freud's view of infant-mother relations and the Kleinian model (followed out from that wartime on in the work of object-relations analysts Bion, Fairbairn, and Winnicott) gave the bigger picture of reunified eclecticism. By air war time, Anna Freud came around to admitting some of the earliest inroads made by identification or unconscious fantasy that she had earlier and otherwise rejected outright in Melanie Klein's thought (which, in turn and by proxy, stood in for a certain unacceptable difference at once between and inside her works and those of her father). Her added insistence t\hat one did not witness the origin or even a more pure form of the mechanisms of projection and identification when watching them as they were happening in the young children one was now able to observe (for example, while they played with dolls) confirmed a reservation that was as Freudian (and that means just as Kleinian, too) as any that Klein was making at the time.

Klein's reorganization of drive theory around therapy with object relations in turn took a backseat to drive when Bion readjusted object relations as subsumable by group relations. World War II was the blender in which, from the perspective of medical understanding or following of models,

Freudian emphasis on sublimation and the homeboy interest in acting out (destruction and restitution) continued to come together over those figures pulled up from the deepest trenches of untreatability who were superimposable onto the war neurotic, whose proclaimed cure remained the primal myth of greater psychoanalysis.

Klein's stress on the early intake of objects (in unconscious-fantasy form) and Freud's turn to the internal and eternal object relations constituting group psychology had exerted an influence that might have been filed away with all the other new improvements one kept in mind while seeing patients had the wartime lab space not provided evidence that "most opportunely confirmed on the grand scale" what Fairbairn had been observing in his private practice just a heartbeat before war broke out:

> Military cases are specially illuminating for two reasons: (1) because in such cases phenomena detected in a narrow field under the high-power lens of the analytical microscope may be observed in a wide field under a less powerful lens, (2) because under military conditions in wartime large numbers of individuals may be observed in an "experimental" state of artificial separation from their objects. ("Repression," 79–80 n. 1)

What Fairbairn saw confirmed was that infantile modes of dependency already getting in the way in early childhood hit the rock bottom line that the neurotic outbreak of internal war, which was making its break out of separation anxiety, always also runs up against.

> My experience of military cases leaves me in no doubt that the chief predisposing factor in determining the breakdown of a soldier (or for that matter a sailor or an airman) is infantile dependence upon his objects. At the same time my experience leaves me in equally little doubt that the most distinctive feature of military breakdowns is separation-anxiety. (79–80)

That's why the war neurotic's "compulsion to return home" means more than just desert ("War Neuroses," 271). Soldiers who have the dependency problem find "great difficulty either in establishing or in maintaining a reliable relationship with the military group on a basis of identification" (278). In other words: "the problem of the 'war neuroses' is not so much a problem of psychotherapy as a problem of group morale" ("Repression," 81).

Freud's *Group Psychology and the Analysis of the Ego,* the direct hit worldwide with all the military psychology experts, raised the superego as the factor to be accounted for in the heightening of group morale. The morale

Fifteenth illustration: Hearse.

Sixteenth illustration: Night of dying. (In German, “Sterbenacht.”)

of this story also covers defense against bad objects (which is the superego's other function, Fairbairn emphasizes). When the authority of the superego collapses in group format, the war neurotic, who coproduced the lapsus, faces the "release of bad objects" and doubles over with "acute anxiety" (Fairbairn, "Repression," 81). A "definite disintegration of the mental structure of conscience (a collapse of the authority of the superego)" issues the unhappy trooper's leave of his senses ("War Neuroses," 286). He gets off at the "infantile emotional level," where he no longer gives his superiors unchecked credit for being trans-parent representatives of the good parent-objects who feel real good inside you when you're good. Instead, on the projective rebound of peristaltically reversed identification, the officers are bad parental figures who lose no love over the private's part in the organization.

That's why war neurotics are so readily deeply injured by the seeming refusal of the military authorities to promote them on fast-forward march (286–87). For both the British and Nazi German psychiatrists in attendance, the first-stage alert was on during the war when a soldier's grievance was, even the first time around, phrased and phased in that stereotypically wound-up, wounded, never-to-be-satisfied way. This brand of war neurosis or, really, borderline psychosis has been brought to us by the superego that has been worn down by the devaluation of group bonds. In the 1946 issue of the *Bulletin of the Menninger Clinic,* Bion reported to American psychiatry on "The Leaderless Group Project" developed in Britain during the war in the course of rendering the selection process efficient and productive (Bion was originally called in by the War Office because the supply and quality of new officers, it was believed, had fallen off). Bion then quickly transferred his group model to the psychiatric hospital, where he encouraged war neurotics to heal or select themselves for one group effort and, thus, by extension, for the greater effort at the front. "The flight from neurotic disorder had to be stopped; as in a regiment, morale had to be raised to a point where the real enemy could be faced. The establishment of morale is of course hardly a prerequisite of treatment; it is treatment, or a part of it" (79). The different takes on the military-evolutionary procedure of selection read out like the divergent plotlines of the two propaganda cinemas of World War II. Right down to Bion's concluding stiff upper quip: "Outside Nazi Germany psychiatrists are not likely to be shot for doing their job, though of course they can be removed from their posts. Any psychiatrist who attempts to make groups study their own tensions, as a therapeutic occupation, is in today's conditions stopping a retreat and may as a result be shot at. But he will lose some of his feeling of guilt" (81). At the point of projection, the two sides of the psychotherapeutic selection contest do, after all, overlap.

Bion went on to invent group therapy at this war time to return disturbed soldiers to the support-group psychology from which they were in withdrawal reaction and thus get back the pathogenic deposit of their identifications. The war neurotic lacks what the young child hasn't got: stable relations of service to the superego (and that means to the group effort). What Bion called "psychiatric disinheritedness" (the name he gave the most prevalent group-psychological symptom that his war neurotics presented to him) runs right up against a boredom line we give ourselves to divert attention from the unconscious forces that are with the interpersonal, the intrapsychic, and the group relation.

By 1948, in "Psychiatry at a Time of Crisis," Bion concluded that group formation or psychologization was now as big a part of modern life as industrialization or technologization. "Forty years ago the channel had not been flown; twenty years ago broadcasting was in its infancy. It is probably true to say that man is more skilled in the mechanics of handling anything from an aeroplane to a mass of his fellow-men than he was forty years ago" (81). Left unattended, group psychology goes the way we like it to when faced with growing leisure time in which to ponder intra- and interpersonal areas of conflict, growth, impasse. Not really wanting to look in that direction, we seek out the diversions and diversifications of the unconscious group, grope, response. Indeed, the psy fi futures that our technological innovations open up remain at the same time stuck on the regressions of narcissistic neurosis.

> Technical developments have a way of repeating early situations. Thus modern methods of travel repeat the problem and stimuli presented by first attempts to walk; modern methods of communication repeat on a more complex level the problems of infant speech. Modern weapons of destruction have produced a repetition of problems of infantile destructiveness. (84)

The downward spiral that first opened up for inspection through Freud's close encounter with war neurosis charts a regression racetrack through technologization or group psychologization on which autoanalysis (in group format) must beat psychotic breakdown to the other side of the finish borderline.

By working the splits and denials that are what's happening in in-group perceptions, Bion soon found himself where auto-analysis leaves you: on the borderline inside psychosis. "The understanding of the emotional life of the group . . . is only comprehensible in terms of psychotic mechanisms"

Seventeenth illustration: Mother excuses boy in school.

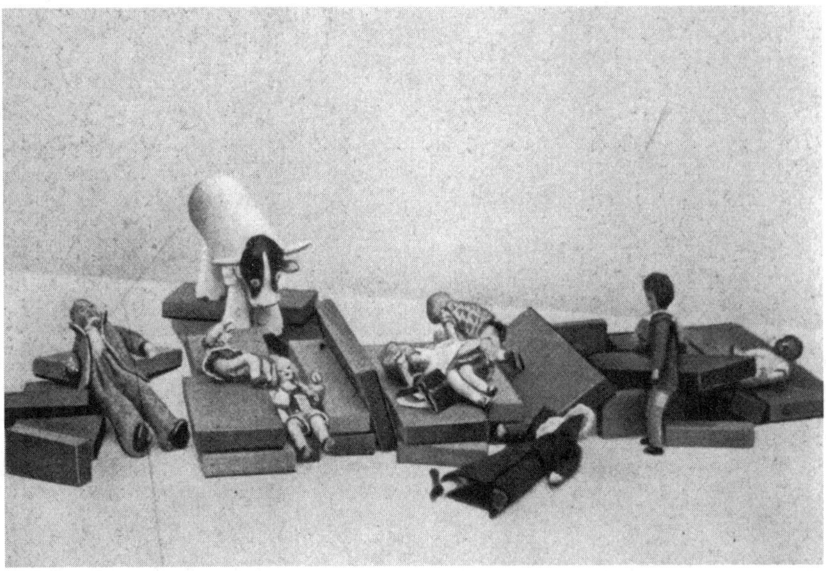

Eighteenth illustration: Bomb (cow) comes.

("Emotional Turbulence," 3). Bion would indeed translate the "entity familiar to members of the medical, psychiatric, and psychoanalytic professions under the usually adequate designation 'borderline patient' or 'borderline psychotic'" as the "emotional turbulence" of early childhood. It's the kind of "upheaval" that cannot be "limited by the physiological boundaries" of individuals because it has already crashed with all the occupants on board onto an "emotional field." The internal child that cases of war neurosis first presented to Bion took a walk on this borderline of emotional turbulence and bailed out over the zone of psychotic mechanisms that group therapy alone could re-cover for community life.

Project Group Identification

In his contribution to the 1940 collection *The Neuroses in War,* Bion's analytic guide to propaganda gives lines to a difference between Allied and German adminstrations that are notches above and below the belt of one intrapsychic development. Let impartiality be our guide Britannia (rather than dictatorial manipulation) in this new field of suggestion:

> Some means must be found by which morale must be maintained without in any way dictating the ends to which the individual uses the capacities which he is helped to retain in efficiency. In theory this means that for those who are concerned with the maintenance of psychological health the first step is to deal successfully with the "Hitlerism" in themselves. ("War of Nerves," 194–95)

Within this scenario of his double devising, Bion has already demonstrated the inside view he first ascribes to the enemy's approach:

> More precisely, one of the aims of such an attack would appear to be to force an opponent to be distracted from reality dangers by fear and guilt arising from phantasies in his own mind.... While he is internally distracted by infantile emotions, his enemy hopes to be able to carry out an attack in objective fact. (181)

But by making all the undercover moves in his promotion of the fantasy of an internal difference between Allied and Axis propaganda as technology or group psychology, he leaves open an unprotected direct access for reality strikes. This move, then, which at least at some level thus duplicated the designing of propaganda ascribed to Nazi Germany, is a demo of the therapeutic side benefit that propaganda brings to its own side:

> But attention must be drawn to the "war of nerves" as an attempt to combine in itself both an aggressive movement towards an enemy and a therapeutic movement in the aggressor. (181–82)

> We suggest that the object of the combatant is to exploit unconscious phantasies, both in the enemy and in himself, in such a way that the enemy is discomfited and he himself benefited. (180)

Bion's performance writes out two wartime alterations of analysis: its "procedure," the time, the time for transference, it takes and sets aside; and the group-size transference setting: "Now that war is upon us, the procedure of analysis is ruled out for rapid large-scale measures" (192). Both alterations or alternations are contained in the Kleinian self-destruct model of, and intervention in, the mutual identification that comes in groups—projective identification—which Bion next turns on the therapeutic reception of war neurosis:

> [The public] might then take a more tolerant attitude towards the war neurosis patient, who often behaves in a way which is unconsciously intended to find an outlet for his deep guilt feelings by producing a condemnatory attitude in his fellows. Similarly, they may regard more tolerantly the anxieties and stresses which they fear in themselves. (186)

In My Side

In "The Treatment of Psychoneurosis in the British Army," H. A. Thorner summarizes in 1946 the World War II therapeutic encounter with war neurosis from the analytic point of view (one incompatible, Thorner concludes, with group therapy): "An account of the treatment of psychoneurotics under military conditions in the Army may serve a useful purpose at this time of transition. Under new and fast-changing social conditions similar methods may come to be applied to the civilian population. It is essential to get a clear idea as to what has been achieved, and what is beyond those methods which I shall call 'manipulative psychotherapy'"(52). This brand of therapeutic eclecticism, which provides preanalytic management of regressed states, is admittedly at least as out there as group therapy (although Thorner holds out in any event for the benefits of one-on-one treatment): "This account will show that the methods applied are in a certain sense the opposite to the psychoanalytical approach, aiming as they do at a change in the patient through manipulation of his external environment" (52). Given the war situation, psychoanalytic treatment "with as little modification as possible to their military patients" produced results not better or worse than the more adaptive, eclectic approaches (which promote development of one's "own technique") (55). It's not just the different situation to which the symptomatizing soldier has failed to adapt—and which certain analysts prove equally rigid about—it's the war neurosis itself that is just not the same as a civilian neurosis (58). In peacetime these war neurotics would never have received psychiatric attention or treatment; they would have been screened as low-maintenance neurotics by general practitioners. They're just such a pill, a-pill-a-day away from adequate functioning in society. So far as military psychiatry is concerned, "the soldier's home is his unit," and the resolution of his problems in efficiency are limited to that frame (52). Where adaptive behavior to this frame cannot be restored, "it may be in the interest of the unit to see that the dead weight of a neurotic is no longer carried, and that he be taken over by a hospital" (54).

It has been Thorner's military practice "to interpret the soldier's material both on the immediate Army level as well as in the transference situation of the consulting room and on the level of the unconscious." These are all extras, however, "of great help where it can be done," but not "the essential part of the treatment in the Army" (56). But his adherence to analysis in favor of blends with weaker insight orientation has to do with his inside view, more in theory than in practice, of the "dead weight" carried at the gunpoint of comparison between the soldier who breaks down and the depressed patient in peacetime. His starting point is the importance of the latent period in the development of traumatic neurosis. The lost-object relationship is at the same time a "time-relationship which exists between the trauma and the onset of the neurotic reaction":

> It is in the latent period that the external danger becomes internalized and thus significant for the ego.... This is consistent with the clinical finding that the analysis of the traumatic experience may reveal an intimate connection with familiar, old-established and unconscious internal danger situations, and from this it receives its energy. (53)

If "it is not the energy of the trauma, but the internal energy liberated by the trauma that is the essential force," then a "further step leads to the connection of traumatic neurosis and depression":

> In both conditions we have a similar pattern, that is to say an external situation, either of an objective danger, or of the loss of an object. The immediate and normal reaction is, in the one instance fear, in the other grief (pain). Instead of a resolution of this reaction either by removal of the external danger or by mourning, in certain cases the reaction is perpetuated, and leads either to traumatic neurosis or depression. In the case of traumatic neurosis Freud uses these words: "The ego which has undergone the trauma passively, now repeats it actively in a weakened version, hoping to have the direction of it in its own hands." (53)

This double inoculation is taken in according to another latency schedule in Thorner's war-delayed reception of psychoanalysis. In a footnote, he suggests that it's only since World War I that psychoanalytic theory has developed to the point of narcissism's introduction, which, in theory (we have seen that Thorner's adaptivity permits splitting off of the practice from the theory), makes civilian and war neuroses essentially the same. Thorner is stuck on the publication schedule of Freud's work, since during the war he was cut off from all prepublication contacts with international psychoanalysis (which was essentially inside or on the side of the Central Powers), a gap that installs itself forever as a delayed, false, hysterical reception of Freud before and after World War I (54 n. 1).

The point Thorner presses in the main text puts depression and traumatic neurosis on one network that transforms external situations into internal ones (like the footnote):

in the case of depression by introjecting an object in an attempt to retain it in the ego, and in the case of traumatic neurosis by internalizing a danger situation in an attempt to master it by ego activity. . . . While in melancholia the external loss loses its importance, so in traumatic neurosis the external trauma may be insignificant, and in some cases its existence may be even doubtful. . . . This relation between depression or melancholia and traumatic neurosis which has been anticipated by Freud in his comparison of mourning and anxiety . . . has never been fully worked out, although it promises to be instructive particularly in the light of recent discussions with regard to Freud's and Melanie Klein's work. (53)

Objection Relations

Edward Glover was the partial-objecting referee of the fight between the queens of analysis. But he took sides with the Freud genealogy, if only to protect the bogus original model of drives against the bogus innovations, the narcissism of small or Klein differences, which were being advanced along the lines of object relations. The conflict sensationalism of the Kleinians was expanding on contact with the actual war. Glover therefore gives the all clear out siren and tells analysts to stick to the only relations they know. In his 1942 survey of war neurosis research ("Notes on the Psychological Effects of War Conditions on the Civilian Population"), Glover insists that the prospect of all-out outbreaks of war neurosis had been an alarmist exaggeration. "But the blitz, when it did come, fell far short of the dimensions anticipated, and it was soon apparent that waves of war neurosis were merely figments of the psychopathologists' imagination" (17). There were two "myths": number one, which was "of an unconsciously apprehensive and appetitive type," was that war neuroses would roll out from under the shadow of air war; and myth number two held that there was no neurotic response whatsoever to air attack (36). Glover, who was there, witnessed "raid shock" as restricted to the analytic setting. Patients who were in analysis at the time of the Nazi air attack indeed reacted with anxiety, but it was an *Angst* that was only disproportionate (in relation to the reality of the situation) according to the transference balance of the in-session relationship. "Psychoanalytical cases with durable analytic transferences stood raid conditions very well" (37). All in all, three groups of individuals under analysis tended to be affected by raids: "(1) the 'anxiety-character' group, (2) the so-called 'narcissistic' type, (3) groups having strong unconscious homosexual organization" (37).

In "The Return of War-Neuroses" Glover takes in the big picture of symptomatizing soldiers and, casting about the unconscious dispositions, finds only one personality type or bundle and one unconscious sexuality. Here he comes, the psychopath, "who has split on the rocks of bisexuality and of unconscious sadism" (124), whose "conduct, although neither neurotic or psychotic, is 'disordered'" (124 n. 1). But the disorderly conduct of psychopaths resembles that of war neurotics also because of the institutional mobilization both states attract or attack through their shake-up of disciplinary and diagnostic boundaries. "Actually the war-neuroses afford a common meeting ground for every sort of psychologist, descriptive, social, anthropological as well as medical. In this respect war-neuroses resemble states of delinquency" (112). Although Glover admits that as far as he's concerned, "very little was learned about 'war-neuroses' in the last war" (117), there's still the one part-insight that surpasses the two whole analysis-compatible models Glover distinguishes (the trauma and conflict models) even as they, whole in one, overlap in theory and practice: "In my opinion the only useful discovery about war-neuroses made in the last war was that what psycho-analysts call the 'unconscious homosexual factor' is of prime importance in their causation" (118).

Glover's review admits by name only Jones as one of the analysts who did write on war neurosis. Only Glover's admission that the two models basically occupy interchangeable places within one thought experiment gives a glimmer of recognition to Freud's thoughts on war neurosis in all their impurity, which Jones and company had to clean up. That a transference crisis is therefore backing up within Glover's decision to go ahead and talk about the world war outside his office is, as always, symptomatized by the willingness to swallow the mixed thinking about homosexuality (followed, as usual, by denial chasers) as the cure-all interpretation, solution, or dissolution of trauma internalization. Glover, who is suddenly out there just wanting colleagues to sign treaties and put themselves on commissions that would guarantee the end of all warfare, finally goes ahead and localizes the breaking out of war neurosis within the half-life of war, which completes itself, comes out, and is overcome at the intersection of impulses gridlocked in the good group bond.

Because Glover does not mean to confuse unconscious homosexuality with the manifest kind, and because he is proposing a plan of prevention and prediction rather than outright selection based on criteria of recognizable identities, the psychopaths must take the heat of the unconscious charge. The narcissistic zone that the war neurotic has crossed with the war zone is represented unconsciously by homosexuality. Even or especially manifest homosexuals suffer from unconscious homosexuality and make the psychopathic crowd.

> The unconscious homosexual situation although an advance on a purely narcissistic state of existence is still only half-way towards a true hetero-sexual attachment to a love object. Homosexuality retains many affinities with narcissism. Hence the infant who passes through a strong "negative Oedipus situation" (or, as the phrase goes—develops an infantile homosexual fixation) tends to suffer from a reinforced narcissism and from the "anxiety-readiness" that goes with excessive narcissism. (118)

> From the point of view of war-prevention it would be greatly to our advantage if we could establish with some accuracy the various stigmata of unconscious homosexuality. But work on this subject is so far in its infancy. Some of the few observations made are, however, extremely suggestive. For example: that those regular soldiers who have come to terms with their unconscious homosexuality and are at home in a setting of sublimated homosexuality, i.e., friendly relations with their fellow combatants, are less likely to break down, or if they do, usually suffer from the most disguised of psycho-neurotic manifestations, i.e., functional or conversion symptoms. (119)

If on friendly terms with unconscious homosexuals in groups, then the conflict internal to these soldiers will be contained or will contain itself. Sublimated homosexuality, Glover continues to specify along the lines of Freud's 1919 differential diagnosis regarding the two ways the two kinds of armies respond to war, would in fact consolidate ties within an army of volunteers; but in the compulsory servicing of world warfare, where the time is too short to develop an equal appreciation of an exquisite if allegorical leaning or yearning, the unaccommodated or uncanny positions homosexuality must take up are all on the war neurosis front (122). Thus soldiers (and civilians too, who in world wartime are in even more neuroticizing straits) must be made at ease with their unconscious or unconsummated homosexuality. For if, as Freud says, group solidarity relies on aim-inhibited impulses, then Glover can again put on his glosses: "A large part of these aim-inhibited impulses are derived from the unconscious homosexual drives of childhood and promote an unconscious bond between each member of the group and the common leader" (122). When there's a break in the group bond, panic defenses are way down: "The whole of the binding energy is suddenly released, and, having nowhere else to go, turns back to increase the narcissistic valuation of the 'self.' The individual then becomes vulnerable to the danger which he could withstand when in a state of group-rapport" (122). And the group bond is what the enemy is always targeting on the civilian side: "Rationing, black-out restrictions, evacuation, loss of wages or employment and so forth . . . *all these forms of hardship are calculated to arouse also unconscious and mostly unreal anxieties or guilt*" (121). Even the instruments of close combat spark psychological war effects of a look in excess of the kill: "It is clear from a study of dreams that war imagery (guns, shells, war-planes, bombs, bayonets, etc.) is excellently adapted not only to symbolic primitive forms of unconscious sexual phantasy but to express the unconscious sadistic phantasies that are associated with them" (121).

The new organization of the group bond makes its disturbances equal part of one evolutionary scheme. But these disorderly partners join in on the rebound back from prehistory, from the missingness or misfiring of the link. To make this group, we have already passed through uncanny war zones on into Freud's second system. War neurosis, for example, is both conflict and contract between ego and superego (or peace ego and war ego): "Almost all psychopathological states are attempts at self-cure—i.e., they are not due simply to a breakthrough of unconscious tension" (125). Given the hysterical look of the war-neurotic outbreak of symptoms, it's Glover's hunch that we should reinvestigate tribal war preparation rituals. With war hysteria, we are brought back to the past history of humanity's development to, and for which, we are still bound:

> We have been led astray by the fact that under service conditions, the neuroses follow the war service.... It may well be that some service war-neuroses are merely measures of war prevention in an inverted order. (125)

In its double movement, between preparation and working through, prevention or predisposition and acting out, the "inverted order" of war neurosis is the time capsule of war's overcoming in miniature. In other words, even though we still don't know how to extinguish war from the scheme of our evolutionary history, "we do know that a good war-neurosis is an effective albeit unconscious means of bringing to an end the participation in war of the sufferer" (125).

There Was No Time like the Present

> Dying is replaced in dreams by *departure*, . . . nakedness by *clothes* and *uniforms*.
>
> —FREUD, "INTRODUCTORY LECTURES ON PSYCHOANALYSIS"

In no time, the Nazi Air Ministry encouraged the psychotherapy institute in Berlin to open a separate section devoted exclusively to the psychological problems going down in the air force. Göring's son (or Göring's nephew), who received his psychoanalytic training in Nazi Germany, specialized in treatment of war-neurotic disturbances in the relations of pilots with their planes. The Air Ministry was the first in the complex to put in the request that the institute take on homosexuality as a psychopathology that can be caused, prevented, and cured. Together with new improvements in the treatment of war neurosis and the application of psychological warfare, eliminating homosexuality through intrapsychic intervention remained up there on the institute's agenda of things to do. The successful treatment of homosexuals was to be the second success scored by the intrapsychic view of conflict: the first had been the theory and therapy of war neurosis that psychoanalysis had advanced for the First World War. The second success story would belong to the reunified psychotherapies (including psychoanalysis) in Nazi Germany.

In addition to all the other savings earned by fetishistic oscillation, Freud gave the movement one more prize: "It also saves the fetishist from becoming a homosexual" (*SE*, 21:154). Another near miss inside fetishism pushes back homosexuality, which, in its various states of resolution or realization, was brought into focus by military psychology's inside view from World War I on as one of *the* enabling factors in the coming out of war neurosis (or in the acting out of desertion, disloyalty, betrayal).

It was the prospect of running out of the reserves that highly recommended the psychodynamic view that disturbance or turbulence in the ranks was treatable or, in the case of pilots, recyclable for rewiring purposes. According to a lecture delivered by Otto Wuth in 1939 to air force and navy judges who were being trained in military justice, psychopaths too are not your usual discards. Among these dysfunctional types there are the asocial ones, or sociopaths, onto whom efficient soldier functions can just the same be superimposed (even though these recruits admittedly remain, characterologically speaking, not good soldiers; that is, they do not contribute to the all-important cult of comradeship). And yes, there are those who under the cover of religious fanaticism, for example, are following the unstoppable command of some hypervalued ideal. But "we cannot possibly characterize everyone who is ready to suffer or die for an idea without any consideration for family and so on as mentally ill" (8).

The problem of homosexuality, says Wuth, fits right into this scan of psychopathic behavior in rehab for military application. The big idea of Magnus Hirschfeld's human rights movement had overvalued homosexuals as being throughout history the pure and noble ones. But Wuth counters that there were greats (like Nietzsche) who also made it, but not because they were sick (which indeed they were), but in spite of their being cases. There is no homosexual disposition, as Hirschfeld had claimed, nor for that matter a heterosexual one. There is only, in the beginning, a bisexual disposition, which is the catchall for both paternal and maternal inheritances. In this bisexual habitat of early childhood, little one plays with his body, but "contrary to the Freudian assumption," not in any genital-sexual sense. The genital-sex drive serves the preservation of the species (just as the nourishment drive serves the individual's preservation). When sex feelings first hit (in adolescence), one doesn't right away recognize the meaning or purpose of what is experienced right off only physically. Masturbation is the only satisfaction the youth knows how to get, based on his earliest preoccupation with his own person. Much of this impulse can then be "spiritualized," replaced by the crushes of worship and fandom. Finally, "the sex drive is redirected towards the biological goal, namely to woman, with whom normal satisfaction is sought" (9). Now, even in this normal scenario, Wuth admits that the "norm represents not some fixed point but rather a flowing boundary line" (9), which is where homosexuality comes in. The misdirection in this case of sex-drive orientation is accompanied by psychopathic variations on all the other drive routes: nicotine and alcohol abuse, keeping late hours and neglecting sleep, dishonesty, and self-destructive tendencies over time or all at once. This overlap between psychopaths and homosexuals, which is part of the diversion they offer from preservation of life, applies to perverts all down the line. To be so far away from the norm also means: so close. Perverts give the norm the slip only by the most extraneous accidents imaginable.

> Thus the glimpse of some object during one's first time experiencing genital-sexual excitement can lead in a sense to a connection with the genital-sexual drive and thereby to fetishism, the simultaneous experience and witnessing of suffering to masochism or sadism. Masturbation can persist, the inclination toward one's

> own sex can be anchored through experiences with comrades or through seduction, and we have homosexuality. (10)

Nazi military psychology worked close to the net to catch the near-miss relations between inoculation against and uncontrolled release of disturbance in the ranks. For example, in 1937 in the pop-psychological journal *Soldierhood*, which was accessible up and down the continuum of the military effort, the reader of Grunwaldt's "The Erotic Moment in the Life of the Recruit" could learn all about homoeroticism, which not only was admitted as being out there among them but was even advertised as a kind of immunizing agent against the other H word with which it overlapped, antibody style, in the mode, again, of near miss. At least by facing the fact of what Grunwaldt calls a "unique vibration between man and man in which one somehow discerns a feminine note" (35), the onset of the toxic spillover of homosexuality can be contained. The Nazis were out to win the future wars that would win the race. That's why what Grunwaldt brings into focus as the "perpetually fluctuating boundary between homoeroticism and homosexuality" (36) requires the kind of all-out (preemptive and intrapsychic) surveillance that only nonphobic tolerance of homoeroticism can bring about.

This pop-psychodynamic approach of total healing can face the fact of homosexuality before which, however, it pulls up short. Because homosexuality was seen as virulent attack on one's reserves, which would be left contaminated by auto-depletion, the Nazi inside view stopped short of covering this borderline from both sides now. Homosexuality was the bottom line of Nazi projections. That's why the fetishistic short stop was one of the key rivets going into the streamlined body of Nazi group protection (or projection).

Kinder-Reich

Fritz and Elisabeth Künkel made a coproduction out of their 1936 manual on how to raise them now that you've reproduced them: *The Raising of Your Children: Manual for Parents and Educators.* Each partner of the couple gets one introduction, and one of two parts of the book; Fritz goes first with his intro, but part 1 belongs to Elisabeth. Fritz: if an individual complains that his environment is curbing his development, a closer look will throw this bawling back into his own court; his majesty limits his capacities and possibilities by keeping them only for himself (7). *Volk* rules: it's what's inside you as hereditary predisposition *(Erbanlage)*, and it also influences you externally as a teacher. "A contradiction between the two is ultimately impossible" (8). One commemoration is allowed to slide inside: a child's "'organ inferiority'" (9) requires a balanced reception on the part of the parents and educators: it's a double commemoration because "organ inferiority" is of course another name for Adler, but then Künkel's tempering of this fact of life by placing its reception first, which is more the cause than the effect or side effect of a sense of not fitting in, recalls Freud's remarks on the Kaiser's withered arm, the one that only became the problem that it was for the world after his mother had reacted to his or her body part with horror. (If you don't use names, so much more goes between the lines.) Elisabeth: There's an inner order to which the child is bound by the rhythm method of individuality. The greatest danger for the child lies in the selfishness of adults who consider only their own order and "neglect or even suppress the silent demands of rhythm and order coming from inside the child" (11). When neurosis develops, we know the cause: "The parents weren't able to carry out the main task of upbringing, attention to the order and rhythm of the child and, through harmonious further development and in gradual and understanding collaboration, assimilate the inner child within the external order of the adults" (14).

Part 1, Elisabeth's, is devoted to "mother and child." She's thus given the task of rendering to the "we" concept what is its duo forum, the "primal we" *(Urwir)*, and following out individuation from and in this bond on the way to the development of the communal "we" of inheritance and *Volk*. The child learns to distinguish between "you" and "I" in the relationship with mother: this is all experienced via the child's entry into language (25). But the mother has her share in the "primal we," too. She'll say, Now we're going to drink something, Now we're going to go to bed, even when the child alone is meant. They keep going we-we until experiences of delayed

Nineteenth illustration: Kindergarten.

gratification teach the child that his willpower is not always the same as his mother's will (30). The *Entwicklung* of the child, his "development" to be sure, but also, literally, his "de-diapering," goes its own way and acts out along the way only at those points where the parents' selfishness or lack of self-awareness interrupts his course forcing the child to respond in kind (34–36). Elisabeth is relieved that in 1936 there are excellent therapeutically correct books available for the younger child: now we can wait until age eight or ten before laying the Grimm reality on them (42). Whenever you punish the young child at kindergarten age, you risk that the step forward that was part of the misdemeanor, and the entry into the community will be cut short. "The child receives through the punishment a shock, a secret anxiety, which will recur with every subsequent encounter with what's new" (45).

Part 2 begins with school, the beginning of the group relations between "child and world." This is when the child learns to think the world of the father and what he represents, community service. There are only two mistakes in the education of the child, either going soft on him or going down too hard. Either extreme may lead to the worst-case scenario: meglo sense of self in isolation from community spirit (49). But even the teacher of first-graders must realize that he's not getting unadulterated "hereditary mass" *(Erbmasse)*, but already all kinds of crooked reroutings and suppressive overlays are there over the top of little one. The teacher must be a therapist,

Twentieth illustration: Unknown children are welcomed. (In German, "Fremde Kinder" could also designate them as foreigners.)

therefore, and not a bio-imprinter on clear mental slates (49–50). The first school years represent the community to the child in all its diversity: levels of income, maturity, town or country (or gown) and so on (51). Only in such institutions of reentry, like most training programs in clinical or counseling psychology, with the focus trained on psychotherapy, does one again experience that first community of radical differences.

Show respect for the humanity of the child, the "wonder of life" that we're here to protect and care for. The child's singing his own song, and it's our song too, but don't keep the rhythm with your fist; it's better to help the song you've got to sing come out of the child all on its own (54). Does your son have trouble with math? Follow one father's lead who used his sizable collection of miniature warships (he was a great fan of naval warfare) to get the boy to forget in the excitement his math trauma and do what comes naturally: figuring out the number of forces on each side of war (57). Don't encourage your child through your own self-esteem to pursue the "external securities of existence" (57). So many exemplary schoolboys end up big failures living out a lame excuse.

It's so surprising how different the children are from each other. Parents have always wondered where they got it, where did it come from. Now with the new *Volk*-focus on racial hygiene and eugenics, it has become possible to speculate whether some particularly difficult child isn't in fact the number that comes up every hundred years or so, bouncing back from some racially alien influence during the date rape Germany was on for the duration of the Thirty Years' War. It's not that the Germans are pure; that's not what the Nazi ideology is out to protect. The kernel of truth that comes out here is that of the inevitable impurity of the German people that we're struggling now to detox. However, Künkel points out, overreliance on the mixed-racial returns from the past as cure-all explanations might be in the service of overlooking what's more likely the case or cause, that the social order of the sequencing of the kids, for instance, already programmed certain differences that can be worked with, through, out (60). You know what you've got with the only child (no sequencing social side effects here). But he's a guaranteed problem. The family is the first and most binding model for community life (as long as the parents behave as older friends, comrades, Oedi-pals). This comradeship inside the family is the basis for all preemptive and future "'healing'" (71). Vain parents encourage their kids to idealize them as perfect models and resist and thus dangerously deny every child's dis-appointment with the ideal (73). The only child goes out into the extrafamilial life of the community either to overrate or underrate the comrades: they're either his heroes or his slaves. If you do bring in another child to break the only-child pattern, try to make it at least a distant relation, you know, like Heidi. Otherwise the little control freak won't learn the bottom line of community relations: blood appeal. The only other type of child that shares many of the negative traits of the only child is the sickly one. (Heidi was faced with a double whammy.)

In 1940 Edgar Herzog criticizes the handling with little care of "Difficulties in Rearing School-Age Children." Before we despair of the child who won't listen to reason or obey threats, let's consider what's behind the lazy or bad habit. "We know only too well that there are children out there whose psychic and physical predispositions are severely damaged. But we adults should take care whenever we no longer can help ourselves and jump to the conclusion that it's the inheritance of a grandfather or uncle. . . . That way we make light of our responsibilities and perhaps endanger the life and future of our child" (3). The first three cases under consideration in this how-to pamphlet concern children suffering from anxiety neurosis. Little Peter is into regression in order to stay in touch with his mother for as long as possible; their separation is deferred and drawn out each day and for years. Fritz had the kind of father who wanted a macho son (or wanted to destroy him under the cover of promoting the little rival's fortitude). School was just the extension of the minefield of his mind that father, who thought exposure to danger was the way to go, had already deposited down and out inside him. He's a coward lying low waiting to be attacked by teacher and fellow pupils; their disdain for him "threatens him like a terrible ghost" (6). He's a stammerer, a hammerer on his father's nerves who keeps on completing or short-circuiting the vicious circle of family and friends. Little Elli identified with the financial and psychic depression that afflicted her parents when she was all ears. She's afraid of failing in the school of life and not graduating with security. All three children have "heartfelt anxiety" (7).

But there's more casework where those three came from. Lazy Lotti was raised to be such a doll. All she cared about was accessorizing the crime her parents perpetrated against her by keeping her in the shallow end. The therapist tells Lotti's mother to get the girl to design and sew outfits for her dolls. At least (at last!) Lotti would develop some taste for concentrated work. A lack or shortness of attention span is the most common denominator in this stretch of cases. "In almost all the cases . . . inattention plays, along with other factors, a big role, and for the simple reason that the child, without knowing it, is virtually hypnotized by a secret interest and therefore can find no more energy for concentration on school work" (11). Ursula is the wild one, compared to her older sister, who's the model daughter: the therapist decides she needs her own "field of application" within which to assert herself. BDM anyone? Yes! She's healed. Sports are the answer for August, too, who's both bully and (unbelievably!) bad pupil. His new homeroom teacher is also the gym teacher, and before August can start up acting up with him, the teacher compliments the boy on his evident strength and birthday-suit-ability, therefore, for the volleyball team. The boy is tamed. In secret he practices hard. Praise alternates with improvement. Soon August sees himself as the teacher's second in command. They see each other a lot! "The prejudice-free behavior and the pedagogical skill of the young teacher saved this boy, almost totally neglected by his parents, from a bad end in degeneration" (16). The same sex story for girls is the arranged affair between Lia, who's a klepto (what she takes she gives away to buy some love time), and a slightly older counselor who for years gives Lia all the loving time she needs. Then there's a whole section entitled "Premature Sex Life." All kinds of sexuality are possible for the normal child. "Even the beginnings of apparent homosexuality in children and teens belong to this realm" (18). It's an experimental realm in which the kid tries to figure out what this life function "wants" (18). Prudish educators are the worst. Everyone loses out in a fight against nature. "In reality the fight should not be waged against the awakening sexuality of the child, but rather together with the child the effort should be made to grasp its meaning, and

Twenty-first illustration: Child on the bridge.

Twenty-second illustration: Housekeeper pulls up the wagon and birthday for triplets.

thereby a way to assume vital control over it. But only those parents or educators who are uninhibited about their own sexuality can help the child or youth out of the distress of having to grow" (19). A "helping leading hand *[Führerhand]* extended toward these youths in comradeship" can work wonders (20). And it's the parents who have to hand it to them. Yes, once the sex clears up, they and their children are comrades. If not, there's something wrong with the parents: "Difficulties in rearing children are in the by far greater number of cases a reflection of parental inner difficulties" (20).

Gerdhild von Staabs, inventor of the sceno-test, contributes in 1940 a pamphlet of answers to the question raised in the title *How Do I Deal with Difficulties in Rearing the Young Child?* N.b., "the time of early childhood is not the paradise adults like to imagine it was in their recollections" (4). If you want to know how adults appear to the little ones, imagine a photograph of the grownup taken from below the belt, looking him or her up (5). It's a giant, all right, but is she good, like the bitch of the north, or plain evil? Then von Staabs addresses the giants: don't crush defiance; it's the seed of a valuable quality that will develop later in life.

Dr. von Staabs turns to the case of a five-year-old boy, "somewhat girlish," who's a stutterer. One day he set out to ask where children come from. All day long he got the answer for his troubles: "One doesn't talk about it." He's ever after getting into machines, taking them apart, inspired by the same question or quest that is now "unconscious" and accompanied by the "feeling of doing something forbidden" (7). It was guilt edge over the top of the speaking interdiction that sponsored the little boy's world and words of stammerama. She turns next to another five-year-old boy who, if he had his stutters, was further gone than was the first example. There was another cause to come back to. His father was not his mother's husband; her ongoing disappointment in the first husband robbed the son of his real father and prompted the fantasy of an ideal father. Thus he carries on his mother's directives and by comparison chops away at the real father. But in the course of the boy's therapy, mother was called on to tell her son the truth, namely, that the father did in fact contribute to the boy's upkeep and was living in another town for professional reasons. The image of the uncaring father was slowly knocked out of the commissions his mother had been earning. The little boy's stammering lifts completely, and with it, the outskirts of his girlishness are overrun by newfound boyishness (8).

Little Helga, the three year old, doesn't take well to her newborn brother. She alternates murderousness with demo mergers with him, all for show of total affection. When mother catches her coaxing him up onto the window ledge, all the while saying that she won't go up there, since she might fall, the adult knows it's therapy time (9). It turns out mother had told Helga that of course the sister would love her own little brother. Helga took her mother's words literally and right to heart: she must be heartless indeed if she was having mixed feelings that she just couldn't accept. The therapist prescribes durable toys for Helga to beat up on. Mother gets told that you can't ask the older sibling to love the newly arrived rival; it's too much to ask, and besides, it's confusing. In sum: the way a person turns out lies in the way one turns them in earliest childhood (16).

Nineteen forty was a very good year for the Göring Institute's child care series of handbooklets on bringing up your "inheritance bundle" of joy. Adolf Weizsäcker contributed with *The Quiet Child*. Uncanny opener: "Nothing is so uncanny to mankind today than quiet. He who understands the loud motion of every motor rarely understands the quiet movement of nature and the hidden strivings of the psyche, in particular the vital movements of the child's psyche" (3). Parents today start Rorschach-blotting up the sudden silent time of their otherwise so lively happy face of the future. Has that bad gene from an uncle thrice removed who was so eccentric made a comeback after all? "In short, out of all corners emerge the ghosts of worry, and the mother now starts harassing the child to get rid of her own unrest" (4). It's apparently difficult for parents to leave a child be, alone, in peace (5). But sometimes the child asks to be left alone expecting the adult to persist just the same. (This is one of those misunderstandings that could lead to abuse charges.)

The child's psyche needs calm while parents today expect constant animation, participation, comradeship, forward march. Sometimes development must make a pass through solitude. From the medical standpoint, every slowdown in development is preferable to fast-forwarding (7). But truth is the child on the racially pure nordic track is more likely to be quiet and withdrawn. Aryans develop late, stop and go, press the pause button then detonate outbursts of growth and development. All this premature comradeship and community enthusiasm for tots is a leftover from the now "outmoded ideal of a big-city-Jewish-mixed-race" (9). This goes for puberty, too. Forcing your fourteen year old into long pants and dancing classes can really mess with the boy's sexual relations, especially with the other sex (9).

Current state interest in making sure the feebleminded among us are kept from propagating themselves and dirtying with their bad blood the *Volk*'s gene pool "plays in the worries and fantasies of young parents . . . a large, indeed an oversize role" (12). But transmitted imbecility is a rare occurrence, and families should calm down. The new hereditary laws were

Twenty-third illustration: Child vacillates between parents.

Twenty-fourth illustration: Child has fallen.

issued to protect the health of German families, not neuroticize them! More often than not, the anomaly in the brood is a victim of neurosis, which only in recent years has been broken down and through to its cure. Neurosis is a disorder in rearing practice; corrective retraining will heal it. A neurotic child can resemble the quiet child. But the neurotic's withdrawal is scared, inhibited, dysphoric. But it remains difficult, without many words to go on, to determine whether the still waters are running into a completely routine blockage soon to be followed by a sudden upsurge of growth and development, or have run aground in neurotic disorder or even are the symptoms of a serious hereditary disease. To this end, psychotherapeutic counseling is necessary—which is why the offering of therapy has grown so much recently to be by now caught up with demand or need (13).

First off, what's going on in the quiet one is a digestion or metabolization of strong impressions (14). This is the focus for our decision or diagnosis making. Neurosis is always another case of indigestion at this level: "Wounds and malformations of the psychic digestive organs lead to a constant un-digestion of life impressions and life goals in general" (14). In German, to stow away, slow down, stare in amazement all come from one word. Just watch how the really big impression can paralyze the young child in all his functions. The rhythm of interior movement and extended movement should be the focus of anyone studying or treating children. "The unconscious ideal of today, schematic uniformity, in achievement as in all other behavior, is modeled after the dead machine and cannot but lead to confusion and inner and outer death, the more we empower it over us" (15). The child's turning quiet is the natural, sensitive answer to new impressions. It's not to the credit of adults that this capacity for being slow on the intake has been lost: "Undigested impressions encrust the adult in a terrifying way and paralyze his freedom and creativity" (15).

In our cities, if the children want some peace, they go to the bathroom and while there take care of all their needs. It's one stop opting for what's natural: "Many people first found in that tepid atmosphere the way to masturbation, that secret whip of our modern, self-destructing life" (16). And thus, by extension, what about the public rest rooms in our cities, what sorts of seduction proliferate there and throughout? "The toilet and the sick bed as the last resort for the child's psyche, the last legitimate place of quiet—is this true image not impetus enough for us guardians of youth to take the problem for once with bitter seriousness, the problem that concerns us here, that of stillness in every sense?" (17).

The biggest mouthful for the inner child's metabolism is loss. Unsupported, the absence of a parent, by death or by divorce, sets up a child—it's

Twenty-fifth illustration: Mother rides with boy on the little dog.

Twenty-sixth illustration: Housekeeper directs a choir.

virtually guaranteed—for neurosis. In our day of leftover urban Jewish intellectual-mechanical directives and influences, true rearing practice is especially endangered in its absorption of essential misses. "We will conquer the ghosts only if we can 'become like the children,'" that is, if we learn seriously how to be still. All the current conquests that are being made by German *Kernkraft* (both "essential force or energy" and, ahead of its time, "nuclear energy") will stay put for reshaping only if we maintain our connection to the true homeland: "the *Reich* of the psyche, which is the *Reich* of stillness" (19).

Soldierhood

> We stand on the shoulders of our precursors and thank them that we no longer need to fight out the etiology of neurosis among ourselves, nor balance out any fundamental differences of opinion about treatment of neuroses or the legal status of psychopathy. We feel however responsible for enriching and polishing what has been handed down to us according to the measure of new experiences, knowledge, and possibilities, in order to contribute modestly to the maintenance and expansion of the striking power of our armed forces and thus to Germany's victory.
>
> —WERNER VILLINGER, "PSYCHIATRY AND THE ARMED FORCES"

Soldierhood was the psychotherapy mag for the pop-psychological *Volk* of readers really into healing and *Heil*-ing. The war's arrest in 1942, its reversal from *Blitzkrieg* to war of attrition, also "arrested the momentum that psychology and psychotherapy had achieved in the military" (Cocks, 225). Nineteen forty-two saw the final issue of *Soldierhood.* But an "arrest" is not necessarily the same thing as a complete reversal. The case of Klaus Conrad (and his students at Marburg University), as we will see further down these pages, demonstrates the arresting staying power of recognizably analytic models in frontline psychiatry even or especially after Stalingrad, after all the consumerism of greater psychoanalysis, as in *Soldierhood,* had gone with the *Blitz.*

In 1939 *Soldierhood* carried the true two-part story by Karl Mierke entitled "Endangered Comradeship." The soldierly concept par excellence, "comradeship" has proven, par hasard, strong enough to hold in place, during the splitting off of soldiers from their civilian units and unities, what now follows the leader: homeland, family, friendship, society, club, and so on. The concept never "raped" a soldier whose own position or disposition defends against loss of distance and related developments in the sentimental cult of comrade-kitsch (130). But the swell of support for the society-wide spread of this soldierly concept has been known to walk the thinning line of mere ceremony, fad, or phrase. The concept has taught the soldier boy how to overcome the selfish ego and, down the scale, all dubious morals. The sacrificial death for the community was the final port or portion of comradeship's calling. The soldiers at the front live and earn comradeship. That's why these are the bonds that are eternal, flaming, and internal. Any true soldier's natural rejection of "pseudocomradeship" gives the proof of this bonding. The aim of comradeship is to inspire all forms of *Volk*-community to unite in the breathing in of its spirit (or ghost).

The word "comrade" comes from the Latin *camera,* which is both the word for "room" (or tent), one that thus enlists double or multiple occupancy, and the word, the same word, for camera. In one focus, comradeship can, close-up, appear "deadly boring," habitual, the surfeit rapport that promotes only *Enge,* the word for spatial tightness or narrowness that etymologically relates to *Angst.* Thus claustro- or closet-phobia joins the various modes of war neurosis ("tent fever," for example). A führer is needed to unmake the many impasses that are headed by certain eccentric types and their off feelings. There's the complainer and the type that's just so negative. With a little humor, the führer can "intervene surgically" to render these eccentrics, who want to stand up and be counted, laughably or pathetically comic. "The main goal remains, however, that through constant perseverance in the group spirit of comradeship a style of experience is bred which in its stability and interiority cannot be shaken by any force of habit" (138). Mierke goes down the list of destructive (literally, "analytic") elements that make it into the hold of comradeship "like slow spreading poison and chronic sources of infection" (138). The selfish type, the self-lover, turns his drives into addictions (the extreme form of habit) that can repression-cook into explosive force (139). This self-love is the underlying "motor that excites all possible lower instincts" (139). It's "the whitewashed ego addiction" that's hardest to identify and treat (139). Cowardice too slides right down the skewer of self-love. Then, over on the psychotic side, we have the schizoid types and the grumblers whose complaints take on a new dementia.

But more generally certain "one-horse carriage types" *(Einspänner)* are usually preferable to outright herd types; their solitary nerdiness reflects an early destiny that was too difficult and which drove them to shift into make-believe. Therapy can work wonders *(Wunder)* with these solo nerdsmen. In his second installment, Mierke opens the second category after the selfish one, which is, number two, the vain type. A kind of "hysterical vanity" promotes paranoid rivalry (189). Ambition will lead these types to mediate between the authorities and all the rest. Then there's, number three, the uncontrolled type, the impulse disorderer. Various forms of anger high in choleric content, violent acting out, and even intrigue belong to manifestations of control-freakdom. Only the führer can protect the society of comrades from all the asocial, power-hungry subjects (194). As the review of threats to comradeship and the instructive means of defense against them that Mierke was mustering demonstrates, what's at stake, at the beginning, is manly action *(Tat)*, by which Mierke could mean, in other words, the phallicity of libido. Comradeship isn't without mood values but isn't a feel-good replacement duty for friendship or romantic love. Comradeship "promotes accountability and staying power in communal creation," which keeps it so close to life and life's practice, its practical side, without neglecting what belongs inside. Everything in and about comradeship "defends itself against service as healing method or space *[Heilmittel oder Heilstätte]* for those inimical to the community" (196). "The idea of soldierly comradeship must be raised up to the ethical goal of all *Volk* community" (197).

Eichberg submits "The Intellectual as Recruit" for the 1938 readership of *Soldierhood*. His conscious resistance to physical fitness notwithstanding, the intellectual represents good human material that must be put to usefulness and developed into the positive bond of belonging to nation and armed services (65). There are true and false intellectuals. The true ones are strivers whose sense of life's necessities adds insight to what would otherwise be understanding all alone. Along with the authentic intellectuals are the more troubling types who are on the one-sided side of science, the side family ambition made them take up. This type overrates intelligence, whereas the born intellectual is always modest. The one-way strivers to the top are the least interested in physical activity, since it can never be an arena in which they will end up walking off the winners. The military can integrate those whose lack of a trophy encourages atrophy only by giving them recognition, inside and out—and then the drill commands. By overcoming his own natural distaste with heroic patience, the superior can turn the smarter-than-you type away from opposition toward the contribution to the group effort that his own spiritual will power represents (which is just about all he has that the military *can* take and put to use). But even under these best reconditionings, he will remain a "foreign body in the army" (67). Then there's another type spelling trouble: the ill or ugly type who transferred all his interests to the life of the mind as one last resort where he might fit in. He quickly feels inferior and not a match for a soldier's life. "Since he got to know the night sides of life, he's weakly, submissive, and easily frustrated, so that he stands in proximity to the dork type *[Tölpel]*" (67). Yet another type gets around in intellectual circles just to circle around. He has no sense of any applicability of what he knows. He's the overlooked and underrated genius who in cities speaks up for the dissatisfied masses. "Intellectual vitality cannot be denied him, only that it isn't of any use to anybody, and the halfway measure is not appreciated by life and certainly not by the military" (67). Basically, with all these types, all you have to do is give them recognition and respect, which is so difficult, but the heroic act of diplomacy does make it possible to include them in the "mobilization of all reserve forces" (68).

What about the eccentrics among the otherwise fit recruits, the 1936 *Soldierhood* readership wanted to know. Military psychologist Deegener is on the lookout for all the ways the way-out types are always trying to get out of the service anyway. They are products of the transitional period, that's still there hanging on and over the totally Nazi history, which has yet to begin in all its purity. Deegener's focus is on the instance of the theatrically failed suicide attempt. This is a sign of psychic shortcomings that must not be ignored. "The necessary conclusion must be as follows: eccentrics *[Sonderlinge]*, who demonstrated that they are untrainable and dangerous and represent in addition a lowering of the troop's morale, must be excluded from the armed services, for it's not the number that's decisive only the quality" (72).

The lout, blockhead, or dork *(Tölpel)* as recruit is the focus of Eichberg's prequel to the article on intellectuals in his 1937 contribution to *Soldierhood*. Eichberg feels the duty of rehabilitation of even these types for the service, as much military as community service. The dork is too clumsy to be of use and puts on the dumb show to keep out of the way of too much activity. But underneath it all, he's clever. He's preemptively nice to all his comrades because he knows he's going to fail as soldier and wants to cover his back. He's actually an experienced misanthrope and thus carries a dose of hatred that can break out "like a hurricane" if he is too severely kidded (243). This psychological view of the dork appears to contradict the layman's understanding of this outsider. But there is a "profound connection that binds these views together" (243). This is the line along which a possible cure or healing can be found. These are sad figures (or sacks) with disordered characters. They are in fact artificially produced characters: "A sheet of ice formed by fear of life and denial of life forcibly keeps back all that's good and useful under the surface, and if you burst through this cover, you'll see something new and green sprout up which has nothing in common with the old stuff" (244). Causes there are two, then Eichberg will be through. Some begin as slow developers who are discouraged early on. Those who were allowed to keep to their own pace soon picked up speed. Among them we find Alexander von Humboldt, Napoleon, *and* Wellington. If traumatized he becomes a slow burner in the vast store of asociality. Then, secondly, there's the dork relative, the geek *(Tolpatsch)*. He too is the product of questionable child-raising practices. Spoiled from a young age onward, he assumes he's commander of his wishes and is left therefore, serves himself right, with no self-sufficiency whatsoever. "This dependency produces automatically weakness of will and lack of energy, and a certain spiritual and physical stagnation is often part of this picture" (245). There are two ways for the geek to approach military life, one positive, the other negative. This lability can be contained as military ability. The negative one, again, is once a failure, forever a failure. The positive and clever one is that the military represents a new start, since no one there knows that my record shows only weakness. Then I will prove myself a man, get married, and visit my hometown and show them how wrong they all were. Love could help the geek onto the positive way. "In the military sense an understanding interest is a full-fledged substitute for love, since with us the emotional standard is a different one" (246). Eichberg even counsels the superior officer to designate one of the fellow men to act as buddy or bodyguard to protect the geek during his healing process up through military integration (247). Then there's the klutz type, the intellectual kind that wears glasses. He's on the same mood swing as the geek. He has neglected his body and lived on the other side of the one way, in his head: "(Spoiled, only child!)" (248). The same method helps this type's inferiority complex, only a slightly more intellectual version will be most successful in this special case (248).

With his name made in therapy heaven, Dr. Gerathewohl explains to the 1938 readership "The Special Nature and Treatment of the Loner." The loner, simply put straight, is the type that "consciously or unconsciously separates himself from the community" (163). The loner shows his hand either by disturbing the separate peace or by fleeing society (163). But loners also form select groups or cliques.

> Finally, let's not forget that inner bonds with extra-soldierly societies make the assimilation in military life that much harder, and that with later conflicts between the two orders the loner existence is only thereby promoted. Then there emerges an idealization of the past, or cliques get formed within the soldierly circle which oppose genuine community spirit. (165)

Loners don't make great leaders, but they lead in the suicide rates. The loner just the same has depth, which is his contribution to the community.

> It is therefore necessary that the community is willing and able to allow itself to be enriched. It must to this end possess a certain elasticity and be standing under the influence of a *Führer* who not only secures their rights over and against the individual, but also recognizes their duties toward him. (168)

Ferdinand Spiegel, *Panzerschütze* [Tank Marksman]. Reproduced from *Die Kunst im deutschen Reich* 5, no. 5 (May 1941): 134.

For another issue of *Soldierhood,* Lüderitz looks into the "Belief in Self-Worth and Subordination." It's the sense of self-worth that makes the beaten-down fighter get up for more. Other beneficiaries are the artist who keeps on in spite of lack of success, the prophet even after his disciples have forsaken him, and the persecuted who must go into exile without support (67). The value of this worth sensation reaches the high point "when we have really surmounted a risk" (67). The worth experienced in this feeling need not be bound to an individual but, even when accessed by the ego, is

Wolfgang Willrich, *Ein Oberst der Gebirgsjäger* [A Colonel of the Mountain Hunters]. Reproduced from *Die Kunst im deutschen Reich* 5, no. 5 (May 1941): 135.

grounded in a "we"; "indeed, we experience the feeling of our own value most intensively in the We-feeling" (68–69).

Under subordination we experience the leader above us as better ego and, through this upbeat bond with the higher personage, an increase and heightening of our own self-worth. And then it comes out: "The submission can also be a more feminine one: I give up my own ego in the encounter with the superior which suddenly appears worthless to me and receive in exchange through the connection a better, more noble ego. The feelings that occupy the foreground are enthusiastic admiration and love" (70). In the military setting, subordination turns on "command" rather than on the "call" resonating in the heart (71). "The command is sharp, hard, and unconditional. It doesn't awaken something in me, but rather grabs as something foreign deep inside my interiority; it forces me to do something that I don't want to do or no longer want; it forces me to keep at it, when I cannot continue" (71). "I answer the command with obedience," which is "in its purest form . . . always 'blind'" (71). How do we do it? "It's the 'we' in us, which demands absolute submission" (71). The "we" goes deeper even than the feeling of self-worth. This depth charge is also a ready position: "Whether or not I am in the position to maintain this state for the duration, as a form of my *Dasein*, depends on the inner readiness for subordination" (72). "Wehrpsychologie" (military defense psychology), the rubric under which the *Soldierhood* selections for this section all fall, could also read, between the lines of the Nazi "we" generation, "Wirpsychologie." But if the we or *wir* is allowed to resonate just one more letter we have here, at the tip of our tongues, and in all the *wir-* compounds too, a sense of mad confusion: *wirr, wirrnis,* and so on. Weness contains a mad confusion of types.

Simoneit lets the 1934 *Soldierhood* readers know that honor *(Ehre)* in the community (of soldiers) is what a clear conscience represents in isolated individuals. Honor is thus more than ideal: it's a "real phenomenon with real, namely, psychic causes and real, namely, social consequences" (118). Simoneit points his finger to the pulsing interconnections between "honor and defense" *(Ehre und Wehren):* "Defense serves honor,—the purpose of defense is, in the experience of the defenders, honor" ("Ehre and Ehrhaftigkeit," 120). This may be a special case of honor, the lower case of the rhyme or collapsus between the two that yields "Wehrehre," a subcategory of honor (120). Honor is not a free gift. You have to acquire it actively, which means you have to defend the honor you're born with.

Simoneit again, still in 1934, gives the soldiers in the hood the inside view of their "life form" *(Lebensform).* You become a soldier not through skills "but rather through the unique aspect of your personality kernels" ("Soldatentum als Lebensform," 65). These kernels are self-evident in children and teens, but all the conditioning of civilization is there to "repress" them (piece by piece by peace) and yield the nonsoldierly life forms by the end of adolescence (65). Thus same-sex youths in love with one another for their own sake of self-worth are really offering opposition to raw soldierly masculinity and allegiance to the spiritual culture as final cause for happiness.

> In comradeship and in love the "you" and the "ego" position themselves ever more clearly, precisely, and with better definition across from each other, and the critical agency of consciousness turns observantly toward its own life processes. The first inward-turning attentiveness gives the young person those delicate animated features in the body image and lifestyle, which stir the sensitive observer so strangely and attract us to youth. (66)

This phase is fleeting in healthy youth. In the divided ones, a conflict arises between the vital tendencies to make love, war, comrades, and a misunderstood cultural inheritance that has turned all those natural strivings into foreign zones or bodies. At that distance from life, the culture vulture circles up and away, majorly, from the soldierly life form. Thus Simoneit has taken us through three phases. In the third one you're already in or out of health. In the fourth phase, a second time for toeing the line, the conscious regulations of will power emerge as final support for a lasting formation of the soldierly life form (66).

Because the surroundings limit the affirmation of vital tendencies, youth learns how to get into insight and comprehend the rest of affirmation that doesn't translate into action; he enters a phase of enthusiastic, fantastic philosophizing through which all teens must pass, though soon one group passes the other and their ways part. Those who quickly find a solution soon embrace a system, a dogma, and build up out of "repression" the youthless personalities of "thin, colorless theorists and pedantic bureaucrats" (67). Those who don't skip too quickly to resolution of the activity of insight keep access open to their youth throughout maturity, an access to excess that is energy-rich fuel. These are the soldiers—of professions, of the intellect—who just keep on striving.

Because the true soldier is insight driven and must maintain and keep animate and flowing this fuel, training and more training are the drill of the soldierly occupation. One must keep to that peak of strength where one functions "as though one were oneself just a means of one's own willpower" (68). Sacrificial duty is the high point of soldierly being's affirmation of the vital tendencies, which are for the most part maintained as tension, not as repression. The soldier is, then, the unique being or teen standing to the tension between life and death that keeps him going, past repression, going, gone.

In 1936 Simoneit tells the *Soldierhood* readers all about "The General Military Service Requirement as Psychological Problem." The two problems that are a given simply because not everyone is equal are the selection process and then the soldierly training procedure. The selection criteria can rise to the top if future warfare can be settled quickly by smaller elite troop formations. But the criteria must grow a more expansive, split-level frame in the event of a longer-term war that includes the whole *Volk*. In the latter case, the less-talented material will require more training time, which increases the tour of their duty beyond that of the already suited-up to be soldiers.

Also in *Soldierhood* 1936 military psychologist Kreipe addresses "The Recruit of the General Service Requirement." As the subtitle goes: "A Psychological Contribution to a Changed Training Situation." His word of advice is to give the recruits their regular dose of recognition; if you don't, the need will "announce itself psychically, but now in the covert form and in the volatile state of being wounded ('I'm only a means to an end')" (97). "It is without a doubt that the armed services today, consciously but also unconsciously, more than ever before in the course of the nineteenth century have found their way back to the origins of general required service and taken up the tradition at that original point" (70–71). The mix of freedom and determination again yields a force field of tension, not to be confused with the hierarchy of repression, such that blind obedience can be given without presenting any contradiction to subordination out of free will and recognition. This dual obedience has thus nothing more to do with what was known in German as "corpse-obedience" *(Kadavergehorsam)* (72). He also advises that one shouldn't jump to conclusions about a recruit's character when mistakes are made or talent in some areas is found wanting: "Even if this were the explanation, one should hold back any interpretation that could bury and shut down the often very tight entries into the interiority of a young man" (72).

For *Soldierhood* 1937 Captain Jordan gives us his less natural view of "The Born Soldier": "'Born soldiers'—soldier conceived as totality—do not exist, but there do exist 'born nonsoldiers'" (114). The only thing all-natural about being a soldier is the selection, the natural process of elimination. He relates World War I stories of misdiagnosed and well-meaning but regularly delinquent soldier boys, like the one who, after he was finally sent to the Marburg institute for testing, turned out to be an "eidetic" ("Eidetiker"), and like the many others who were synesthesia types (most commonly recurring among the Jews) (115). These latter types were "'psychically slimy'" (116). But there are two synesthesia types. Number one doesn't count the slimers; these types can maintain themselves through bursts of energy, but they lack the essential enthusiasm. Jordan feels that, in general, the disintegrated types might be part of the war work force but not the armed forces. The other requirement for soldierhood, other than vitality, is self integration, but integration distributed differently, with each difference displacing the aptitude towards some specialization, say in radio communications, or truck driving, or artillery, and so on (116).

In 1938 the readers of *Soldierhood* were asked to entertain "Thoughts on Obedience." Captain Meier-Welcker seconds the great notion of required service through which "the soldierly sensibility has largely merged with the spirit of the whole *Volk*" (69). Now that military service has been raised to a duty of honor on the part of the citizen of the state, the notion of obedience cannot but show some of this spread across the middle.

What about "Soldierhood at the Front and Religion in World War," *Soldierhood* readers want to know, and the military pastor Otto lets them in on it in 1935. The religiosity along for the First World War was grounded more in interiority than in the supernatural. The "Last Hurrah" sermons were soon out of place as the war wore on. But what had staying power, inside and out, was a kind of cultic fetishism: "Apologetically soldiers would say: 'Even if it doesn't help, it can't hurt.' All kinds of objects, grenade splinters, sticks, 'souvenirs' took on the character of amulets and were revered as such" (62). Comradeship group levels out all nearest and dearest relations as one continuum of loss and soldierly commemoration: "I experienced father and son in the same company. The son fell. His father stood at the grave without showing on the outside any essential difference between this loss and all the others. Father and son were at the same time complete comrades" (62–63). The pastor remembers being called on by a freethinking type to support his pacifist position with the corresponding commandment. But the pastor responded as commandant: "I tried to explain to him that he was guilty of the death of German comrades and of the death and destruction of the German homeland, that he was killing just the same, even or especially when he refused to kill the enemy. He couldn't or didn't want to understand" (67). The pastor didn't add the final slice to the total pileup of ingredients he wants the objector to swallow: it should also be, for all the same reasons, necessary to eat the dead meat.

Colonel Scherbening addresses "The Company Leader and His Soldiers" in the 1938 pages of *Soldierhood.* "A successful pedagogue *[Erzieher]* can only be that person who knows his own human material and has grown together with it" (168). A leader needs to go to the front line of his unit every day and look each man right in the eyes. He can see in the answering look what's the "pulse beat" of the individual and of the whole. It also establishes the leader and his gaze as the tribunal before which the men cannot hide, pretend, but thus at the same time can feel safe. It's a therapeutic gazing (168). Never make fun of your men, take every personality seriously, show respect. Don't forget their birthdays! On occasion give them interpersonal (rather than the above-mentioned intrapsychic) attention: as in relaxed eye-to-eye discussions just between the two of you (169). Prepare the attention span of the men for instructions and lengthy drills. Don't let them get bored! On the other hand, they must be made to relax before inspection (170). If you must punish a soldier, make sure that he knows that it means more than it hurts, and that he knows, therefore, forever, what is meant (171).

Karl Kreipe considers "The Significance of Sense Perception (in Particular Seeing and Hearing) for the Soldierly Service." Kreipe reassures the 1934 readers of *Soldierhood* that the question of these abilities is not exclusive to the "anatomical-physiological organ question" but rather raises the "psychological function question" (10). The difference in range or acuity between the primitive or natural peoples and the citified types who will be filling the ranks of future total war efforts (coming soon), concerns specialization and repression. The more modern man is shut down "for stimuli which do not concern him, which have become meaningless to him, whereas he is open to all the external world stimuli which hit his sense organs, which are important for or threatening in his life in the city" (10). As became clear in World War I, modern civilized man is not useless when it comes to certain sensory functions, but they can and must be trained into him; it's not his eye that doesn't see (11). A certain amount of guesswork of one's own is required in using the techno-instruments that allow us to measure or estimate distances. That's why the psychological assessment of all functions is all-important. For pilots the ability to hear from what direction sounds are coming (with or without apparatus) is a more fundamental requirement than overall sharpness of hearing (13). Sense perception is not an "isolated mechanical process" (13) but rather a process typical "for the whole psycho-physical behavior of an individual" (14). Thus "the characteristic sense perception becomes symptomatically significant for the essential type of character" (14). Because "inter-individual" factors exercise determining force upon the whole, "the mode of behavior of an individual will yield important information about the faultless perceptual identifications via the apparatus, so that a psychological total picture of the personality is essential to the determination of aptitude, just as in turn peculiarities of sense perception give the psychologist important information for the characterological diagnosis" (14).

Dr. H. Strauß gets called in by *Soldierhood* 1937 to consult "On the Psychic Effects of Mine Detonations." First historical coincidence or explosion:

the first battlefields covered with the psychological casualties of war, those of the Russo-Japanese War, were also the first modern resettings of mine warfare (which, while ancient in pedigree, had been out of circulation since the end of the eighteenth century). Mining war technology was turned up full blast for World War I. Luis Trenker captures his war experience in the "unforgettable" movie *Mountains in Flames* ("Berge in Flammen") right down to one's captivity by or abandonment to "enemy technology" (61). World War I was big on "undermining" *(Unterminierung)*, especially the strongholds that weren't holding up much longer under enemy assault. This key word, "undermining," gives us the psychological moral side of mining: the aftershock under it all of explosion, but also an underlying preparedness we take back up with us from early encounters with mining technology in which we dug ore but also disaster (the cultivation of mine entertainment as shock absorption seems to fall within the period of its laying down and low as weapon). And Strauß comes right out with it: the experience of mine detonations borders on "primal fear which inhabits the deepest subconscious in man and which is aroused by the destabilization of his profound connection with the earth" (63). Mother Earth opens wide and devours her children to the accompaniment of "uncanny sounds and shocks, that is, balance disturbances" (63). The readily available result: "severe psychic trauma" (63). Thus two sets of reflections are required: one concerning mine attack, the other defense. Basically monotony is the only filler in this kind of warfare, and that doesn't absorb the shocks. It's up to the leader, who must recognize the psychic burden inherent in the situation and thus understand how to address directly and "mobilize the psychic forces which have the greater influence on deciding victory than do the physical factors" (64).

In *Soldierhood* 1939 there are two contributions titled "On the Fighting Spirit of the Tank Defense Troops," which are more back and forth than back-to-back. Dr. Dirks and Captain Engels have different opinions. To be on the defensive in a proactive war is a drag—on inner psychic resources. But there has got to be the sensibility or predisposition to match, Dirks believes. "This alternation between waiting and observing at increased tempos of charge with termination in goal-directed, relaxed combat presuppose very specific psychic qualities" (14). Because enthusiasm in all the fields of warfare is so vulnerable—what swings up must swing down—only "the training of a heightened sense of duty must form the kernel of all weapons training" (15). But in the tank defense troops there's an added note required: the development of an "ethos of protecting" (15). It's a question of getting into your weapon in all its functions, links, and limits. Psychically the

Elk Eber, *Combat in the Outskirts of Warsaw.* Reproduced from *Die Kunst im deutschen Reich* 5, no. 5 (May 1941): 131.

attackers who are out there winning are better off; those who defend what the advance has crossed in its forward movement give staying power to what's been accomplished, but is the silent partner behind the man. The silent partner must ground his sense of self-worth in himself and, by extension, in the weapon he knows inside and out. Dirks concedes a final thought that the situation would be greatly improved if the tank defense troops could be coordinated with the attack formation at times when not needed for defense duties (17).

Captain Engels wonders what the gain for the military could possibly be if its whole body is allowed to break down into part-objectives with their own psychologies. This is certainly not to be recommended in the

Franz Eichhorst, *Poland Fighter.* Reproduced from *Die Kunst im deutschen Reich* 4, nos. 8–9 (August–September 1940): 232.

case of the so-called ethos of protecting (75). Every soldier must be primed for attack, and that enthusiasm for forward march and winning must be introduced and at all times maintained in every member of the whole military group. Only if the weapon is aimed at destroying the enemy is the soldier-operator animated (77). The ethos of every soldier is the aim of the weapon, and of the whole struggle: annihilation of the other side. But then Engels suggests that perhaps a change in name rather than in ethos for the outfit might help put everyone at ease. He drops his alternative into the footnote below: "tank hunters" *(Panzerjäger)* (78 n. 1).

It's 1937 and Simoneit is back on the pages of *Soldierhood* to give advice "On the Panic Problem." "One part-objective of psychologically directed defense training of the *Volk* wants to protect itself is the raising of its resistance to panics" (64). But Simoneit drops one key element, the reversal of charges, in the midst of his typologies of what to look out for in future research: "Within the system of general psychology, panic belongs to the group of psychic infections. There are normal and pathogenic psychic infections" (65). Inoculations, anyone?

Let Me Introduce You

An extensive receiving line and welcoming committee was set up for the protection of psychotherapeutic interests and the projection of therapeutic correctness to the top of the holistic agenda of National Socialism. Internal reunification of the psychotherapies required at least as many remetabolizations as did the overall alliance with the new Germany. We begin reading the meter of reunification in the attempts made by complete outsiders to form compromise formations with a new upsurge of interest and investment in psychotherapeutic healing in the Reich. Thus by 1943, W. H. Becker could fill an article on the psychotherapeutic treatment of the mentally ill with covert eclecticism. But even as he tries recycling preanalytic methods, such as hard labor and injections that only inflict pain (and that is their point), he finds he must close with the therapeutic salute:

> In spite of all the modern specific methods of treatment, psychotherapy still enjoys a sovereign status in the care of the mentally ill, and the mental health physician who is the most proficient in this area of psychic influence, whether from gradual accumulation of knowledge or out of inborn intuitive talent, is, now as before, the best. (277)

A negative example can give itself away as marginal displacement when it overshoots the mark or march of the new order not on one but even on both counts. The question of J. Bresler's "Is There a National Psychotherapy?" answers itself in the hysterical mode. The exclusions are too interesting: whatever German psychotherapy may be, Bresler knows it's not psychoanalysis, that chain of "transcendental anxiety factories and lapsus-offices" (13). But his rejection of all Indian practices of tension release is so total that he must pursue his point down into the footnote underworld where the *Volk* of Buddhism is held up as an ongoing national misfortune. The German Institute included in its eclectic mix psychoanalysis to a degree that can be measured against the other exclusion: from 1933 onward yoga or yoga-based methods were actively recruited to form combos with German psychotherapy at large.

Hans von Hattingberg's 1933 review of the three schools is eclectic on an even keel with many textbooks today. But he has his quarrel with the harder sciences that resist analysis the way they resist philosophy. Hattingberg imagines the scientist sizing up philosophies as socially integrated cases of paranoia ("Zur Entwicklung," 329). But imagine again, before going on to say that the three-pack of analysis represents a return of philosophy within the sciences. Freud, for one, wasn't far removed from antiphilosophical quips shot from the hip. He insisted that his science was not just science nor another philosophy, nor their synthesis. Adler and Jung in fact demonstrated, to Freud, the short fallout of philosophical system building. One wonders how Freud could ever cosign Hattingberg's view that neurosis is where a person encounters the problematic of free will (329).

The analytic principle, technically speaking, is one of "disturbance" *(Störung):* "The procedure is directed in contrast to the fundamentally tranquilizing suggestion toward analytic demolition of a merely superficial balancing act, one that has paralyzed the vital forces" (330). Freud dog-ears his corner of this market with master/slave inoculations: "The devil is to be exorcized through Beelzebub" (331). Adler doesn't recognize any higher authority (like drive power) over and above him. Basically he tells neurotics that they're not so unique, which apparently convinces them to stop the retraumatization and take their part in the activities of the group. Jung's just the greatest. He doesn't stop with the sexual meaning as bottom line but finds the deeper meanings. This is especially important when it comes to reframing perversions (Freud's school couldn't get around the "central perversion" of masturbation, which squeaks between the legacy like an embarrassment) (333).

In his *Characterology,* a 1936 primer for the new era that guides us through the most supported development in psychological theory of that time, Paul Helwig stipulates from the get go that although "psychoanalysis" is racially alien, it cannot be "scientifically dismissed." Its Jewish background can't explain what's wrong with the theory, but it does explain the "natural" aversion that Aryans must overcome whenever getting into that way it has of raising questions. So it's not the drive model or any biological force of argument that's the turnoff. Only those stuck on their own one-sided views (Helwig is referring to the closest competitors in the analytic field) can get hung up at this level of the psychoanalytic intervention. But in particular it's the tendency of "disenchantment" *(Entzauberung)* that does concern Helwig: "This is nothing but" is the scientific motto that psychoanalysis has become in toto (212). Past all-out skirmishes between resisters and the doctrinaire notwithstanding: "Today there's a doctrine in psychoanalysis that stands at the center of our scientific culture" (213). But resistance is no surprise, since every psychoanalytic formulation is designed for its resistibility. Wholesale attacks on art, artists, and ethical and religious values (on the cheap) follow out this ad campaign: it's the nothing butt of the Jewish joke. "But at the same time there is no teaching more important than that of psychoanalysis, none more objective in its basis, more deserving of our attention" (213).

Let the paraphrases begin. Helwig cuts to the psychic reading and healing of mechanistic, causal modes of thinking. Then he goes through just another paraphrase. He separates that center of basis in Freud that's still so important worldwide from the manifest tendency to look at what's placed up high from underneath (up skirts, for example) (214).

When it comes to the ego, another useful concept, Helwig's coverage slips and slides onto Freud's World War I reformation of the ego state under lab conditions of war neuroticization. He describes an ego always at war on two fronts:

> Psychoanalysis thereby gives the ego a double front: one toward the outside and one inward. The latter takes the form of a "censor" that resists the drive and prevents the actual drive tendency from becoming conscious.—This part of the psychoanalytic teaching is methodologically and in content the most important and interesting. (215)

Resistance is again provoked by the alleged noncongruency of what we think we want and what we really want. But this unresolvable break or lag is only true of disturbed individuals. Resistance can serve a therapeutic purpose: the purely intellectual side, say of dream decoding, requires a dynamic understanding, too, affective processing that resistance to the therapist brings about with the release of transferences. The solution must be poured out of the patient who can never be force fed by intellect alone.

The concept of libido is useful when cleared of the misconception that it equals sexus (although the latter does develop out of the former). By libido, Freud just means that "X" factor, that scientific conceptual character without qualities that holds the place of the drives (216). Sex is thus just a way station of the drives in their course of development: but it's also the "basic colony of all drives" (217). So far, so value free: yes, power does come driving up from below, but the higher authorities are still in control. At the same time, it's true, the drive underworld just will not be ignored. The ego must show solidarity with life's nature. "Turned into the ego's enemy, the unconscious makes the ego itself 'inauthentic'" (218). While Helwig still holds out that there is too much negativity (and too much freedom) in Freud as in his "Oriental" friend Adler, for the opening of his Jung section, he basically praises the favorite only for returning to Freud and pushing aside the disciples who've been getting it all wrong on the cheap.

The party outline Helwig tried to follow is given less ambiguously and ambivalently by A. Hanse, who decries the recent past as convulsed with mass delusions collapsible back onto the ego-centric self addictions: in review of psychotherapy's recent past, Freud is name-called pornographic (at once too intellectual and too sexual), Adler is roll called the better pedagogue (but Jewish too), and Jung is named with a reputation for improving on analysis by not getting stuck on the pasts of individuals. In his "Foundations of Psychotherapy," Matthias Göring, the leader of the three-way reunification of Nazi German psychotherapy, gives it to Freud both ways, coming and going. Why do physicians and psychologists today resist the concept of the unconscious? Because around the turn of the century the disposition of science was thoroughly mechanistic: the psyche or soul had to be taken apart experimentally. In medicine, individual organs took center stage. That left little room for the unconscious. In the preceding paragraph Göring has already said that Freud was not the first discoverer of the unconscious (false advertising!). Now in a paragraph following the historicization of a mechanistic worldview, Göring asks: "And what did Freud then do? He forced the unconscious into the mechanical mindset. He connected the unconscious to genital development and established his system on that basis. The mechanization of the unconscious was too much even for the German scholars. But rather than dismiss the mechanistic theory, they rejected the unconscious" (1443).

Carl Müller-Braunschweig's "Psychoanalysis and Worldview" gives countertestimony on behalf of his training (Müller-Braunschweig was one of the official analysts who joined the Nazi German merger of one therapy for all and all for one therapy). The alleged psychoanalytic overvaluation of sex reflects a misconception. Now Müller-Braunschweig gives conflict its overdue (he knows he's not fighting some losing battle to preserve psychoanalysis). He quotes Freud's attack on the so-called wild analysts, who promoted sex and more sex as the only cure (two of them, Schultz and von Hattingberg, ended up his colleagues at the German Institute). Then there's the charge that analysis is just so destructive. But in fact whatever alleged breakdown occurs through analysis of a psyche, both in theory and in practice, is also a breakthrough, not a dissolution but a genuine resolution. Psychoanalysis guarantees (and here Müller-Braunschweig lets its war record speak for itself) that it can turn weaklings into vital people, the inhibited into self-assured types, and those hooked on a fantasy life into solid citizens who really look you in the eye. Psychoanalysis is the *Volk*-sy Oedipedagogy that leads the way in turning out new citizens in the one size of fitness for all.

Fritz Künkel weighs in his words of community healing (which is basic Adlerian) in an article of explanation: "Soul-Healing Knowledge," which is the Nazified or Aryanized term for "psychotherapy" (in three *German* words). The study of psychic suffering has advanced in recent years to the point that the "borders between disturbance of organic functioning (brain injury, tumor in the nerve substance, poisoning etc.) and an actual psychic illness (anxiety neurosis, compulsion neurosis, hysteria) are often difficult to determine in complete clarity" (294). But the dividing line between neurosis and psychosis can be drawn, "which for the successful war against the psychotically ruined inheritance substance *[Erbmasse]* is unavoidable requirement" (294).

Madness and genius don't go together, but neurosis and talent do. Nor is there a trace of race mixing and contamination in neurosis. Often the racially purest peoples, like the Scandinavians, are more neurotic than the mixed breeds. Neurosis may accelerate degeneration but is not the same thing as the degeneration. We (the parents, instructors, and, when all else has failed, the therapists) have to decide if we want creative spirits for Germany today and tomorrow or hysterics and obsessive compulsives (296). The neurotic has been crippled in his capacity for participation in the big "We." Thus "inferiority complex, false relations with the greater community, lack of gumption, and therefore craving for securities emerge" in the neurotic. "And the actual root of these character twistings and all the sad consequences which later must follow is, we find, always and again, anxiety readiness *[Angstbereitschaft]*" (296). All kinds of bad habits, addictions, even "perversions" originate here (297). That the alcoholic doesn't take full responsibility for his self-abuse but experiences it as a foreign power over him is actually a good sign. His yearning for community belonging under higher authority thus expresses itself (297). In this yearning lies the hope for healing. AA all the way!

The "we" is first broken by the parents, and thus the selfishness or egotism of the child is a response to the only break he gets (297). "The healed neurotic can thus often become a valuable and perhaps irreplaceable member of the We; he immunizes the group against a new break down: he is (if only his healing has been conducted in rigorous fashion) a man of knowledge, a specialist, in questions of loyalty" (298). Now if that's a transference interpretation that doesn't beat all.

In treatment the physician establishes the "we" with the patient, their working relationship, their community service and comradeship. Community feeling comes into the neurotic's life of psyche. Baby steps! Another "we" break should not be risked during this inoculative procedure. But the therapy must go beyond pseudo or apparent props of healthier adjustment that outside therapy circles characterize religious sects. It's always only part of the same apparent harmony that can bind active to passive neurotics in what looks like a relationship for life (299). Differentiation or individuation moves from the primal "we" *(Urwir)* to the community "we," in session via mega-transferences that lead to therapeutic disappointments in a setting where further flight has been contained. For couples therapy, it can mean that "out of the childish spoiling community of two marriage partners can develop a mature combat community of two adults" (300).

Viktor von Weizsäcker, the leader after the war too of the psychosomatic-medicine legacy of the Nazi era, resituates what's new in 1934 about the current call for a new spiritual decision making that's of an individual's own making. This is not part of the materialist, so negative view of man as sick animal suffering instinctual and hormonal imbalances. Nor is it a piece of the romantic understanding of wholeness as a hole that mightier nature opens wide for man, who, because his powers are only psychic, falls in. Man isn't "finished" in either sense.

No one is weak, tired, irritable and so on because he is sick; the sickness is caused by the so-called side effects, which come first. Organ-focused prevention and restoration were the words to watch in standard medical work; its ideal was causal therapy. "Substitution for what was lacking, resignation before what's irreplaceable, nonrestorable, determined the way in which physicians understood their calling to heal. The characteristic signs: operation, artificial limb, the chemically effective substance, serum, hormone" (83). The countermovement progressed through the psyche or soul, which is also, however, "the organ through which we are connected up with one another" (83). Psychotherapy is still the answer. The neurotic was disturbed in his development and can therefore be straightened out; psychiatry in the former era only now ending used the cover-all notion of psychopathy to stigmatize the casualties of faulty upbringing, a symptom of psychiatry's own laziness in observation and description, always quick to make moral judgment to pick up its own slack. Making people fit for work is the new order's goal. We've thus graduated from the causalism of disease (with its attendant industries of insurance and restitution) to the "finalism of human-social integration" (85). Integration is a better word than totality for what's on the agenda. Now we have formed "a solidarity of all therapies in the simple idea of the healthy person" (85). Psychotherapy and social work are the two supporting columns of medical-political action.

It's sheer materialism to try to cut out the disease even from the social body: ultimately such strategies of isolation isolate the sexual act and make it less reproductive. The so-called neurotics often have more spunk to offer the hereditary mass. The normal ones are often really "normopaths" (87). To the list of goals or objects of psychic intervention can now be added, alongside conflict or loneliness, "unhealability" (87). "Treatment, medical attention, is not, however, just restoration to normalcy. To treat means rather to make a history, to join with the patient, in order to make a piece of life history" (88). "The physician in our time has a political duty. I call it a political duty that one no longer treat the patient as a sick person but as an individual currently unable to work who must be led and counseled" (89).

Schultz was always a mixed bag of techniques. He's most famous, to this day, in Germany, for his autogenic training, the form of self-hypnosis that grew out of his eclectic encounters with yoga. His mixture of how all the Nazi German therapists, all together now, could refer to the basic parts of the new reunified psychodynamic therapy and theory had DSM-like currency. Take, for example, his 1942 survey and manual *Maintaining Psychic Health under Specific Consideration of the War Conditions.* Through the centuries, science progressed to the point where the organs were "the letters of the sentence. All that was lacking was the text so that the whole could be read. And this text has in the last forty years been given many different names by the leading researchers to characterize their work" (10). One encoded reference to psychoanalysis (the stand-in or stand-up's name is Friedrich Kraus) is along for the "depth person" (10), which Schultz reformulates in psychosomatic terms for today's audience as the "*total psychic disposition of the patient*" (10).

Medicine today may adopt a holistic throwback to romanticism, but without the blurry bloatedness of that era's speculations. This starry-eyed quality of the past gives way today to a "secure basis of experimentally tested knowledge" (18). "Above all, we stand today at the sarcophagus of materialism, the limits of which we with all our lasting achievements can clearly evaluate" (18). Life is again a "primal phenomenon" *(Urphänomen)* (18) rather than an "isolated corpse-like organ" (19). Untreated anxiety can lead a patient in convalescence following completely successful surgery just to die anyway: one might call it a case of "psychogenic operation death" (19).

The book seems packed and backed up with a 1942 cottage industry of retroactive phrasing and phasing of the history of greater psychoanalysis transposed to that of psychosomatics. But if he simulates a transmission or tradition to get around psychoanalysis, he's at least consistent about it. In

1942 this history is streamlined bare bones to pick. In his 1936 textbook *Neurosis, Life Crisis, Medical Duty: Clinical Lectures on Psychotherapy for Physicians and Students,* the whole false or hysterical-seeming history of all the names except for what we might consider the right ones is entered in full. But then, in a separate and secondary section, coverage is granted Freud and Adler with an air of objectivity. His only criticism of Freud is that while deep work is often necessary, there's always something alienated from the here and now about the archaeological bias of psychoanalysis. Schultz shows us his "But" of resistance: "But even the surface has its depth." Schultz switches to Adler by making it brief: "It was up to Adler . . . to make a system out of this question" (58). If nothing else, this textbook shows that it almost goes without saying—and by 1942 will remain legible only between the lines—that the most severe neuroses and psychoanalysis are a match made in long-term therapy heaven. There's no way around it, whether names get dropped or what. In the 1937 edition of Schultz's autogenic training manual *Das Autogene Training (Konzentrative Selbstentspannung),* references to countless analysts (whose names were of course no problem for the original 1932 edition) continue unabated. At a glance, it's as though they're all there still in 1937 and nothing really happened. From the start, Schultz (in the 1932 manual, too) included the homegrown listing of precursor German therapists and theorists in first place; it wasn't a put-on that adapted to a Nazi situation, but already pre-Nazi Germany was the balancing act he performed together with the main corridor or list of his field's history. By 1942 the balancing act is over, the main corridor of names just bombs away. But the entire field was saturated (or, to borrow one of the Nazi German diagnoses, contaminated) with the influence of these name brands.

In 1942 Schultz summarizes his repair job of the taxonomic proliferation of neuroses that grew up between the world wars at twice the usual speed owing to splits and mergers between psychology and sociology: neuroses of childhood, adolescence, and then job neurosis, pension neurosis, and so on. But neurosis is always some kind of psychic indisposition that can then be broken down according to the personal participation of the neurotic in the etiology of his condition. There are "foreign neuroses" *(Fremdneurosen),* which are anxiety of influence only. A neurotic woman adopts a healthy child who soon develops a neurosis: bingo, that's a foreign neurosis. Then, the "margin neuroses" *(Randneurosen)* are bad habits wedged right in there between body and psyche: like eating too quickly and sucking in air. The "layer neuroses" *(Schichtneurosen),* which are psychogenic turn on impulses that are not conscious to the patients. Thus the gentleman currently under Schultz's treatment has the sweats whenever his functioning (which is otherwise, in business, family, and sex, of high or full value) crosses what looks like stage fright. But it's the perfect but terribly forbidding father who still makes the man sweat when he enters the public space of recognition, self-assertion, contest (and, in turn, of possible humiliation before the witness and judge) (45–47). With "kernel neuroses" *(Kernneurosen)* the afflicted no longer just have their neurosis; they are the neurosis, too. These illnesses flow out of the deepest contents of the person and can be called "characterogenic" *(charakterogen).* Without exception there arise such "severe malformations of the personality through abnormally severe destinies in early childhood."

> The first six years of a person which on the average lie before his conscious recollection are of the greatest significance for the formulation of character, more supporting evidence for the view that has triumphed today in Germany of the family as the irreplaceable cellular unit of the organism *Volk.* (48)

Similarly, state support for a minimum number of children per family gives therapeutic aid to the only child, who without siblings doesn't have an adequate foundation for living in communities (49). The family and the community are invoked at the dividing line between hereditary, untreatable psychopathy, and the kernel neuroses, the latter demanding cases nevertheless representing a worthwhile investment of therapy time. That's what professional psychotherapists are good for: to "clean up" the neurotic mess that was dropped on healthy "hereditary substance" (60). Kernel neurotics are always charges of a "psychic work of healing that includes the unconscious and is long-term (depth psychotherapy)" (54–55).

As we approach the kernel, the perversions too come under the charge of deep work. It never fails: in early development there will be masturbation, and there will be same-sex crushes. And it doesn't really matter if anything gets consummated or not. But in normal or healthy development "the first real love experience with a representative of the other gender" picks up the baton and wins the race (108). These developments, fundamentally psychic, can get stuck all over the place. "A person is closest to himself and also his fellow gender members are relatively familiar to him, especially if he has no sibling of the other gender. The step toward the other gender is in a sense the bridging of a contradiction, an adventure, discovery of new land. Such a step however requires courage and joy in making discoveries. This joy is given the natural person because, through his early-childhood experience of mother love, he knows how nice it is to be loved" (109). The only child with a "witch mother" and a father of the genre "'bunny men,' with long soft ears, pink paws, great big eyes and long eyelashes" would have to do the next best thing forever, getting into his own sex (109). It's as plain as the nose on bunny's face just how difficult it is to help these aberrant developers out (110).

Considering the retraining, reraising required in the treatment of kernel neurotics, and keeping in mind just how long it takes anyone to learn how to ride or sing or become a soldier, then it should come as no surprise that the therapy can take years of working together. But the results we now know are many happy returns on the investment in what was basically valuable human material.

Secret Wartime Report

> Hitler shares with many an actor the fact, that he is apparently queer and unbearable behind the scenes, to say nothing of his bedroom. He undoubtedly has hazardous borderline traits. But he knows how to approach the borderline, to appear as if he were transgressing it, and to turn back on his breathless audience.
>
> —ERIK H. ERIKSON, "HITLER'S IMAGERY AND GERMAN YOUTH"

> In regard to virile heterosexuality, the Nazi "doth protest too much." As an aftermath of trench life and due to chance eccentricities of leaders there is a latent homoerotic quality pervading the movement.... A psychoanalyst could enjoy many happy hours of carefree speculation concerning the depths of the Nazi mind.
>
> —CLIFFORD KIRKPATRICK, *NAZI GERMANY: ITS WOMEN AND FAMILY LIFE*

Walter Langer was another psychoanalyst who got "mixed up with an outfit like the Office of Strategic Services during wartime" (Langer, 3). It was end of summer 1941, and he decided to volunteer for propaganda work, more out of the sense of restitution to be performed than on account of any know-how. Like Bateson, Langer had the sense that the war crime of the Entente propaganda had to be undone.

> I had never concerned myself with the problem of psychological warfare, but I had served overseas during World War I and had been far from impressed with our blatant psychological warfare endeavors. (3)

He was astonished to find the developing organization of U.S. psychological war efforts completely open to psychoanalytic perspectives. After a few running starts on projects that weren't finally funded, he ended up with this psycho-biography project which made him a "psychological bedfellow to Adolf Hitler" (10). The report he wrote up on Hitler went the secret and confidential rounds for some time. On social occasions, his introduction to some diplomat or official would light up a look of recognition that showed that the steamy study had circulated that way, too. In 1972 it could become a basic book uncensored in its public, pubic display.

Langer's dossier on Hitler explores many insinuations (originating not only in his own analytic work) that Hitler was homosexual. Langer determines that the homosexuality was repressed in Hitler's case, subordinate to his greatest masochistic delight in having women piss and shit on him; his special women friends tended to go suicidal under the pressure to perform. Eva Braun, the sole survivor of a date with Hitler (until the dual exit), made several suicide attempts.

As he builds himself up in the course of every speech he delivers, Hitler achieves once again the reversal of the sex fantasy:

> The steady stream of filth he pours on the heads of his "X" audience is the reverse of his masochistic perversion that finds gratification in having women pour their "filth" on him. (204)

Two souls in one breast take turns, the second achieving in the course of the speech the overturning of the first.

> As one surveys Hitler's behavior patterns, as his close associates observe them, one gets the impression that this is not a single personality, but two that inhabit the same body and alternate back and forth. (127)

> It is this transformation of the little Hitler into the great Führer, taking place under the eyes of his audience, that probably fascinates them. By complicated psychological processes they are able to identify themselves with him, and as the speech progresses they themselves are temporarily transformed and inspired. (129–30)

But repressed or not, the homosexual connection is made right through the double whammy of speech transformations, which represent the first adjustment he made to the posttraumatic peace. Before the war he lived in homo flophouses, wearing cast-off clothes of Jews (he even looked Jewish, Langer says). After his discovery of the power of parole, his new rerelease on life after the war trauma, everything got reversed to make room for his being so special:

> The Jews now played the same role in the life of Germany as his effeminate, masochistic, and perverse adjustment had played in his own life. (194)

But Hitler had no problem associating with known homosexuals even in this born-again phase of his nondevelopment, a free association that Langer checks off as remarkable, if not revealing. The final connection slides into place:

> In this connection it is interesting to note that homosexuals, too, frequently regard themselves as a special form of creation or as chosen ones whose destiny it is to initiate a new order. (174)

Heil Homosexuality

There's the joke about two analysts in Berlin who meet on the street after 1933. One greets the other, "Heil Hitler," and the other says: "No, you go ahead, I haven't the time to heal him." This uncanny cohabitation of healing and hailing within a supersavior economy swims into focus on the bottom line of Nazi projections and does some more overlaps there with the production lines of the internal enemy or public enemy number one. The homosexual toed this line between scapegoat and mascot because the Nazis were getting with a program of "transcending" homosexuality to get themselves off the dead-end racecourse of the "self-impaled" artist and "homunculus." The resulting savings in libido could be reinvested in the reproductive future of the race—its male-female law and ethos of life—which apparently was not a natural that could be left alone, unattended (Cocks, 206).

The joke's butt was secretly on the line through an economy of interchangeable parts: Hitler was a World War I shell shock victim. The pun-filled encounter on the streets of Berlin describes a living end of the movement or era of "greater psychoanalysis." When in his introduction to the collection *Psychoanalysis and the War Neuroses*, the year-old proceeds from the 1918 conference that had decided the military selection of psychoanalysis, Freud announced the share splitting of the war bonds issued internally and eternally by the ego's own divisions, the narcissistic zoning of ego libido, which Freud had already discovered peacetime inside psychosis and claimed for analytic theory in his reading of the Schreber case, was soon being taken too interpersonally, even by his analytic followers. The homosexual positions and dispositions punctuating the psychotic reformulations of libido or "capacity for love" (*SE*, 14:306)—literally, in the Schreber case, the transitive sentences bearing the verb "love" (*SE*, 12:62–65)—described sexual identifications dispersed across an intrapsychic force field that blasted apart, in fact and in theory, the couplification of Schreber's sexual difference or identity. The proximity of homosexuality to narcissism and narcissistic neurosis was not a one-on-one fill-in-the-blank kind of proposition. But in World War I studies of symptomatizing soldiers published by such members of the analytic in-group as Karl Abraham and Victor Tausk, it was the candidates for varying degrees of homosexuality who were selected to fill in and fall in with the interpersonal columns of the war neurotic disorder. In the contexts and corridors of institutional resistance, the sexual etiology of the neuroses had produced shocks of recognition that got everyone

The nine photographs that accompany this essay are from a private collection and were taken from 1944 to 1946 at Camp Somerset, a camp for German prisoners of war in Maryland. They depict several plays performed by the prisoners for other prisoners and for the U.S. guards.

stuck on what just takes two. In the in-group effort to outflank the resisters and uphold the sexual and unconscious dimensions of neurotic symptom formation, analytic overcompensation sought out designated drivers for the interpersonalization of drive. In other words, the society-wide transfer of the intrapsychic model was at the same time supplementally transferenced with homosexuality. The claustrophobic and closetphobic Oedipalizations that Deleuze and Guattari symptomatically diagnose as "perverse reterritorializations" were stowaway on this passage, while homosexuality was mixed up with all the static and traffic-jamming coming out of the model's internalization (and technologization) of traumatic conflict. This doubly or endopsychically registered homosexual component—one part psychopathology, the same part its theory and therapy—was back with Nazi psychotherapy's escalating administration of inoculations against the breaking out of the "perversion" of war neurosis.

As a group, the reunified psychotherapists had already been given the Nazi hit list of therapeutic goals to put up in the institute. In addition to psychological warfare (which was on its own in the group-psychological register), the agenda of things to do counted a trio of overlapping targets: war neurosis (and war psychosis), infertility (or phantasmo-interchangeably, frigidity), and homosexuality. But even under the category of group psychology or psychological warfare (or total war), analysts were picking up on the homosexual (or perverse) impulses in soldiers who tended to turn around into spies, informants, or deserters. Military psychology would

have to try and catch homosexual impulses where they breed. The preemptive strike of psychological interventionism had been called in.

The calculation of homosexuality as a risk was introduced into the American military complex in the context or contest of catching up with the Nazis. In Farago's 1941 *German Psychological Warfare,* Nazi psychologist

L. Fritzsching is introduced as an authority on the "psychology of individual surrender."

> Fritzsching . . . describes this "reversal of the military conscience" as "perversion." He analyzes the psychological process leading up to surrender: The soldier goes to war with a definite attitude toward friend and foe. . . .
>
> Suddenly, the negative influences of military service and combat begin one by one to cancel out these preconceived ideas. Anxiety and other negative factors, resulting in simultaneous physical disturbances, reverse his way of thinking and he becomes inclined to overestimate the enemy's power while underestimating his own strength as an individual and as a member of the military community. He reorients his thinking to that of the enemy and is being irrevocably drawn toward a state of mind where the thought of surrender is pleasurable and often an outright psychological necessity.
>
> It is due to this frame of mind that the war prisoner is usually gay after his capture and willing to "tell everything to the enemy intelligence officer." The sudden relaxation of tension hatches high treason.
>
> Fritzsching's advice is to explain this psychological process to soldiers during peacetime training and thus to expose to the soldier himself all the subconscious elements leading up to sur-

> render. His knowledge of these factors usually immunizes him thereafter to voluntary surrender in combat. (Farago, 43)

The kind of treatment schedule that goes with the inoculative approach at the same time requires greater tolerance of the fact of homosexuality. The Nazi establishment came to face the facts with a phobia-proofed and psychoanalysis-compatible attitude, the good attitude to have within the first pop-psychological culture of all-out healing.

The inoculations that were being downed in Nazi Germany treated a wide spectrum of war neurosis that was at the same time group-sized both to fit the scope of the perversions and to be subsumed in turn under psychopathy. But the simplicity of the formula was the very measure, measured inoculatively in reverse, of an epidemic of perversion that was easier to cause than to cure or prevent.

By all Nazi accounts, there was once upon a time in Germany a biodegradable core of 500,000 homosexuals that was infecting with its antigenerational contagion the surrounding masses of top men innocently standing by.

> Himmler fantasied with dismay that 2 million men, a tenth of the German male population—and possibly even 4 million—would be withdrawn from the genetic pool of the nation and fail to reproduce because they were "contaminated by this frightful malignancy." (Johansson and Percy, 235)

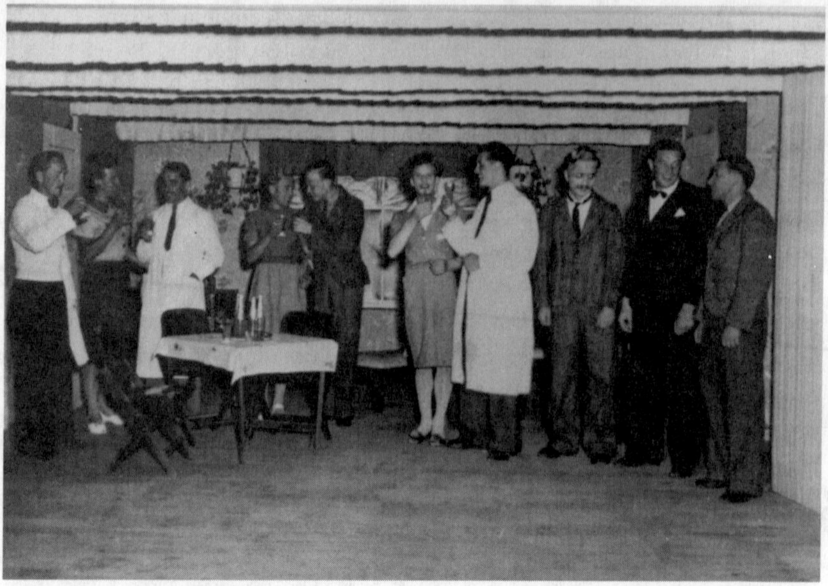

Among men, homosexuality spreads. Which is why the majority of German homosexuals needed no prison, camp, or oven, but only therapy.

In a 1935 interdisciplinary group effort entitled *Psychotherapy and Castration,* the multiauthors proposed therapy as the one option that should be kept open as alternative to castration and sterilization (the two cure-alls for every biogenetic threat to the future of the race). "We will demonstrate that in a number of cases large enough to command our respect it was with the help of psychotherapy alone that the sexual deviant and moral offender could already be favorably influenced" (Böhme et al., 26). Homosexuality belongs to an interdisciplinary field of interventions over which the bio-proponents of sterilization, castration, or elimination compete with psychotherapists for best results. The editor of the 1935 volume is on the side of psychotherapy: that's why the efficacy of castration as a method of healing homosexuals is dismissed right off. But the ambiguity of the "and" in the title covers the divergence of scientific opinion offered inside the volume. One contribution (143) is not convinced that homosexuals, who, like the bisexuals, cannot be assumed to be 100 percent reproduction proofed, are not a threat to the national gene pool of applicants for procreation. Even when they are straightened out, it's only the suppression of homosexuality that has been accomplished, which is not the same thing as healing a person inside and out. The editor runs a footnote commentary throughout: when it comes to sexual aberrations, the scientific community doesn't want to be tied down to a difference between healing and suppression. The work that went into this volume (which cites by name both psychoanalysis proper [56] and Wilhelm Stekel's brand [73] as methods successful in healing homosexuals) has by 1935 already led to insurance coverage of the treatment of the illness of homosexuality. The authors hope that what goes for homosexuality will be made available soon for the treatment of exhibitionists and bisexuals (45). The 1935 collection can only attribute the ignorance of homosexuals regarding the cure and coverage available to them to the lasting influence of Hirschfeld, whose worldview had clearly not panned out: Why, look at them; they suffer physically and psychically; they are not happy people (*Psychotherapy and Castration*, 74).

From Hirschfeld's doctrine of the third sex to more recent discoveries of a brain drain that slides heterosexual men out from under homosexual males in whom the head that's given them packs some larger part, the homosexual rights movement has at times preferred biodestinal theories of homosexuality and accepted their offer of a safety zone from moral and psychological operations. But when the bioblinders are set on elimination, the homosexual right to exist has been protected and projected by psychotherapy as living proof, according to the bisexual constitution, that there can always be change for the better. The racism of the Nazi community helped Aryan homosexuals out: if the genes were right, then how could there be a tight fit with racial inferiority? Neurosis existed—precisely because it could be cured.

Schultz Complex

J. H. Schultz was a good choice to prepare us psychologically for air-raid idealizations—as the ultimate therapy for true Germans—if only because his autogenic training *(autogenes Training)* was already such a hit the spot of self-soothing in a few easy lessons. This streamlined version of yoga, that plugs the old mastery into the recent history of hypnosis and suggestion, remains, together with the sceno-test, the seemingly value-free transmission from the era of one psychotherapy for all. Before the Nazis took over, he was close enough to psychoanalysis to be considered one of the "wild" ones (Hans von Hattingberg was also on this blacklist). Recent news flashbacks have outed him as a little too selective when it came to determining which homosexuals were treatable in therapy (the "little-brother" types) and which (the "mama's boys") just weren't ("Bluthaftes Verständnis"). To that date the historical record counted analyst Boehm as unwilling star witness to this selection program (and the stress was always on his trying to save another one of them whenever he could).

In 1917 Schultz was publishing on the front lines of psychoanalysis, the thin line walked by introductions: *S. Freud's Sexual-Psychoanalysis: A Critical Introduction for Court Physicians, Physicians, and Lay Persons.* O. Binswanger took a station break from war neurosis service to supply the introduction. Dangling from a bunch of gripes, Binswanger nevertheless can give Schultz's introduction project a line of praise: "since I am convinced of the scientific—or rather, as I have shown elsewhere more fully—the heuristic value of this research method" (3). Schultz gives a thorough paraphrase with some time out for humor: "The Child . . . has the same interest in sexual matters as psychoanalysis has, and is preoccupied with the problem of generation, of birth" (25). He rules the little Hans case hands-off: "All the mechanisms were asked into the child" (27). Nor is Schultz too convinced that the zeppelin can be equated with the penis (28). But it is as sexology that psychoanalysis is on our mark, set to go to all those aberrations for facts-of-life understanding and, where no one's looking, treatment: "What is really unique and new about psychoanalysis lies exclusively in the 'sexual theory' with all its consequences for conscious and unconscious life" (29). Schultz then quickly rejects all apodictic definitions of homosexuality by Stekel or Sadger and notes that fetishism is so close to "normal sexual life" (33). It's really amazing, especially with his introduction of Binswanger as witness for the defense, that the war spirit is left out of this rundown of Freud's theory. But then he closes after all with humorous dismissal of the

J. H. Schultz in the room of the director of the German Institute, M. H. Göring. Reproduced from Brecht, *"Here life goes on in a most peculiar way. . .": Psychoanalysis before and after 1933,* 148.

allegations of war specificity to outbreaks of mental illness in soldiers: "You might as well blame the train administration for a peasant lad's schizophrenic disorder that breaks out after his first train trip and which gets recycled in the delusions as some reference to train travel" (39).

Well into the Nazi period, Schultz writes "On the Psychic Life of Youth." With youth or in adolescence one gets with the rhythm of life: this should be our model, not the already constructed model of organism of cells: "We are guided here by leading exponents of German biology today. . . to see not the dead objective corpse-organ as the basis of representing life but rather that in the force field of living being, the organs—as v. Bertalanffy expressly underscores—are only 'slowed down functions,' dynamic condensations that, as though in slow-motion tempo, give the appearance of being formed" (88). It's function over form, organs, machine parts, the works. Adolescent development can't be viewed as "continuous, progressive flow, but rather as a series of salient metamorphoses" (88). For "stormy" teens, "time consciously fills infinite space, since the whole of life still lies ahead, undisclosed. Space expands, as one can recognize in the strong interest frequently shown in questions of foreign countries, outer space exploration and more of the same" (89). Internally the movement is ego only, but then, as the body builds up harmoniously (with rhythm), there's the we of the community, the *Volk* (90). "Deep down inside the adolescent wants to be led" (91). He's a we-ego but he self searches: that's why he often appears "difficult and moody like an ill person during the incubation period of an infectious illness" (92). Youth is full of itself, full of contradictions. That's why there's a "split" between "purely material sexual primitive bodily experiences, often masturbatory in nature," and "romantic yearning relations with the other sex" (91). But since we're given to do splits, sexual aberrations, "so-called perversions," do follow pretty regularly from our teen passion play.

J. H. Schultz's *Gender, Love, Marriage: The Basic Facts of Love and Sex in Their Significance for the Individual and for the People* was the sex education manual operation fully authorized by the German Institute of Psychological Research and Psychotherapy. Schultz starts out by reassuring his readership that masturbation in childhood and, next in line for early developments, same-sex intimacies are within the norm. "One's own sex is closer to us than the opposite one, and it depends on many purely extraneous circumstances how long and how explicitly this period of normal youthful goal uncertainty will take" (56). The homoerotic crush doesn't have to be consummately sexualized. What's more, these attachments are often between the more masculine boys and the more feminine types ("girlish looking boys with delicate skin, rosy cheeks, large feminine eyes, tender limbs and soft hands"): so it's just the dress rehearsal for going straight (71). Serious researchers view a small number of homosexuals as selected by inborn inheritance, but even this minority report is controversial (97). It's the psychic consequence of parental misguidance by a cold "witch" of a mother and father who's a softie. Show me this couple, half soft, better half cold, and Schultz will show you a homosexual (96–97). Schultz moreover takes the European view of homosexuality as akin to stuttering (99). "Lapses in the area of love life, the so-called perversions, are fundamentally always treatable through an appropriate professional treatment of psychic illness (psychotherapy), and this is that much more the case, where the problems have been brought on by tragic vicissitudes of fate, especially during childhood, in otherwise completely healthy and fully valuable individuals" (98). To acclimatize his audience to the evidence of diverse perverts who are everywhere that you innocent bystanders simply overlook, Schultz goes on a techno-digression: "How many people ride the electric street car or in a truck or plane without giving the workings of the miraculous technologies the slightest thought" (97). But human development, sexual and otherwise, all the way to the solo heights of Goethe or Bismarck, is "infinitely more complex, miraculous, and mysterious than even the most impressive technological accomplishment of the human spirit" (97).

The German language helps Schultz do his 1936 PR stint for psychotherapy within the new order. Anxiety *(Angst)* is etymologically related to *Enge:* narrow straits, tight squeeze ("Das Leib-Seele Problem," 291). And there's only one German word (in Freud, too) for psyche and soul: *Seele.* In keeping with the spirit of changes, then, the medical discipline is born again through the "rediscovery of the soul" (292).

> Here too there's interplay, since the scientific exploration of nervousness ("neuroses") and the medical healing-treatment through psychic [or soulful] means ("Psychotherapy") in the last half century were in turn the pathbreakers for realization of the animated vital unity of man. In the last decades it could be seen in controlled hypnotic experiments conducted at the leading clinics in all civilized nations, in particular in our fatherland, that all the activities of the human organism . . . are open to influence of psychic functions; it doesn't matter whether we're considering a sick or healthy organism; what's decisive is only whether the functions are altered. Only beyond the functions, when local or total destruction of resources *(Zerstörung des Bestandes),* in other words, localized death, takes over, only then does the possibility of psychic influence disappear completely. (292–93)

In 1940 Schultz soulfully defends his discipline's usefulness at every age or stage. He understands that physicians mistake the patient suffering from a kernel neurosis *(Kernneurose)* at first sight for a degenerate. But these neurotics are really fully valuable stock; they were just misguided and got stuck in childhood. Healing these types means restoring valuable human resources to the community gene pool. In fact it's often the strongest who are most vulnerable to damages, for example, catching parents out in a lie. Parents are the "axis" of the child's being; if the child is struck here, then apocalyptic, end-of-the-world prospects open and shut his case (the image Schultz uses is *Götterdämmerung*). Schultz consults Adlerian colleague F. Künkel, who calls the decisive crisis a "*Wirbruch,*" a "breaking of the 'we,'" inside the child; this "we," the very "bed" of his little ego, goes crack ("Der seelische Schutz," 214). Then there's the "catastrophe" of puberty: it is not the masturbation that creates problems, but certain interventions in what comes naturally to youngsters can prove very damaging. It leads to impotence, the secret meaning of unexplained suicides or nonmarriage or marriages without offspring (215). The fallout is the noncontribution of these fully valuable specimens to the future of the *Volk.* See a therapist!

Next year, in 1941, Schultz has slightly altered his strategy. Now he gives the psychiatrists certain hardened psychopaths as bad stock but keeps in exchange the psychoneurotics, who can be healed and restored to the eternal, internal life of the *Volk*. (By this date, psychiatrists were getting nervous about the rise of psychotherapy's value in the new order; pretty soon, if they were given only the discards, then after the killing stopped, they'd be out of business.) Schultz is emboldened to give "depth psychology" its due in the concise history of psychotherapy out of the same holistic spirit that spawned National Socialism. But while he looks forward to cooperation with psychiatrists who can point out to the therapist which psychopathic patients are just waste, he jumps the gun of elimination and declares the majority of homosexuals to be "kernel neurotics" ("Psychopathie," 229).

Council of Marriage

Schultz proposes the "Psychic Reasons for Infertility." Psychic reason number one is a deficiency in the will to procreate *(Fortpflanzungswille)*. But this number is dedicated to those who still come out sterile, unfruitful, even though the *Fortpflanzungswille* seems "genuine and serious" (22).

> Let us remind ourselves briefly of the basic facts of bodily function. Next to local functions, the whole oscillation *[Gesamtschwingung]* of the organism and that deep psychic, dissolving willingness to give oneself is also necessary so that the symphony of love can resonate in both equally and evenly. It's just in this so important and so delicate area of life that every observation falls short that seeks to understand the processes of life only in derivation from the organs. Always ancient, time-honored forces of nature and the most profound human experience interpenetrate one another. (23)

Certainly gender certainty and self-affirmation must be ready and waiting. But guilt feelings get in the way. "Here the deeper cause of sex incapacity can be located in unnatural child raising practices that were inimical to the senses and prudish, and can be fixed through a medical psychic work of healing (psychotherapy)" (23).

"Above all things love must seek out the whole other person, not individual particulars or parts" (24). Along these parting lines, Schultz can conclude, checking off two problems at once, that the so-called perversions are in truth cases of varying degrees of infertility. (Again, he throws in the safety net: don't confuse perverts, who are neurotics, and thus healable, with the untreatable birthright of psychopathy.)

Hattingberg considers "Marriage Crises from the Medical Point of View." First off, couple conflicts are to be expected during this time of transition between two epochs. So don't be embarrassed. However, when you come into my office going on and on about how great your marriage is, I have to wonder about the hidden tensions. Perhaps this exchange is only the first-stage alert. When the crisis advances further we reach a highpoint in the development of "a type of neurosis for two" (909).

Modern or "more conscious" citizens may think that marriage is outmoded. But they're wrong: it's still (more than ever) the "germ cell" *(Keimzelle)* of the *Volk* community. It's also a good format for doing individual work on one's inner self. We especially need marriage the more conscious we become (910).

Crisis is therefore not a fatal sign but, like fever, the signal of healing processes battling the trend toward sickness. There can be "development through love." For couples as for individuals, "Freud's essential error" was to derive neurosis (which tends to overlap with incapacity for loving) as a "consequence of a repression of sensual love wishes" (911). Yes, in the Platonic sense, there's a basic bisexuality that is worked through during adolescence. "When the developing youth leaves behind the neutral stage of childhood and takes on a gender role, that signifies the *erection of an order of values*" (912). Because "only through the other do we come upon ourselves." But we defend ourselves against ourselves via the other, too. But it's the least resistance on the evolutionary scale that gets tipped toward a new relationship between man and woman with every new marital crisis. This new relationship is what the big fight is all about. Outside the rocky ride of the new relationship in the long run of the species, equality or equi-finality in the individual couple is finally guaranteed by the third player. The meaning of marriage resides in a principle of thirdness. It's the children who bring this principle to life.

Werner Kemper puts through his emergency broadcast on "The Psychic Component in Sterility": work groups are being set up all over Germany to assist in cases of childlessness. All perversions are "developmental disturbances of the psychic capacity for love" (399). Although millions of women do conceive without orgasm, there are enough who don't. According to Kemper, therefore, the wanting orgasm in women is our biggest problem. Kemper calls on the Germans to fight the good fight against coitus interruptus. "Highest commandment of psychotherapy in the fight against sterility will be and will remain the constant awakening and maintenance of the will to the child" (399).

Finck shares his thoughts on "*Volk* Health and Love Life" in 1934. It has not been a very long time now that knowledge of how reproduction works is generally available. But what has always worked is representation of mother as carrier of procreation, as "symbol of the eternity of the race" (287). And this is all you need to know:

> But when we know that we are as individuals nothing, only the transitional vessel for a temporary preservation of our hereditary mass *[Erbmasse]*, only one link in the chain of the clan *[Stamm]*, then the significance of all these side effects of the great natural process, which uses us only as means to an end, shrinks considerably. We learn to estimate marriage from the point of view of the race, see how all possible factors interpenetrate one another,

> personal, economic-social, *Volk*-sy ones, to allow the ideal image of harmonious marriage to emerge. (289)

Before the Nazi revolution, women were like spiders, capturing any man they could for the sake of marriage (290). Now selection rules. Race mixture is in the family's way. It's always an extreme case of perversion, fixation on earlier stages of development, before the emergence of the will to the child. Sex education for teens was a Jewish plot that had terrible consequences. The Jew can't help being sexualized; it's just the opposite for blond beast boys. Those subconscious undertones with which northerners can swing are not available for Jewish reception. For the Jewish set, what's erotic can't be background music but must be blaring on top. No beauty of the body for the Jew: only fast-food appetizer. Every "swinish habit dressed up in a scientific coatlet could refer to the psychoanalysis of the great Jew Freud" (293). *Jud Süß* was a novel only a Jew could write (and only a Nazi German director could turn around as the screen memory of the deeper more primal race crime). Northerners are slow to develop; Jews are always sexually precocious (294). That's why there's always a "danger of psychic infection," which becomes that much more dangerous in its stealth, its slip into the "subconscious" where the drives and fantasies are engendered that are foreign to one's kind, one's race. Obsessive or perverse sexual "associations" are foreign bodies in the Aryan unconscious (294). Historically the Germans have been infected by some race mixture: they must steel themselves against all foreign thoughts. Let the purification begin. But down into the unconscious the race is on to outrun the impurity to the source where the Nordic track can begin again.

For the Aryan, duty always comes first: the primal drives are there, and we must get used to them, but the race is what's kept foremost in one's mind. The value of one's own personality resides in the family, the race (292). "The whole of one's love life must grow together with the consciousness of duty to our race to such an extent that it can no longer be separated from that consciousness, also not in the subconscious" (292).

Mohr Therapy

> As far as psychotherapeutic technique in particular goes, all methods, to which we have recourse, can also be applied to what are for the most part physical afflictions, and yet one must remember that there are only a few methods, which to a great degree aim at the root of the illness, where the somatic and psychic are almost indistinguishable cohabitants. That is hypnosis and autogenic training, as Schultz has described it, on the one side, and analysis in the widest sense on the other.
>
> —FRITZ MOHR, "THE BODY-SOUL-PROBLEM (FROM THE POINT OF VIEW OF THE PSYCHOTHERAPIST)"

The World War I experience on the front of greater psychoanalysis convinced not only Fritz Mohr that every psychic disturbance or aberration could be cured or adjusted, that most breakdowns could be avoided, and, finally, that a major portion of the so-called physical illnesses remained accessible to a psychic fix on treatment ("Aus der Praxis der Psychotherapie," 1119). In a series of articles published between 1915 and 1917, Mohr hails Freud's war-conditioned contribution as a new energetic eclecticism in therapy culture ranging from the mobilizations of hypnotic suggestion and electroshock all the way to long- or short-term analytic therapy. Even if, as Mohr observes, the practitioners of this eclectic spread of techniques may want to avoid the name "psychoanalysis," Freud's model was still the underlying one that was being used by one and all. Indeed, the detractors of the name brand were at the same time operating with the Freudian notions of flight into illness, gains from illness, and repression (1118).

In 1944 Mohr extended therapeutic correctness and coverage to homosexuals, defending their rights as neurotics against their fixation by the Weimar homosexologists which thus had them tagged out for extinction.

> For decades it was considered completely settled that in the development of homosexuality only physical predisposition and chemical changes in the hormonal process (based on anatomical divergences), in other words, purely bodily factors played a role. One boldly claimed (in particular the sufficiently well known Magnus Hirschfeld) that homosexuality is always given at birth, has nothing to do with pathology, the homosexual is as far as the rest of his behavior goes often a completely normal person, indeed in certain urban circles he was even granted an almost finer

> and higher status than the average man. Only gradually as all attempts to arrive at an organic, clear, and certain diagnosis of homosexuality failed, and after one came to recognize that the claims of many homosexuals that they had been homosexual from childhood on, had never had heterosexual experiences or even feelings did not hold up, was the way open for another perspective. At the same time the results of depth psychology had clearly shown how an infinite number of items that seemed only physically explicable were in truth basically psychically determined. With that, room was also made for a completely new view in regard to homosexuality. ("Einige Betrachtungen über Wesen," 1–2)

Mohr's opening case study came to him in 1940 via the local prison hospital. Caught in the act several times running, the patient now can remember all the way back in adolescence and, indeed, in early childhood only a lack of libidinal interest; what's more, the little there was was heterosexual. When he was seventeen a gym teacher's pep talk about the sexual abstinence that wrestlers must practice before their matches was his biggest sexual turn-on to date. In 1918, while under the influence, he was for the first time seduced by a fellow soldier. Then there was a hiatus populated by barmaids. But when he entered his next all-male institution, the German version of the boy scouts, he was actively recruited by one of the boys for a mutual masturbation session. On the way to his current prison term and his sessions with Mohr, he kept on being caught being come on to by boys who got younger as the years went by.

According to Mohr, homosexuality isn't so much a sexuality on its own as it is a way around an ego-libidinal blockage "on the way to the girl," which a series of traumatic experiences has set up along the dotted lines of repression-trauma that went down in early childhood. But that means that what's coming out in homosexuality isn't sex: it's self-esteem. This takes the homosexual back to the origin of his neurotic component, which "was there" right from the start and through which his homosexuality becomes accessible to the intrapsychic view master.

> So we see in this case, as I have often been able to observe, that the sexual component plays far less a role in homosexual practice than does the need to prove to oneself that one is held to be particularly valuable, thus receiving in the other's evaluation of you the confirmation of your own value. (7)

Mohr therefore cracks his homosexual cases war neurosis style by blowing up the neurotic component of the patient's makeup put on in early childhood. But in the big picture, the component part exceeds the whole: homosexuality "is a partial manifestation of a neurosis in which the bisexuality that indwells every individual makes its appearance in an abnormal way" (13).

> By grasping these connections at first intellectually between his actions and experiences from childhood and adolescence he no longer related to them uncomprehendingly as if faced with a demonic power that one cannot confront because it is so enigmatic and uncanny. But that is the precondition for a gradual inner change. It is accompanied by a series of inner convulsions. . . . In the beginning it was clear that the intellectual process could not alone effect a change, and only gradually did the inner convulsion bring the new insights into deeper proximity with the rest of his psychic life.
>
> The result of the enlightenment and the depth-psychological disclosures was in this case quite a good one. (8)

Beaming up the endopsychic messages from another patient's dream, Mohr introduces his inside view of homosexuality into the present tense or tension of the Nazi worldview:

> The seemingly purely sexual wishes are in truth only a symbolic expression of his wish for acceptance into the totality of life and for the consolidation of his psychic totality. After all, sexual disturbances are in fact always disturbances in relations with the totality. If he wants to take control of his sexuality, he must accordingly reorder his relations with life as a whole. The dream was thus trying to tell him: Transform your physical wish impulse into the psychic one of connectedness with the totality of the world and of the people. You then have the guarantee that your homosexuality will dissolve itself within this higher relationship. (13)

That's why treatment "must aim at effecting a change not through direct attack on the patient's homosexuality but rather by directing itself against its basis, the asocial attitude in its totality" (14–15). This approach is designed for patients who do not on their own wish to be transformed. Mohr considers the prospects for these resisters:

> We all know that the results one obtains with the neurotics who do not come to treatment of their own volition are always extremely questionable. Here the state has prepared the way for our psychotherapeutic work through its severe treatment of

> homosexuality insofar as the extremely uncomfortable position into which homosexuals have today been brought promotes in a larger number of such people and to a greater degree than ever before a wish of their own to get out of this situation and a willingness to be treated. The state and psychotherapy thus in this regard go completely hand in hand. (16)

Mohr is grateful to National Socialism and, ultimately, to psychoanalysis for supplying a basis of operation that does not need to castrate, sterilize, or eliminate. The more impressed Hirschfeld's followers and their bio-psychiatric enemies were by physical conditions and conditionings the less is Mohr: "The only treatment that brings truly lasting results is the depth psychological, the analytical one" (16). In 1921 Mohr saw a patient who in his fervent wish to straighten out had already been through a series of radical treatments. One surgeon agreed to remove one testicle to cut the drive in half. Then a vasectomy was performed on the remaining one. The patient was next advised that just one more operation, which would transplant someone else's testicle in the missing place of his own, would cure him. He cruised the prisons looking for Mr. Volunteer. In deep despair over always coming out of jail without the pair, he checked in with Mohr: "What many unindicated surgical interventions failed to accomplish could be attained through a relatively simple psychotherapy in a rather short period, namely a transformation in sexual matters and a normal capacity for work and life. He married later on and engendered a series of healthy children" (15).

At the end of a psychoanalysis-compatible rundown of the neurotic constitution of sexuality and of the way treatment can bring unconscious factors (identifications, sadistic components, etc.) to consciousness, Mohr gives a final portrait of the healed homosexual. The entire shoot, it turns out, was arranged for a family album out of place in the total picture of Nazi Germany: "His false tendency to see in love only a power problem is thus dissolved and he comes to understand that in true love both halves must be equal partners" (18). What a fragile thing is healed homosexuality reserved thus for the democracy of true love: the one-sidedness of perversion is free to spread inside the antidemocratic institutions of the all-male bond. Mohr's first case study of healed homosexuality was already working close to the net where male bonding and homosexuality are caught in a near miss. Consider how the patient's willingness to go straight is typecast:

> He himself says that when he joined the boy scout movement he was fleeing culture back to nature. Homosexuality surely did not consciously play an essential role here but rather it was his hap-

> piness at being fully accepted into this circle, at being able to play officer and be together with natural people. His pronounced aversion to the type of homosexual you could come across back then in certain big city bars also fits in here. (8)

What also fits in here is the synchronization of the onset of his homosexuality with the concluding year of the lost war. In 1918 the war bond between natural people spilled over into homosexual excess. First comes a depletion of outwardly directed heterosexual libido, then comes the upsurge (back in the barracks or inside oneself) of the basic need for self-esteem. The drunken one-night stand belongs to a demonization of the homo front, where libidinal depletion or excess no longer toed the line of the war effort. The "knife in the back" view of how the German soldiers lost the war is too hot to handle. But it's a demonization that's so far away (like all projection) but also (this time around) so close: homosexuality is a contagious disease that can strike down millions of all-natural men and thus deplete the future reserve or resource of the generations coming soon.

Hands-on Reproach

It was Heinrich Himmler's sense (inspired by Hans Blüher's popular World War I work on the homosexual erection of extrafamilial institutions) that institutional life (especially as it was then being radicalized inside out through the Nazi revolution) was not naturally on the side of generation. And it was this sick sense that backed his all-out confrontation with the contagion of homosexuality. It was a projective affair. Out on the streets and down the corridors of institutions, the main target of the Nazi sweep was the very origin of homosexual excess (and access): mutual masturbation or, in short, masturbation.

> Before the Röhm assassination, very few cases of homosexuality came up in the Hitler Youth, but afterwards they became shockingly frequent. The reprimand index *(Warnkartei)* of the Hitler Youth. . . . shows that between 1934 and 1939 about 25 percent of the 4,800 youths expelled from the movement were expelled for homosexuality, in addition to those expelled for "moral offenses," some of which were basically homosexual. . . . Youths were stuffed into the over-crowded prisons as punishment for mutual masturbation, for which penalties of 2 years and 6 months were handed down even before 1935, when the penalty was raised especially for "seduction." (Johansson and Percy, 234)

In the 1935 volume on the merits of choosing psychotherapy over castration, the authors come down hard on the masturbation problem (indeed, in the case studies of healed homosexuals, the lessening of masturbation is always the indicator of the beginning of a good prognosis):

> Mutual masturbation in adolescence is definitely a very serious danger. Let every educator be alerted to this loud and clear. Most of them never free themselves from this experience. (Böhme et al., 125)

Mutual masturbation comes out of the "development of masturbation which bears association, no matter how one chooses to think about it, with homosexuality" (56). Masturbation is what keeps bisexuality coming: "Masturbation still after puberty, masturbation during marriage is the rule" (72). The development of masturbation—in other words, mutual masturbation—must be eradicated: "It drives woman out of the sexual imaginary; it carries man into the imaginary as a valid partner both physically and psychically" (74).

Udo Wendel, *The Art Magazine.* Reproduced from *Die Kunst im deutschen Reich* 4, nos. 8–9 (August–September 1940): 242. This average-to-repressed middle-class family unity examines together the nudes in *Die Kunst im deutschen Reich.* The photograph should bear the title *The Inoculation.*

The intrapsychic controls that had fine-tuned the healing of war neurosis started flipping through all the channels when Freud's victory through analysis was escalated into a total libido therapy to go with the Nazi war effort. The analytic breakthrough reversed itself and went into autodestruct on all fronts. In other words: even the autoerotic origin of sexuality was to be scrubbed down and blown up.

Hugo Lederer, *Wrestler.* Reproduced from *Die Kunst im deutschen Reich* 4, no. 12 (December 1940): 373.

According to Mohr's scan of this handheld imaginary, the homosexuality or mutual masturbation (or masturbation) that catches on and spreads externalizes or acts out a purely psychic contagion that has been gathering momentum on the inside through displacement by association:

> At age 10 or 11 he masturbated with some other boys out in the woods. When he was 12 he was propositioned by another boy who asked to be sodomized. Although he was willing, he was not encouraging, and so nothing came of it. Characteristically the homosexual inclination toward the 12-year-old fellow student

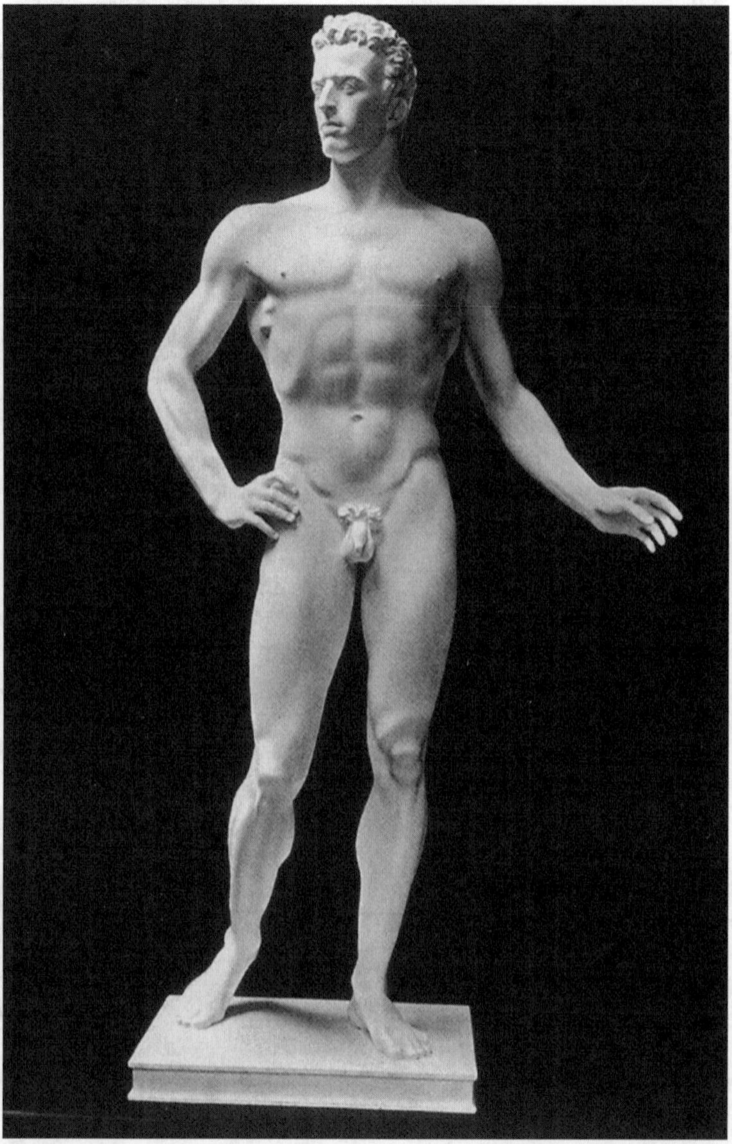

Arno Breker, *La Vie Active.* Reproduced from Charles Despiau, *Arno Breker,* 91. From a letter he wrote in 1942 to a former student on the Russian front: "May providence give us the strength to crush completely in this year our hardest opponent. Cheerless is only that this inferior race has cost so many sacrifices, since we require immense strength for the powerful tasks that await us after the war." Reprinted with permission of the family of the letter's recipient.

> went over to his 23-year-old brother and from him on to another brother. One sees here clearly the purely associative displacement of such sexual feelings. ("Einige Betrachtungen über Wesen," 11)

Once it goes into intrapsychic orbit (off the prefab launching pad of early trauma reinforced after the fact by the penetration-or-identification proposition that failed), the circle jerk starts turning on one and the same axis with the internal recycling center of libido with no place to go. Mohr concludes that with homosexuality it's the traumatization brought to us by missingness or abuse that creates a limit (backed by internalized and self-addressed rage) that redirects all libido through the stricken and stuck metabolism of self-esteem. That's why there is a connection between the fast-food mania of Mohr's patients' object choosing and the melancholic condition that corners and covers them from the outset. This is Mohr's way of saying that the shortness of the attention span he observes going with the all-male object choice does not serve substitution. What goes around and comes around inside the homosexual consumerism of objects is the one irreplaceable relation (to the body, that is, to the mother's body). It's as though this is the way every mother's son would infinitely prefer, if left to his own devices, that is, out from under the pressures of heterosexual couplification, to come and go. But once you're backed up against that one limit, the off-limitness of the mother's body, there are in fact two and a half ways to go.

The halfway measure (as Freud called it when diagnosing the kind of double vision that sets fetishism oscillating between neurosis and psychosis) covers the repress release of homosexuality inside psychosis. Before World War I showed Freud the way transference could expand even on contact with the narcissistic neuroses to create a no-man's-land or borderline where psychotic shutdown mixes with accessibility to treatment, the broadcast of psychosis was coming in on the three channels of a mixed reception that was the native habitat of homosexuality in Freud's thinking. It was the place where the disintegrative release of unresolved homosexuality (or sublimation breakdown) was conjoined with melancholic grief mismanagement and the projective rapport with technologization. These prewar connections (from Leonardo da Vinci to Schreber) were premature articulations of the inside view of war and trauma that would lead Freud to reorganize his thought along the lines of a psychic war economy that set ego against double, life against death.

But the two full ways to go are also too ambivalent by half. In German the "way" to the girl can also mean "away" with her. To follow the detour around the mother that father sets up and enter matrimony, you must go

Josef Thorak, *Female Nude.* Reproduced from *Die Kunst im deutschen Reich* 4, nos. 8–9 (August–September 1940): 265.

the way of substitution of incestuous and same-sex ties. Freud says the problems a wife encounters while trying to preserve a first marriage still come from relations with mother; the marriage problems the husband faces cross the heart of the couple and hail from father. Freud's double reading of the taboos on virginity and menstruation lines up father and wife as the primal parents of a coupling that must be conjugated as nonoriginal: the father's premier penetration of his daughter-in-law outlaws the son's wish to be or be with an original. That's why each time husband hangs with the regressions that go down with group or adolescent psychology, wife heads off at the impasse yet another invasion of the couple by the matricentric

Arno Breker, *La Grâce.* Reproduced from Despiau, *Arno Breker,* 79.

group. The ambivalence of this tension goes all the way: the couple that the group cannot admit or leave alone is at the same time the group's reproductive agency, its future. That's why homosexuals are always the mascots and trendsetters of group psychologization, and that's why they are the suicidal and sacrificial stars of mass (both communionist and consumerist) society. They're the way to go, and they've got to go.

Lesbianism beams up into this context or contest as threat only through the (homosexual) confusion of frigidity with infertility. All women get attributed to them a confusion or lack of direction of desires that's the static on the male-to-male transmission going through them. It's like: what don't they want (and who really cares anyway). That's why women (straight or whatever) can make their careers fantasizing and theorizing about the male bond. Look at Leni Riefenstahl's *Olympia:* these are a woman's fantasies about the male-to-male transmission that rub the backs in the sauna scene all the way to a near miss with homosexuality. It's what all-natural males in paramilitary outfits like to see and hear. But they've got to be careful: an excluded woman's fantasy about their bonding happiness can always infect them with the contagion of mutual masturbation or homosexuality (which loses the war that loses the race).

The Women

> And since flight is not a natural function of man; since it has been won by centuries of effort; since it has been climbed so arduously, not simply stumbled upon; since it has been slowly built, not suddenly discovered, it cannot be suspended as the word "freedom" is suspended in the mind. It rests, firmly supported, on a structure of laws, rules, principles—laws to which plane and man alike must conform. Rules of construction, or performance, or equipment, for one; rules of training, health, experience, skill, and judgment, for the other.
>
> —ANNE MORROW LINDBERGH, *NORTH TO THE ORIENT*

Leni Riefenstahl has been likened to test pilot Hanna Reitsch as the other woman who did not fit a certain down-home model of Nazi antifeminism. Riefenstahl was into planes but left the flying to Udet, even when she was playing the pilot in *SOS Eisberg*.

> Action! We start—Udet flew a few loops, then cut the motor and headed toward the iceberg increasingly losing tempo. I closed my eyes, and when I opened them for a split second, it seemed to me that the iceberg was collapsing on top of us. Then came the crash—a spark and the machine was in flames. With the speed of lightning I jumped into the icy water, Udet followed a little later, since he couldn't appear in the shot. (Riefenstahl, 175)

But the pilot series set another trend that kept up the tension with the breeding requirement, which resembled a kind of techno-segregationist movement for women that was, along the way of upward displacement, lesbian-social. Beate Uhse, who flew fighter planes from the factory to the front for the Nazi German air force, started her postwar sex-gadget-love empire by selling contraceptive information she lifted from medical books. A certain German wish not to reproduce is what she sold hard and fast on the clicking heels of the lost Reich. But this wasn't only a postwar wave she was riding out. The birthrate was already hitting all-time lows in Nazi Germany, going down with the shock of recognition between comrades and then their war widows.

Erika Hantel, who belonged to the growing equal opportunity for women as therapists in Nazi Germany, was able to pursue on location her interest in the psychology of the Nazis. She extended her specialization

Beate Uhse promoting the opening of a new sex shop. Reproduced from Roland Müller, *Beate Uhse: Vom Mut einer Frau*, 72.

during and after the war to therapy in factories that, by fixing a focus on "accident neuroses," for example, entered the same continuum or assembly line of trauma internalization and technologization occupied or cathected by the war neuroses. During her thousand years, Hantel did a stint as consulting psychologist at an airplane factory. The postwar era, which the Americans would lend to the society-wide cultivation of "human relations," would be reclaimed by Hantel as the still new field for women on the sidelines of relations between men and machines.

Beate Uhse as a young student pilot in the Third Reich in 1937. Reproduced from R. Müller, *Beate Uhse*, 60.

In 1947 Hantel argued that these cyborgian influences, which were mutual, she was sure, modeled the breakdown of relations between the sexes. The polar tension between men and women was no longer productive at this moment in our technological development. Women, eccentric outsiders, and the unconscious ("blind spots in our psyche") had been left unattended by (and thus exercised remote control over) the superficial, fetishistic concentration of phallic, omnipotent energy and thought within machine relations. "All those disowned violent emotions, all the originally warm feelings

Beate Uhse and her special Jamaican friend. Reproduced from R. Müller, *Beate Uhse*, 83.

that had to be pressed back, live on in women as ghosts" (*Verborgenes Kräftspiel*, 43). But these are the side effects of an evolutionary transition: Hantel encounters this misfiring link to the future in a worker-patient suffering from attacks of dizziness who was formerly a long-distance pilot. He is the "exemplar of a new human species"—"the flying human"—or at least "a human with a new psychic balancing disposition" (49). It is her countertransference that first tunes in his new wavelength: as he leaves the session she is overwhelmed by feelings of endless emptiness onto which her sense of warm empathy next washes up. He wasn't a pilot fulltime in his former life: he had a half-life on the ground as a *Hausfrau*. The sheerly phallic space he regularly traversed as pilot pressurized him to develop a feminine space for polar tension release and relaxation. Thus Hantel prescribes that her patient must fly again and cook and clean. "The machine devours the human and transfers its properties to his psyche" (51). But because man isn't only machine (because he is also woman), the new balancing act between the sexes, airborne all the way, is the transitional phase of a future distribution of sexual difference across intrapsychic air space.

While the triumphs of technologization (Hantel continues in her 1953 book on psychology for industry) leave out the influence of the feminine and maternal, the recent war has at the same time outnumbered manpower

Beate Uhse, still her own pilot at age seventy-four. Reproduced from R. Müller, *Beate Uhse*, 49.

and turned the population of women into an overabundantly unused resource and reserve. This recalls a model resolution of the "women's question" posed already during the middle ages crisis when an imbalance in sexual difference emerged in excess of the even chances for couplification: in the twelfth century a priest, Lambert le Buegue, established special colonies and collectivities for women only to house the excess as the access women could now have to each other. Hantel was already grooving on the feminine aside to the historical war record during World War II (indeed, her only wartime publication that's part of the 1953 work features this feminist fantasy). "The Bueguine concept released energies which would have gone under with pain, grief, and fear for one's life. It unconsciously transformed a situation of danger for women into productive life, and resolved a women's question through the purely feminine disposition of interiority" (*Brücken von Mensch*, 92). Within the original 1942 version, Hantel points to a woman of today who, following the loss of husband and all his sons to the war effort, turned her home into a special place for women whose spiritual and intellectual work she advised and guided. "Such a decision is the birth of the maternal principle in woman, who remains faithful to herself as woman in a time of greatest need. Such an example, reduplicated and carried out in many variations, would be the beginning of feminine women's colonies, informed by a completely practical but yet moral notion of leading and helping, connecting and shaping" (93).

Colonization

In Britain the air war occasioned a necessary remobilization of psychiatry, a bit of good luck that doesn't stop there. What was accomplished thanks to the second chance world war gave British psychiatry should never again be one time or wartime only. Even or especially in peacetime, issues ranging from industrial concerns to all the conditions of group psychology will still need to be treated. For the future, John Rawlings Rees therefore recommends more of the same: a "broader application of analytic understanding" (137) to be administered by "shock troops," "mobile teams of well-selected, well-trained psychiatrists" (133).

On Emergency Island the group response would also raise the ghost of a sexual meaning closeted inside war neurosis: save the war bond of comradeship, spear homosexuality across the heart of group psychology. In 1946 Fairbairn spearheaded the object-relations move to give cases of perversion the group rate. In fact, his first postwar application of the lab work with traumatized soldiers followed the bouncing male bond from the breakdown of defenses to sexual offense. The wartime distinction between individual treatment and rehabilitation or maintenance in group format could be recycled, no problem, to make perversion's untreatability accessible to theory and, then, practically speaking, to adjustment according to a group plan.

Fairbairn uses Freud's time-release caption, the one that says that neurosis is the negative of perversion, to locate the difference between perversion and psychoneurosis. But to appreciate how far Fairbairn is going with this formula, we must turn it around within the extra dimension of Freud's second system until it reads: perversion is the negative of psychosis.

> What the sexual pervert does is to capitalize his perverse tendencies instead of repressing them, with the consequence that they not only become overt, but assume a dominant position in the structure of his personality. The resulting situation may, to use psychiatric terms, be summarized in the statement that the sexual pervert is not a psychoneurotic, but a psychopath. (Fairbairn, "Treatment and Rehabilitation," 291)

> Characteristically he regards his perversion as a personal asset, although he may disguise this fact for reasons of expediency.... Basically he despises the standards of the community of which he falls foul... and what he seeks at the hands of the community

> is not cure, but reinstatement. This desire for reinstatement in the absence of cure is perhaps the most characteristic feature of his attitude. (293)

Fairbairn relieves the inconsistency he's still having with his opening analogy between the psychoneurotic soldier and the sexual offender by confining his comparison chopping to both their lapsed group memberships. To confirm that the pervert's therapeutic habitat is the social group, and that only group therapy can raise the morale of his case history, Fairbairn draws attention "to the frequency with which individuals addicted to certain forms of sexual perversion form groups of their own within the community. This is, of course, particularly common in the case of homosexuals; and it is characteristic of such groups that the difference between their standards and those of the community is not necessarily confined to the sexual sphere" (293). That's why the therapeutic potential of special interest grouping must be uncovered in new, remote-controlled groups.

> What appears to be required therefore, is the establishment of special communities for offenders—settlements with a group life of their own, in which offenders can participate, and which is psychologically controlled with a view to its gradual approximation to the life of the community at large. (294–95)

Missing the war experience with neurotic soldiers, Fairbairn takes better aim with the civilian population of perverts: "The establishment of such settlements would have the advantage of providing a unique field for the scientific study of social relationships and the factors which determine the nature of a group" (295).

In his review article on Fairbairn, Winnicott described without comment (and thus became silent partner in) the extention of the rehab practice with war neurotics to include the special handling of sexual offenders. This selection of perverts (that is, up front, homosexuals) for the first postwar support groups and, thus, for group-therapeutic assessments of group psychology coincides with the introduction of acting out as the idiomatic phase or phrase of pop psychology or adolescence that is still with us. Acting out comes to symptomatize for the postwar era the all-new conditions of latent homosexuality, homosexual panic, and the double bind of homosociality. This introduction of acting out into group-level interaction is itself only another form of acting out in groups. Only by skipping a beat and getting stuck in a groove on the war record of psychoanalysis can homosexuals be advanced as the true veterans of the psychological war effort.

TAKING PART

Buffoonery

At the U.S. end of the war, Abram Kardiner's work on war neurosis, which Judith Herman reset as the therapeutic standard for all the accounts she's settling on behalf of psychotherapy, poses the male-to-male bond both as problem leading to the coming out of neurotic conflict and, inoculation style, as resource that contains the impact of trauma in self-protection and self-healing. This is pre-Oedipus: the male bond, the free gift that comes with military group membership, is now the only complex that's up for treatment. In his 1949 report back from his World War II application of a happy medium of psychotherapeutic techniques that openly depart from the psychoanalytic model to which every departure is still owed, J. G. Watkins offers some of the earliest examples of confrontation in session with a patient's "latent homosexuality," hidden but seen in the symptom support it gives unconscious behavior. Watkins asks himself, "Could this understanding be initiated into X without creating a panic?" (337). But then he goes ahead just the same and provides the buffer zone of a denial-style explanation designed to get the aggressive impulse off.

> Have you ever heard some soldiers tell how they enjoyed beating up a homosexual who approached them? Why do you think they got such pleasure at mistreating the man? It was because in so doing they were able to deny the existence of feelings which they themselves had deep down inside. (339)

No way is the patient or any of the other soldiers actually homosexual. But male bonding plays too close to the net of near misses with homosexuality not to act out rather than, horrors, remember its sexual senses. Latent homosexuality and acting out together suspend a safety net that must catch the approaches of homosexuality, which, as William Menninger poses the problem in his 1948 study, was classifiable by 1943 as constitutional psychopathy (*Psychiatry in a Troubled World,* 225). Indeed a 1944 War Department directive "provided for hospitalization of those who were deemed reclaimable. . . . Included in the category of 'reclaimable' were those who were guilty of first offenses, those who acted as the result of intoxication or curiosity, or 'those who acted under undue influence, especially when such influence was exercised by a person of greater years or superior grade'" (229).

The preemptive strikes already against the coming out of the homosexual disposition or component at the same time opened up the border with actual homosexuality. Take—to this shifting borderline—one of Menninger's examples of acting out or tension release in military groups: "An interesting sublimation has been excellently described by Janis as 'homosexual buffoonery'" (224–25).

> In the barracks, usually when the men were getting undressed, one frequently observed play-acting in which various persons "kiddingly" assumed the role of overt homosexuals. One soldier, returning from the shower room in the nude, was greeted with catcalls, salacious whistling, and comments like, "Hey, Joe, you shouldn't go around like that—you don't know what that does to me." Joe responded by coyly draping a towel around himself wriggling his hips in feminine fashion. Some of the men joined in the buffoonery by playing the role of the appreciative spectator: "Ain't he hot stuff though!" "C'mon, take it off." Others acted the part of active solicitors for sexual favors: "How much do you want for sleeping with me tonight?"; "Come into my bed and I'll give you the time of your life." (225)

Menninger lifts the locker-room activity sheet verbatim out of Irving Janis's "Psychodynamic Aspects of Adjustment to Army Life." But the coy boys adjusting their towels just a heartbeat below the tan line do this regularly in the Janis vignette; in Menninger's transposition, all the sexual tension is past tense, "history." Janis: "Joe will respond by wriggling his hips in feminine fashion after coyly draping a towel around himself" (Janis, 171). Menninger: "Joe responded by coyly draping a towel around himself and wriggling his hips in feminine fashion" (*Psychiatry in a Troubled World*, 225). Someone's diction is showing. But what Menninger leaves out is the real possibility made explicit by Janis (who's not the one with two faces) that some guy on his own could play the buffoon as "a channel for substitutive sexual gratification" (Janis, 171). Janis stresses that this outside chance of someone getting off under these covers produces the guilt feelings that would arise if it weren't for the unanimity of the group's acting out. The extremes to which the buffoonery is carried are the guarantees it comes with that none of the participants would be caught dead crossing each other's minds with actual homosexual thoughts. This so-called "acting out of homosexual play," which belongs to the special effects of the group projection plan, absorbs the shocks of recognition that go down in the one-on-one. But a history of shell shock comes up between homosexuality and its latency, its acting out. The psychopathology continuum or column was made to close ranks (to heal!) from war neurosis through perversion to psychopathy and back again. The therapeutic lab space that first opened up under the air pressure of total war finally contained only one kind of bonding happiness (or was it happiness envy?). It was the new phallus that bisexuality, latent homosexuality, and acting out filled or suffused up to the group level where no actual homosexuals could get off.

Back in the U. S. of A.

R. C. Anderson is all afterglow on the upbeat: the war gave so many boys the opportunity to realize their wish to fly that it "is as though all the little boys of a bygone generation who dreamed of being cowboys actually had become cowboys" (18). (I take it these ghosts are friendly?) Back in wartime there were three types who really took to the skies: the lover of flying, the schizoid, and the psychopath. But fellow flyers will look on a true lover of flying as "somewhat apart," too: "They speak of him as 'having the bug,' 'being plane-crazy,' et cetera" (19). When it comes to facing stress, the schizoid, who's in it for the solitude, and the psychopath, who loves the height, both fall apart way before the true lover of flying, whose focus is the plane itself. "To such a man the sheer joy of flying, of 'being a part of his plane,' is enough to compensate for any attendant anxieties for a long period" (26). Anderson refers to Grinker and Spiegel and to Douglas Bond but isn't fazed out of what at first reading appears to be his couplified and heterosexual phase of gadget-loving development. For Grinker and Spiegel, the attraction a plane holds for the pilot is, simply, unmitigated and unidentified narcissism. But on double take, does Anderson take his plane love straight, or does he rather see the pilot take off from the straight path up and away into out space?

> Not infrequently, such an individual makes sexual analogies with flying. The wife or sweetheart of such a man is truly an "aviation widow." These men are devoted to their aircraft and tend to personalize them and identify with them. Bond has spoken of the libidinization of flying, which occurs in this type of flyer. (20)

In *The Love and Fear of Flying*, Bond doubly names the bonding of sameness as the circuit of this libidinization:

> Perhaps it is precisely this narcissistic quality of the fantasy that provides the protection against trauma so noticeable in devoted airmen. For when there is a close blend of flyer and plane, there may be no room for the insertion of a traumatic factor that might separate them.
>
> The narcissism, the relative indifference to women, and the pronounced rivalry among flyers all point to an unconscious homosexuality. . . . The fact that the homosexuality remains unconscious is very striking. (26)

Unlike the bomber crewman, who is closer to the hatch that unconsciously overstimulates associations with birth and defecation (22 n. 8), the pilot, for all his narcissistic grounding in the fuel injections of unconsummated homosexuality, flies all clear of more occasions for neurotic breakdown. "The freer use of aggression and the greater joy in flying fighter planes are factors which account for the observation that fighter pilots, as a whole, are far less emotionally disintegrated by combat than are bomber crewmen" (39). But when war neurosis does strike the pilot (and his machine) in the form of phobia and panic, the lab opportunity for watching what's happening in slo mo (precisely because the pilot is so well defended against shock) is not to be missed:

> Because the aircraft is a very delicate instrument for the measurement of anxiety, and because the phobic condensation makes certain that the anxiety will be manifested in the aircraft, it is possible to study the very earliest beginnings of the formation of a phobia and to watch its development. The spread of such a phobia is remarkably similar to the spread of an agoraphobia. (43)

But what is suspended for observation on the wings of gadget love comes down most commonly to a loss in the category of buddy love, which scatters death wishes back at the pilot.

> The death wishes of men suffering from combat neuroses become strikingly evident upon exploration. (72)

> The phobias for combat or for flying that we observed all began with the reversal of the formula "nothing can happen to me" to "some disaster must happen to me." . . . The commonest cause for this reversal was an identification with a dead or a wounded companion on the basis of unconscious aggression. This identification universally manifested itself as a phobia for flight. (81)

Bond's parting shot is reserved for the U.S. military's faith in selection going into war. It may be the very measure of before and after 1941 relations between psychoanalysis and the U.S. military-psychological complex.

> One wonders whether some emotional reason did not underlie so unrealistic a system. The remarkable pretense at prediction of success and failure in combat, common to medical and line officers alike, suggests a widespread defense against the emotional impact of combat—the denial that mutilation and death are in themselves strong enough to change a man, and the assertion

that more important factors are whether he has wet his bed past the age of six or whether he can take orders or whether he is a competent flyer. It seems very likely that some such defense was at work, for combat dominates an army to an almost ludicrous extent and gives final meaning to being in the service. (125)

Boring

> A pamphlet entitled "What's the Score in a Case Like Mine?" is being distributed to Army Service Forces hospitals in the zone of the interior to assist medical officers in the treatment of military personnel to be discharged from the service because of psychoneurosis. This W. D. Pamphlet 21–35 provides information which has been found helpful to such patients in recovering and in adjusting to civilian life. A copy will be given each patient at the time it has been determined he will be separated from the service for psychoneurosis . . . except in cases where the attending medical officer considers this contraindicated.
>
> —"PSYCHONEUROSIS"

In 1945 *Psychology for the Armed Services* entered the college level as textbook for military psychology classes. The first words of "Acknowledgments" by editor Edwin G. Boring: "This book has no author" (x). In content if not in form, now more suitable for the 1945 public forum, the book had a service record as a 1943 handbook for use in the armed services that was the work of sixty correspondents. In fact the college version builds up on a service past entombed together with the unknown authors: "It was based in first place upon the content furnished by the sixty collaborators for *Psychology for the Fighting Man*. . . . While the present text is indebted to all of these sixty persons, it does not seem proper to reprint their names. They must rest content with being its unmentioned ancestors" (x). A whole National Research Council Committee (at the same time a subcommittee of the Emergency Committee on Psychology) prepared and sponsored the textbook.

The book's mode of operation is to call on all together now to listen to reason. "Personal Adjustment" recalls for all of us that life is about "changing things or people—making something in a factory, . . . getting a girl to like you" (344). Following the civilian slide of change right into home base, there's the military portion of change that's self-related: "The other half of life is changing *yourself*, adjusting yourself to the inevitable, the unalterable and the necessary" (344). Psychoanalysis (which goes unmentioned) is along for this mobilization of the self:

> When one comes to consider the adjustment of the soldier or sailor to the many new requirements which military service lays upon him, it is convenient to keep in mind the distinction between his

> *social needs* and his needs as an individual. These latter are sometimes called his *ego needs.* Man is fundamentally egoistic. (345)

Because the soldier can have no immediate future plans in the eternal present of readiness for combat, every longer stretch of waiting around during the many latency phases of warfare can be unbearable (or boring?). To come up with an alternative to the time killers sex and drink, a whole network of correspondence courses has opened up for degree work in your spare time (349). That's the course of action the 1943 handbook took to get into your schedule, syllabus, and curriculum vitae.

As for all extracurricular activities that are left once the new requirements of camp or campus life have been fulfilled, "there is a loss of privacy. His life has suddenly become public. If he looks much at his girl's picture, his comrades know it" (346). But they're looking where? Or is another connection, made further down the textbook pages, the one to look out for? "Military life, moreover, is so public that masturbators are likely to be found out and made the butt of joking" (403). Move over, there's more. Because the punch line could end up in your butt. (Don't give me the difference of coeducation! It's still same sex in the locker-room space of possibilities.) Where there's public, there's private parts, too: "The absence of normal heterosexual opportunities in the services increases any tendency toward the establishment of secret homosexual relationships. A man of strong sexual drive, who in more normal conditions of life never dreamed of homosexual relations, may be seduced to them" (407).

Among the many resources of personal adjustment that get homespun together, there's insight, too. Take this remarkable example of insight in action:

> The man who invented the sewing machine was baffled by the fact that he could not get a machine to hold a needle, with a point on one end and the eye in the other, and have the needle go all the way through the cloth to pull the thread through. Then he dreamed that he was being chased by men with swords that had holes in their pointed ends, and at once on waking he had his needed insight. Put the needle's hole in its point and fix it so that it can go back and forth. That is the way inventive genius depends on insight. (351)

What he needs, as in Kafka's torture-writing machine, in his wartime story "In the Penal Colony," isn't the insight he gets, not directly. What other swordlike items have holes at their pointed ends? Gadget love intervenes to get around the anxiety production of homosexual dreaming by threading the pointed end of the needle of his machine.

But for the majority of relief seekers from frustration there are two attempts regularly made to adjust to the frustration: defense mechanisms and escape mechanisms. Now Freud gets named: "During the last forty years, under the original stimulus furnished by Sigmund Freud and psychoanalysis, these mechanisms have been studied, understood and given names" (352). But whenever the Boring squad gives the rundown, the drill, of mechanisms, the psychoanalytic ones are doubled by extras from the ranks of eclectics who follow psychoanalysis but have their own ideas, too. Among the defense mechanisms, therefore, we also find "exhibitionism" and "compensation" (353). Compensation's coverage gets overfilled with an example of how complicated the problem of anti-Semitism is, in particular in American contexts of adjustment. It's an example that comes within earshot of the reference to Freud. Compensation has the Adlerian ring of inferiority when superiority is asserted to cover up the other, deeper sense of self. Thus the compensator always also perpetuates a trauma. By acting superior, the compensator attracts criticism that wounds his already low self-esteem and thus gives even higher rise to the superiority act. "Thus a vicious circle is set up" (354). Vicious also because the responsibility for persecution can only be collective.

> A great deal of the prejudice of Gentiles against Jews functions in this way. The able and competent Jew finds himself unfairly discriminated against by many of the Gentiles with whom he has contact. He feels inferior because he does not command their respect, yet, assessing his own qualities, perhaps correctly, he feels competent and not inferior. At first he may try to compensate for his handicap by aggression. But the Gentiles turn out to resent the aggression, partly because it fortifies the prejudice they may already feel toward Jews, partly because it is apt to get mixed up with the Jew's deference (an escape mechanism) which is a logical mechanism to try next by way of appeasement for the prejudice. Deference and aggression are, however, contradictory and the Jew then appears to the Gentile as inconsistent, insincere, a pattern which any majority group can readily force on a minority group. Hence the Jew's attempt to adjust to the prejudice has eventually the effect of strengthening the prejudice. That tends to make the Jew try ultimately to escape from the Gentiles, to associate primarily with other Jews where he finds no prejudice,

> but the prejudiced Gentiles do not like this any better. They become disturbed because they see the Jew helping to form a strong cooperative group of persons toward whom they are already ill-disposed. (354)

While the Boring squad also granted that many homosexual and bisexual men who make it into the services often do make excellent soldiers, and while the textbook also admits or permits that frustration can promote various kinds of homosexual adaptation, including temporary solutions for otherwise heterosexual men that are not held against them, the final word is that there's a huge social body of complications out there just waiting for homosexuals. It's just stupid to be a minority.

The textbook functions like a handbook for internal use when it comes to war shock. Leaders and fellow soldiers are asked to be on the alert for symptoms of war shock or, better yet, for advance signs of impending shock reactions in themselves and in everyone else:

> The first thing for them to watch for is anything that makes a man stand out as awkward or queer among his fellows, anything that makes him look odd to the other men, that sets him off as "not belonging." Does he stay by himself too much? Does he go for long periods without speaking? Is he known to other men as having queer ideas? Does he find conditions intolerable when other men manage to accept them? Is he a problem in the outfit? (366)

Thus a community service opens up around an open column of advice entrusted to and led by the leader, but equally open to fellow soldiers or citizens as guideline for recognizing and turning in suspects (for their own good or betterment). The gadget-loving detail that also comes out of such sometimes murderous mutual identifications gets honorable mention, in conclusion, among the rules for building up immunity in the armed services: "Give them also understanding of themselves as psychological machines, so that they may handle themselves wisely and know what is the matter when the mental machine goes wrong" (370).

Consensual Text

Neuropsychiatry in World War II is an act on improv nightmare for resisters acting out independence that has no other grounds for declaration: "Improvisation and empirical data were the keynotes of our therapy. Psychodynamic understanding of the significance of breakdown was not part of our armamentarium" (U.S. Army, *Neuropsychiatry*, 2:461). Here are some more combos that label their psychoanalysis covers as originals, started from scratch, not off the record:

> Perhaps the most important contribution of military psychiatry of World War II has not been stated. This concerns the subtle or gradual orientation of psychiatry as a result of wartime experience toward considering the emotional problems of the individual within the context of his group and his social culture, instead of almost exclusive preoccupation with intrapsychic conflict or pathology. (1:759)

> There are basically two schools of thought on psychiatric treatment in combat. One believes in appropriate psychotherapeutic intervention to provide emotional catharsis and to recover amnestic memory losses; the other, that recovery is essentially a function of social support, and that any kind of psychotherapeutic intervention is contraindicated. (2:635)

> The relationship between the patient and the physician was always considered to be the primary recovery force, regardless of the methods or devices used. Hypnosis and suggestion succeeded only where the therapist was skilled, sure of himself, and capable of establishing a quick positive transference. (2:649)

In the midst of anything-goes, the all-importance of the transference in the healing of soldier-patients, even if it's only a quickie, reminds us that it all still comes down to psychoanalysis (even when the psychiatric unit gets named, as happened in one case, "The Fitness Center" [2:93]). Narcosynthesis serves as a short-hands-on version of psychoanalytic therapy in the wartime zone: "It is not certain that the technique actually performed anything which could not be carried out by more or less prolonged psychoanalytically oriented psychotherapy, which of course was rarely possible in the forward zone" (2:906). The independence declarations are couched in highly ambivalence-vigilant assessments. The United States overrelied on selection procedures for the Second World War to put the screen on and block from consciousness the nonstop techno-internal receptions of war trauma. "Some Freudian-oriented psychiatrists considered the fear of death and mutilation to be a recrudescence of childhood fears" (2:128). In theory this fixation on the past is codependent with the defensive use to which overselectivity was put. We should consider, to boot, that the psychiatrists charged with selecting out all those in any way so predisposed to develop neurotic reactions in the war zone were at the same time given only five minutes max to exercise their extreme selection: "This indifference in providing sufficient time for such a difficult task perhaps best illustrates the denial of the psychiatric problem in World War II by reliance on a token process" (1:743).

The metabolization of psychoanalysis demonstrated by these examples went right into the writing of this history of psychiatry's war experience:

> In June 1945, Brig. Gen. William C. Menninger, MC, developed an original outline for this history. A few months later, after several revisions and changes in format, Lt. Col. Malcolm J. Farrell, MC, produced the outline which was generally accepted at the time and followed, but with little success, for attempts to complete the work failed, until 1957 when the project was again resumed.... [Then,] discarding this approach, the old history outline of Menninger and his associates was resurrected. (1:xv–xvi)

Menninger then has the final word, as when, in chapter 5 (which he coauthored), he makes himself laugh last and lastingly:

> Incidentally, contrary to the popular jokes about the mysterious jargon of psychoanalysis, their presumed obsession with sex and the couch, most psychoanalysts in the Army did outstanding work and earned the high regard of their colleagues and superior officers. (1:84–85)

Group therapy was all over the place and up for grabs. Psychodynamic leadership was promoted, but frequently psychiatrists improvised, made it all up as they went along, playing it now as lecture circuit, now as talk show that he would always host (he was the host with the most transferences) (1:323). But not unlike the primal repression that Freud could never let go, there was always, at the beginning, an introductory offer of drug- or hypnosis-induced memory abreaction with plenty of rest and talk, an offer made only to be withdrawn—into the group. "The 'mothering' period of treatment ended in 24 to 48 hours. Then men were encouraged to take part in group activities.... This was... done voluntarily, as part of the team effort to bring about improvement in the immediate environment" (2:648).

Even after selection had picked out the obvious candidates for breakdown, the pressure cooker of war brought the less-obvious candidates quickly to their breaking point. As bad as that looks, it was also good news, to the extent that early treatment always guarantees the best prognosis (1:255–56). The rate or ratio of breakdown cannot be altered by selection criteria: "To circumvent the escape mechanism and remove secondary gain from illness, it became evident that it might be necessary to retain, rather than discharge, known psychiatric noneffective personnel" (1:39). Preselection, together with the rapid turnover from health into neurosis back again into health, introduced a breakdown-proof economy that, however, since at the same time 100 proof, supplemented itself with the development of research projects on, and the opening of, entire military units set apart for psychopaths (who were in the army anyhow).

> The question of disposition is very important, and I think we must be much more hardboiled. They are here. We are going to redouble our efforts in every way to find some place where they can be fitted here. (2:201 [Colonel Thompson's memo of 25 March 1943])

The fit could get so good that new problems developed when we ran out of wartime: "Here was a complex problem: an individual normal or useful in combat, yet pathologic in peacetime" (2:106). "The severe personality deviates presented the same insoluble problems in the North Pacific Theater that they presented throughout the world.... As noted previously, these patients were deprived, because of conditions in the theater, of their usual mode of response; that is, acting-out. With this unavailable, other manifestations of their difficulties came to the attention of the psychiatrist" (2:722). Psychopaths found "the airborne way of life acceptable" and made expert paratroopers: "Command levels appeared to be lenient and often supported and encouraged a degree of acting-out behavior which may not have been tolerated in other Army elements" (2:382). Character disorders may be just what the Air Force ordered:

> In observations among the combat personnel in the Air Forces, including pilot officers and officers in responsible command positions, character disorders approaching the delinquent type occasionally occurred. At times, these disorders were helpful rather than harmful in adjusting to the peculiar conditions encountered in the combat air force, provided, of course, that adequate ego defenses existed to prevent the individual from being overwhelmed by anxiety or from destroying himself. (2:901).

In 1945 Lt. Col. Fred F. Senerchia, MC, gave a good summary of the Neuropsychiatric Service he saw during the war. Directions notwithstanding the temptation, too many psychopaths were being admitted; and if something constructive wasn't done with them fast, they would start undermining morale. It was decided they should keep themselves company. So a special company was activated for them only. Thus the psychopathic patient could be "processed rapidly and returned to duty to be handled administratively by the line" (1:285). Nor were the psychoneurotics dismissed out of every hand. The need for a new diagnosis of "borderline psychoneurosis" arose before acceptance. So when the psychoneurosis was pretty "mild" and the soldier not incapable of doing his duty, some psychiatrists helped him out by not putting the true diagnosis on the record, which spoke for itself (1:198). How sane do you have to be to serve? Personality defects need not get in the way (1:274). Nor were homosexuals always a problem. If they were caught, another kind of transference, transfer to another regiment, might be the only consequence and all-clear to follow (2:637). At a completely isolated Alaskan outpost there was one overt homosexual who was in a "panic" a short time after his arrival. His fellow soldiers, a "rough-and-ready group" (one might say "amoral in character"), had been holed up there for so long that they were ready to give it to the crack. The outlet associated with the homosexual gave the gang of men a sexual assault charge (the account closes with a general court martial for "the 10 men implicated") (2:701). U.S. military policy boiled down to a therapeutic distinction: homosexuals who were "non reclaimable offenders" would get the "blue" discharge (which signified "without honor" but was given in lieu of court martial) whereas those deemed "reclaimable" were admitted to hospitalization. The result: this womb inseminated with reclaimed semen.

The pilot was the first warrior recommended (by psychiatry) for solo status as long-distance syndication, as group of one, of all the fellows (who, if too close, dead or alive, were just the placeholders in his face of his own mortality timer).

> We found more success in splitting up a crew and distributing the men among other crews in instances where a number of men had been lost in bailouts or ditchings. This removes a source of depression and a constant reminder of the harrowing experience they have been through. (2:879).

Pilots tend to know that they experience a fear that's in the mind:

> One feature which tends to distinguish the neuroses of the flier from those of the average person is the strong conscious compo-

> nent which is usually present. Often, this conscious element is the presenting one, such as "I'm scared to fly." (2:882)

But phobia and conscious fear do double duty as symptom, too: "Such a symptom may be a clever disguise for the true underlying situation, especially important to bear in mind in the phobias of fliers" (2:882). The importance, given the seat the pilot occupies, refers to a process whereby the phobia can go destinal, especially when the address is shared, identification style, with a dead friend. In general, for the whole service of military communion, guilt is often just one more way for the psychoneurotic to stay in touch with the group: "The expressions of guilt . . . served as a continuing effort to remain identified with the values of the combat group" (2:133). But at the buddy level, this guilt is a real downer for the pilot and the flight team that depends on him. The pilot's fear of flying can soon become a takeoff "in the best Hollywood fashion." Each flight is going to be his last, this one has his name on it:

> Often, identification with a dead friend who was a "better pilot than I" may strengthen this conviction. The flier takes off on every flight unconsciously saying to himself . . . "This is it." (2:883)

The pilot's depression lies low, playing dead; but it does not, just the same, have to represent punishment for death wish benefits, but can also be taken as straight identification (another frequent flier advantage?).

> The more severe forms of reactive depression in flying personnel are usually the result of identification with dead friends or the assumption of responsibility for the death of others in crashes and collisions. Very often, the true underlying cause may be repressed hostility toward those who are dead. In the opinion of this author, however, such ambivalence is not necessarily present, and straight identification can occur without it. (2:885)

Rather than go for the phobia, the pilot who's in a depression with his dead friend is such a drip: "Those who develop depressions in such circumstances are usually somewhat immature and narcissistic in their personality makeups" (2:885). But if the makeup shouldn't be overlooked, it's because it won't be ignored. The plane, still according to the logic of prosthetic extension of the pilot's show of narcissism, soon doubles as "a convenient instrument of self-destruction which may explain some 'unexplained' crashes" (2:885).

The adjustment mechanism of acting out in groups therefore packs bad backfire for the pilot:

> The activity of combat flying was for many men a form of acting out. . . . Flying . . . is an activity which is rich in unconscious meanings and motivations as one would suspect from the frequency and nature of dreams dealing with airplanes and flying. (2:923)

But after the experts have all been cited, including Freud, to establish "the importance of acting out as a defense against depression" (2:923), one more tailspin is given the formulation: suicide is just as good a defense, especially in the covert form so available to depressed pilots.

> The presence of strong unconscious tendencies toward self-destruction was demonstrable in air force flying personnel. These tendencies, if not checked by adequate character defenses or, if remobilized by stress, often led to suicidal or uncontrolled homicidal acts, which were considered to constitute acting-out behavior as a defense against a depression. (2:928)

Getting to Know You

In "Dug-Out Psychiatry," Albert Mayers offers the hardest bulletin to bite and swallow:

> It is hard to imagine the American Army as an institution producing radical change in the field of psychiatry, but this is an accomplished fact. It has provided psychotherapy for the "normal" person—a vast change in psychiatric orientation—and it has used psychological methods in procuring better personnel, more skilled workers, and better oriented soldiers. It has also provided methods to improve and test group mental health. Finally, the lessons which have been learned in mental maintenance can be used in the greatest of all postwar problems—psychological rehabilitation, not for the veteran alone, or for the negroes, or for the displaced factory workers, or for the Germans, but for all. (389)

One of Mayers's anecdotal examples of the inroads of psychological methods in and through the military features a praiseworthy second lieutenant who improvises treatment of his antitank platoon while they're in the staticcling situation of waiting:

> When the weather was bad, and the men only went outside for guard duty, he had those indoors cut out Mickey Mouses which were utilized in making Christmas cards. . . . the one concern the Lieutenant had regarding the situation was whether he had done the right thing, psychologically speaking. He was chiefly worried about cutting out paper dolls, because he had never heard of rugged combat soldiers engaging in such childish behavior. The entire situation was reviewed as to what else could have been done from the psychological point of view, and the Lieutenant was reassured that since his plan had developed satisfactorily, it had withstood the pragmatic test. (386)

Between the occupational therapy and the passing of a test there's the lieutenant's transferential netsurfing with group mascot Mickey Mouse that wipes out on an undercurrent, turns around and calls Mickey a doll, and submits to the judgment of higher authorities. Mayers describes a spontaneous admission of relational therapies ultimately based on a new tolerance for the abnormal: "Due to the stress of battle all officers and men realize that there is not so much difference between what is called a 'normal' person and the men with combat exhaustion. The ultimate result is that all people soon feel a kinship with the abnormal person which is seldom perceived under ordinary conditions" (387).

Edward Billings and company drew their findings on war neurotics, homosexuals, and malingerers from two columns: one hundred army psychiatric patients from column A, one hundred enlisted men from B.

> When one inquires into the reasons of the patient for volunteering, one often obtains a quick clue to a basic maladjustment in civilian life. For example, 7 of the sick soldiers volunteered specifically for medical treatment, 3 to "make a man of myself," 2 to cure homosexuality, 2 because of unemployment, 2 to avoid quarrels with the family and 1 to "get my memory back." (287)

Patrolling the downbeat, depressive trends tend to reflect the stress factors specific to military adjustment, from inability to take kidding back to latent homosexuality and then, still moving in place, to withdrawal from alcohol and back to nonadvancement up the ranks (292). While a few cases are known to the authors of disturbed soldiers who were able to put their intrapsychic conflict on hold for the duration of the wartime experience until they all broke down peacetime, in most cases psychic disturbance in uniform canceled the soldier's functioning part in the war effort. The infraction of malingering, nearly impossible to determine, "particularly when it is well known that hysteria and overstatement are not mutually exclusive" (294), is the false alarm to set: "Actually the simulation of health is a more common and more difficult problem than malingering" (294).

Both overt and latent homosexuality rate low as good adjustment factors. It's not a good sign that all the triggers of their nonadaptive responses reiterate those already pulled for the depressed types. Caught between "failure of sublimation" and "lack of opportunities for continued homosexual relations," overt homosexuals who, when they were sitting pretty, were ridiculed to boot for any "obvious signs of feminism" were doomed to maladjust from the start, even without the added pressures (295). "In general, maladjustments in sexual development offered one of the better clues to total adjustment, for one of the more complex factors of maturation is steady and adequate progress to a sound heterosexual relationship, with the responsibilities of a wife, home and family" (295).

S. K. Weinberg treats the marginalized fallout of optimum team cohesion—"goldbrick," "goof-off," "wise guy," "sadsack," or "foul-up"—as "temporary lapses or phases of a soldier's assimilation to the army," as, therefore, transitional objections to assimilation that the whole group can process toward an even greater adaptability (271). Deviance "awakens the desire for conformity" (272).

One more for the Allies to watch out for: Bingham Dai presents the case of a Chinese patient on the theoretical basis of keeping up with Jones on the psychic state of divided loyalty to the state in time of war. The patient was bisexual, but his identification with his father and through him with the Japanese was hot. He once again passed though his early homosexual resolution of the Oedipus complex. In this case, the superego delivered homosexuality as the punishment that sex attracts or that is itself sexually attractive.

Furer

Margaret Mahler's "pioneering task of trying to conceptualize childhood psychosis with the frame of reference of psychoanalytic theory" (*On Human Symbiosis*, vii) is just a few beats out of sync with two corners of a context, Klein's work with children and the next generation's work with soldiers and teenagers. But before that, at the precursor level, there's less ambiguity. Mahler gives Victor Tausk's 1919 study of the psychotic delusion of machines of influence plenty of referrals. Tausk's work is propped up by the immediate context of psychoanalysis meets shell shock (Tausk contributed two pieces to the war neurosis effort). It was soldiers, not women and children, who were first.

Tausk's "On the Origin of the 'Influencing Machine' in Schizophrenia" was his exploration of the techno and occult fantasies making up a delusional system in time for world war (and inside the same window as Kafka's "In the Penal Colony"). Mahler took this lead back into infancy and to the real-time developments that can be espied when the little ones are kept under surveillance. Mahler adds a mother and child reunion where Tausk was left reading, in the delusional system of his patient Natalija A., the encrypted mummy that the patient was tuning and turning into under the influence of a "cinematograph." Back in prehistory or real time, Mahler sees mother and infant prying one another loose via "identification through partial introjection" from their "hitherto 'omnipotent common orbit'" (205–6). The psychotic infant is the one that can't separate from mother during their voyage through the same space. As a result, bodily sensations are "experienced as if the body were powered by more or less demoniacal, ego-alien mechanical forces (the introjects), and whatever object libido is available is in turn vested in inanimate objects and/or quasi-animate machineries" (209).

During World War I the movies offer shelter from the wipeout of catatonia following your direct psychotic connection with our otherwise subliminally and sublimationally veiled technologizations. In the fifties, Mahler's new assembly of words to express the way development comes and goes represents an all-out symptomatization of the emergence of electronic warfare out of the world war dyad. When it comes to "emotional refueling," for example, she's following Furer (17). Then there's also "the infant's constitutional 'sending power'" (151), its innate "signal equipment" (34); baby doesn't coo but participates in "mutual cuing" (34): Mother is now a "beacon of orientation" (231) for the "checking back" or "scanning" function (17, 16), now a "buffer" zone (231) and "holding" pattern (18) that holds out a "protective shield" (16), now "home base" for "refuelings" stops (69), now the diplomatic receptionist with whom the infant negotiates "customs inspection" (17) and, finally, "rapprochement" (23). When the infant has been "helped . . . to become ready to 'hatch' from the symbiotic orbit smoothly and gradually—that is, without undue strain upon his own resources" (18), and in contrast to the combo of premature hatching and bad mirroring (19), then the thought that crosses the mind, the road, or the skies is not just the chicken and the egg but also, in the order of what came first, the "bombs away" of air war (which, back feeding the kids, drops "down the hatch"). As already implicated in what falls from above, mother's good or bad mirroring, a "'mirroring frame of reference,' to which the primitive self of the infant automatically adjusts" (19), is also tuning in techno-channels of military history and TV guidance. The terms Mahler has collected in part hail from a detritus of anxiety left over from the total world wars (as in refueling) but largely already participate in an electronic replacement of these limitations and fears within a new techno-order of feedback. The case presentations also occupy this transitional space, one footnote in depletion technologies, the other in the switchover to electronics. For example, in the case of Steve, when the orbit still holds and you've got no body image, even as the hands, on the one, on the other, are there anyway, there's always the television set and then the set of responses: acting out and mirroring in front of the tube.

> Steve sought another mode of compensation through histrionics and addiction to TV and movies, mirroring all the actors. That is to say, he tried to compensate for the deficit concerning the visual part of his body-image demarcation by his voyeurism and by attempts at mirroring identification. (207)

Stanley, another one of Mahler's orbiting charges, has had his fill of introjects. He is symptomatically in sync with the same live era, but within an infrastructure of feedback and all-out computing that gets around repression even as he therefore doesn't make the cut of selection.

> It seemed to the observer as though the boy were switching himself, as it were, from one mode of behavior into the other. Once he had switched himself "on," it often seemed as if the motion were generated from within him, as from an engine—an engine gaining momentum and running so powerfully that the child had no way of stopping it. . . . Stanley's attempts to reach some

> kind of homeostasis and adaptation to reality expressed themselves in numerous other ways, all of which were mechanical and machinelike. (219)

> Stanley commanded a fabulous memory, but this memory at close examination turned out to be a storage of disconnected engrams, unorganized as to the qualities of essential or unessential. . . . The most essential defense mechanism for normal development, that of repression, has failed in Stanley's case. (220)

Mahler's study of psychotic infants confirmed Tausk's World War I focus on the projective-cinematic mechanisms whereby the wasting products of aggression get ejected outside the body, which is thus constituted complete with inner/outer boundaries. But she went one step further, earlier, into a zone where no researcher had gone before (except for Melanie Klein, who, however, according to Mahler, was all over the place with fantasies that just can't come up before the first year of life). Mahler followed out a libidinal movement from an original autistic shell to the outer ego shell of the sensorium, the move that's required before the projective extensions of the bodily or bound senses can begin. She preempts Tausk by going back before him in developmental time to a period of preprojective identification that's as quiescent as a corpse, dead or alive. That's why this early stage really functions only as a coordinate or orientation beam for where psychotic regressions in a psyche so young could be going. It's no known phase of development to which a psychotic child or infant regresses. The way back to these "preobject relations" (81) can, however, be analogized, first with traumatic or war neurosis on the downbeat and, next, on the upbeat, with fetishism: "With his own baby book Stanley behaved like a traumatic neurotic who tries to overcome a trauma, bit by bit, through endless repetitions" (89). Mahler evokes and pushes to the side of her more primal concern the notion of "separation anxiety" associated with the object-relations research on war neurotics and acting-out adolescents during the Second World War. The phase and crisis she is addressing is way earlier than the development required before separation anxiety can be experienced. In fact, when this anxiety emerges in the course of her work with psychotic children, she is given a transferential indicator that real improvement has taken place (234). Mahler's innovation then was to build into her theory of the mother and child union a kind of reserve tank for supplying the psychotic regressions of young children with a place to go. By focusing on an identification that's "on" even before that already early birth of development or technology out of identification's alternation with projection, Mahler enters mirror stage left. But unlike Lacan's electronic compatibility with psychosis, Mahler's souped-up model covers a place of tension between the TV cathexis and the projective kind represented by film or photography. Mahler's patient Alma lives with her own doubling reflections (and thus with her mother). But just as often she's completely inside what she calls her "live reflections":

> "It is as if I have to live with my reflection (like when I look in the mirror) [the mother in herself] and I have to face my reflection when I see people because they are my walking or live reflections." The fusion of all three representations—self, mother, and world—is expressed in her own words: "What if I am the living reflection of my mother and when I look in the mirror it is a double exposure." (128–29)

What the patients externalize in between techno war zones is the psychotic fetish, an inanimate object that holds the child's emerging and reemerging investments. "In our experience, children who are brought to treatment with such a stereotyped, yet outward-directed and focused activity have a better prognosis" (165). Although psychotic children are not candidates for group therapy with their disturbed peers, they do benefit from a kind of acting out (or psychodrama) in which the uncontaminated or unconditional support they need from their "auxiliary egos" is performed by "a team of adults." The team spirits "represent diversified substitutes for the pathological symbiotic object, thus diluting the impact of the pull to merge and the dread of fusion. Continual infusions of borrowed ego strength may have to be given for a long, long time" (182). But already with the making of the fetish, these kids have helped themselves—to a new link with what's missing (comparable to the connection afforded by transitional objects or even, in fact, by the missing link) (111). The psychotic fetish takes off then as the nonprojective connection with the earliest form of shell shock, the collapse across the threshold halfway back inside the autistic shell.

A Couple of Fetishes

In *The Spirit and Structure of German Fascism,* Robert Brady diagnoses Nazi "science" as "a fetish of 'co-ordinating'" (39) at the out-of-focal point of many boundary dissolves. Inspiration or intuition and scientific truth do overlaps together as "inspired truth":

> All sciences and "culture" must be co-ordinated and made to serve the purposes of the "leader," "total," "corporate," "master" *(Herren)* state. Propaganda is the method. Propaganda knows neither right nor wrong, neither truth nor falsehood, but only what it wants. (42)

There is no "objective," "universal" scientific validity: every science shows national and racial determination (the universal notion just belongs to the particular Jewish perspective that knows how to get around until every other POV is spread thin). What's more "there is *no clear line between science and non-science*" (49). If science is a tool that's always only spiritually or emotionally charged and directed, then the only "science" around is the one that's missing: psychoanalysis *as* the science of transference.

Published in 1944 for the Netherlands Government Information Bureau, A. M. Meerloo's *Total War and the Human Mind: A Psychologist's Experiences in Occupied Holland* examines a group war neurosis that developed out of the Nazi occupation or cathexis:

> It will therefore be understood that in the first three months of the occupation the people of the Netherlands passed through what I might call a collective neurasthenic phase. Just as the presence of an infection in the body is not necessarily the signal for immediate illness, so it is with a great mental shock. There may be a period of incubation during which the effects of the shock work subconsciously: sooner or later, however, the shock will influence the conscious life of a man in one of two ways, producing either complete mental breakdown, culminating perhaps in suicide, or else stimulating the mind to resistance. (18–19)

On the German side of this relationship there was always the "almost neurotic urge to form a unity" (29), even when the order, coming from on high, came crashing down: "The courage of this highly organized, immensely disciplined army is the courage of hysteria. I have seen planes brought down in flames, the crews of which went to their death shouting *Heil! Heil!*" (60). But How? How? Did he see that? We've touched down on the abyssal ground of internal conflict. The problem, as Meerloo indeed could observe in a setting of collaboration versus resistance, is that "we have within each one of us the seeds of democracy and fascism, and thus the struggle for the democratic or authoritarian attitude to life is fought out in each individual" (52). That's very "Dutch date" of him. But the Nazi is the young one:

> Germany as a nation is young and self-conscious. The German's sense of collective unity is a primitive one, it is a participation mystique. It overrides individuality altogether and is felt as a kind of ecstasy. Deutschland, in fact, becomes the fetish, the All-father, from which the German cannot detach himself. . . . The presence of these primitive tendencies in the midst of a civilized community has led to a remarkable state of tension in the individual. The German takes flight from his emotions in an iron discipline, in a passion for system and for thoroughness. (29)

The fetishistic oscillation between civilization or intellectualization and the cooped-up emotions that the German has flown between—in other words, neurosis and psychosis—runs its commentary through the modern history of German philosophy according to Meerloo.

> The two most important German philosophical schools of the years following the last war provide good illustratrions of this. Between 1920 and 1924 Vaihinger's *Theorie des Als-ob* had great influence; this theory of "as if" was used as a philosophical glorification of hypocrisy. It may be said that the whole Weimar Republic acted "as if," while underneath was a fermenting mass of irrational feeling which presently sought its theoretical justification in Heidegger's *Existenz-philosophie*. Thus there was first the glorification of pretence, followed by the justification of existence and of expansion. The theory of *Lebensraum* may already be found here. Even a philosophical system may have an emotional background, and it will be well for us to remember this when we are deluged with a flood of German semi-philosophical propaganda after the war. (73–74)

PARTING

Mummy's the Word

> A deterioration of morale that has gone to very serious lengths can show itself in negligence in the burial of the dead.
>
> —W. R. BION, "THE 'WAR OF NERVES': CIVILIAN REACTION, MORALE, AND PROPHYLAXIS"

Burton Stevenson began organizing his war literature in 1915 around an affair of espionage. At the end of this tour of literature, in 1918, he entered the mummy complex where cinema, psychosis, and war traumatizations were conjoined at the rip and roar of psychological warfare. In his 1915 *Little Comrade: The Romance of a Lady Spy in the Great War,* Stevenson focuses on an upsurge of all-maleness that will wrap up the woman agent in the cross-dressing of a wound: "'How easy it is for a man to do things!' she remarked to nobody in particular. 'Never speak to me again of woman suffrage!'" (40). Europe, "top-heavy under the burden of her awful armaments" (8), has suffered the little sexual differences to come unto her. When spywoman finally turns herself into a boy, she requires her fellow agent, despite his masculine protests, to cut her hair to regulation wavelength: he's now more turned on than ever (150). But her original come-on to her accomplice came via the slipper fetish she let slide into his suitcase to pump up his interest in her feminine sex: "A woman with a foot like that—" (63). But he doesn't put the foot in his mouth, nor does anything appear to melt in his hands. It's all in the spirit of metabolization in the blender of identifications of all the energy sources that must fill the slack and close ranks. Thus the only "tingling" admitted between two comrades is the one every soldier is into while awaiting "the order to charge" (101). All the "theories" (including or excluding the sexual-research ones) were up for testing in the new world war zone:

> Oh, this would be a great war! It would be like no other ever seen upon this earth. It would be fought in the air, as well as on the land; in the depths of the ocean, as well as on its surface. At last all theories were to be put to the supreme test! (109)

But whereas the 1915 war correspondence between desire and identification could only enter an espionage contest that was a total promotional, Stevenson's 1918 follow-up, *A King in Babylon,* assigned work of trauma control and preparedness for the long haul that took it all back, back to the mysteries of mummy. For long stretches, on the mark between split-off time zones, the war presses for cinematic replay within the metapsychological plot of all mummy fiction: the crypt frame that gets held up between reincarnation and reanimation. The terms of this contest sit well in one corner with mourning and substitution, and, in the other, fit melancholia precisely.

Director Creel's wish to make his mummy movie takes the crew away from U.S. studios across the maritime war zone to on-location sightings of ghosts in Egypt. That's what happens. But what recurs is the screenplay of the wish for many eternal returns: "Every member of the company... would appear both in modern togs and in those of ancient Egypt" (*A King in Babylon*, 39). Even actor and actress feel the undertow of attraction and danger picking up spectral momentum from a past life: "It was as though, looking up casually to greet a friend, she had found a spectre confronting her—a spectre which she had reason to fear and hate" (50–51). But what glides just beneath with the shock of recognition is internally related to, say, the fear of submarines that kept one actress from joining the crew's expedition to Egypt (26). The leading lady who has somewhere an obscure sense of her own reincarnation-destiny is spooked when she meets for the first time, once and forever, the leading man and somehow, according to her own double standard, recognizes him: "'I must go ashore,' she said, in a voice thick with terror. 'I cannot go on. It is impossible'" (50–51).

> A man who had been at the front told me one day that whenever a big shell comes screaming toward the trenches and explodes, there is always a moment of suspended animation, as it were, while the men wait to see whether they are dead or alive. I doubt if any bigger shell was ever exploded than that set off by Mlle. Roland, and I can still see that ring of astounded faces staring at her. By some freak of second-sight, my own face is always in that circle! (52)

Already reeling with mobile references to the film medium, the director's name, Creel, also belongs to the U.S. propaganda meister of World War I. George Creel founded the Committee on Public Information, which formulated inside views of the war (and ultimately the Fourteen Points) for enemy consumption only. Looking back in 1947, Creel has final cut of the war record he replays for all the good memoirs:

> Putting the Committee on Public Information together was like asking the Babylonians to build a threshing machine. (160)

> How could the national emergency be met without national unity? The printed word, the spoken word, motion pictures, the tele-

> graph, the wireless, cables, posters, signboards, and every possible media should be used to drive home the justice of America's cause. Not to combat prejudices and disaffection at home was to weaken the firing line. There was also an even greater task beyond our borders. . . . Not propaganda as the Germans defined it, but propaganda in the true sense of the word, meaning the "propagation of faith." (157–58)

Creel made the Fourteen Points into an "article of faith," the kind that political disappointments (like the Versailles conference outcome) could never compromise. But Woodrow Wilson's self-appointment as savior was boundary blended with the genuine article and its worldwide acceptance. He belonged to the war-neurotic model that was still hot off the repression. According to Freud and William Bullitt's analysis, which for Freud was set to go by the *Dasein*-rhyme between his own and Wilson's birth years (Freud and Bullitt vi), the Treaty of Versailles, the retreat from the Fourteen Points, forced superpsychic savings on Wilson who, however, on balance, had already broken down:

> It became self-sacrificing of him not to fight. By this somewhat circuitous route he managed to bring further support to his conviction that he had sacrificed himself for the welfare of humanity, and therefore resembled Christ. . . .
>
> Thus, most satisfactorily to him, he escaped from the inner conflict which tormented him. . . . A man may repress knowledge of an unpleasant fact into his unconscious; but it remains there struggling to escape into consciousness and he is compelled to repress not only his memory of it but of all closely associated facts in order to continue to forget it. His mental integrity becomes impaired, and he moves steadily away from the fact making greater and greater denials that the fact exists. . . . His mental life from April to September 1919, when he collapsed completely and permanently, was a wild flight from fact. This mental disintegration is an additional indication that in the second week of April 1919 he could not face his femininity and fear. . . . At the crisis of his life he was in fact overwhelmed once more by his passivity to his father and by fear. (263–64)

The dual diagnosis of Wilson's crackup is matched, according to Erikson, by the buildup and letdown that just as swiftly took down the Germans:

> When the last offensive had failed, Wilson, the enemy, in one of Germany's most sudden change of ideals was endowed with almost metaphysical trust, a blind belief in previously "foreign"

> values. His failure prepared Germany's complete break with the "outerworld." (Erikson, "Hitler's Imagery," 489)

In Stevenson's novel, the film work digs the site unseen of ancient burial alive; the discovery begins to give the historian who's along for the expedition the filler missing from a gap of five centuries in the account of ancient Egypt; and it gives away the screen story that Creel can now complete: "'Buried alive!' he cried. 'Whoopee! Professor, you've given me the one word I needed. I've got the story now! . . . There was one weak point in the story. . . . But buried alive! It's perfect. . . . It rivets the whole thing together into a water-tight, unsinkable bit of logic!'" (*A King in Babylon*, 134). In the technological mode, an excess of connections has opened up. The mummy has already been reunited with ghosts, vampires, and, in passing reference to an external namesake, Jekyll and Hyde. The missing and misfiring link of premature burial sparks connections and finally builds, as monument to and containment of itself, the unsinkable carrier on which the crew prepares for and survives *Titanic*-style catastrophes: "We felt a good deal as the passengers must feel on a ship which has just shaved past an iceberg" (139). If the narrator "had always thought that cartouche meant cartridge," and Creel that the transcript from the crypt "sounds a good deal like shorthand" (165), then it only follows that the film crew waits to see if the professor's find, the "missing link" inside the granite tomb of a living testimonial, will be "a monkey or something" (163), "with or without a tail" (186). The missing link is a tale from the crypt that doubly registers the war trauma of burial alive—"half unconsciously" (56)—within two separate time zones. The Egyptologist on the expedition diagnoses the male lead's possession by the part he plays in the reincarnation pageant as "manic" and therefore as endopsychically "clairvoyant" about "the secret of this place" (222).

As the two leads both fall into a deep sleep that unnerves the crew standing by, Creel wants to put an end to "those hysterics" (226) but is warned by Egyptologist Davis—whose insider's knowledge of the mummy complex represents (as always with the occult specialists in monstrosity fiction) the analytic perspective—not to wake them and give them yet another shock.

> "We burn more nerve force sometimes holding ourselves in than letting ourselves go," Davis pointed out. . . . "They both seem to be very highly-strung and extraordinarily susceptible to suggestion." (228–30)

Davis's therapeutic attention spans evolutionary wavelengths. The story on him is that "he has a theory that every time we yield to unreasoning fear, we are setting the race back toward savagery" (235). That's why the so-called ghost sighted at the end was really an ape: "It's a breeder of lunatics, that's what it is—this moving-picture business! You're mad, both of you! It was an ape, I tell you!" (309). Evolutionary linkups to the missing, filmy buildups of technologization and trauma time (live burial) all go the rounds within a gap in history and admit in the place of the stopgap of unmourning and missingness the future forces of selection (natural and military), invention, and psy war. Ferenczi closed his "Psychoanalysis and the War Neuroses" with consideration of evolutionary returns or linkups within war neurosis. Recent research, he observed in 1918, had produced with the right stimulus a small traumatic response in infants who would spread their limbs and then pull them back together as though semi-encircling someone or thing. Ferenczi sees here the clasping or holding-on reflex of monkeys and thus an "atavistic regression of the reaction mode in the face of sudden shock" (30). The functional misfiring of the war neurotic was only near missing the link that was there to the evolution of the doubled ego taking up position between neurosis and psychosis, the ready positioning for technologization (of trauma).

In Seabury Quinn's "The Man in Crescent Terrace," the grounding support the mummy phantasm gives the control panel, the machine, and the same wavelength of trauma confirms this phantasm's reserve supply relationship to a certain military complex. But the mummy also has a certain techno-look, which means it's running down those mediatic feedback tracks of the visible and the blind.

> The mummy was attuned to catch the slightest sound vibration, like a delicate instrument. (88)

> The mummy came on relentlessly, or more exactly, insensately, with the utter lack of caution of an automaton. (98)

But the "council of war" (93) the hunters of mummies and mummy creators must call (just as they call in a certain Grayson to assist them who was "formerly of the British intelligence" [94]) already takes us to the border. The mummy hunters organize themselves so that they "shall have two parties of two each for reserves" (97).

While they have separate followings, the genres of monstrosity nevertheless cosign each with the other in the corners of their respective works. Within the big picture of unmourning, the different occult figures occupy distinct phases or phrases. The vampire's trace is already breaking up the shutdown of mourning to which it owes its projective makeup. The mummy complex is stuck on the split between the corpse and the eternal and internal relations of long distance, between the object dead on its feet and the ready position, takeoff, and itinerary of flight. The light or life show of technology-compatible motion that a mummy seconds—*Ba, Ka,* astral body—is always on the verge of dropping back onto the mummified corpse, absorbing the spot of an instant of disappearance that can only be preserved. The spot that the narcissistically disturbed is always in gets blotted up by the endopsychic double track around it: inside viewing too much raises delusions of archaeological excavation or entombment on one side and delusions of technologization on the other, until it's curtains for the concealment of the psychic apparatus's dysfunction or functioning. We watch the apparatus inside us in mummy-techno-projective stereo.

The mummy phantasm owes its reception to the same agencies and mechanisms that brought us the case of Schreber's psychoticization or media-technologized thought control. Source and symptom alternate between melancholic attachment and psychotic delusion—but the alternator itself belongs not to Freud's first but to his second system. The primal origin of the mummy-techno-phantasm lies not in the still personalizable inside-out disorders of the psychic apparatus but in the nonmachinic conditions of what Freud called group psychology. If the mummy has been set up as the first artwork—or, like the automaton, as the material realization or end product of a narcissism (of an ego-body bond) that art is supposed to sublimate and psychosis simulate—then its place even in art holds in reserve technology's displaced origin.

Between the auto-analytic breakthrough and its alternating state, psychotic breakdown (which the mediatic reception of the mummy phantasm tunes in) the endopsychic part and portrait of the dysfunctional psychic apparatus arose to the attention of psychoanalytic theory. It was the cases of Schreber and Ratman and in the *Gradiva* rereading that only those analogues drawing on archaeological and techno phantasms were awarded endopsychic status. In 1918 Tausk followed his work on war psychosis with his analysis of schizophrenic patient Natalija A., whose persecution was inflicted by an "influencing machine," a coffin look-alike that happens to be a repro of a body (especially on the inside: the machine's batteries recall organs). By virtue of its telepathic and remote-control connection to the patient, and because, quite simply, as the patient admits, it kind of resembles her, the machine is her double: it projects her body back from the stage (to which she has regressed) on which it was a body-genital. This body-genital or machine runs independently of her ego. The fantasy that the whole body is a genital belongs to the "womb complex" (Tausk, "Über die Entstehung," 277): "The psyche increasingly approximates the womb" (272). When libido regresses behind the stage of identification, all contact with the outside world has either been given up for lost or reclaimed on the terms of the new world of two-dimensional externalizations, hallucinations, and mummifications. In the discussion following Tausk's presentation, Freud commented on the connection between the influencing machine and the significance of Egyptian mummification. The placement of the mummy inside a shell modeled on human form corresponds, Freud pointed out, to the "later" conception of the return of human life to Mother Earth—a return to the womb through death. Tausk has last say with the observation that mummification or return to womb is one of the four primal fantasies: it emerges as pathological reality for the psyche developing backward, where it gives symptomatic expression to schizophrenia. As Freud pointed out, the spiritual death the schizo undergoes as return to the womb rehearses or repeats the physical death that the mummy must pass through on its way back. This staggering of analogy leaves time for or performs what in psychoanalytic theory is always mourning's work on the death that, according to Freud, is never one's own but belongs always to the other. The detour through or around the dead other is narcissism's rerouting into power relations that can never return to one's own body. This, Freud says, is technology.

Hi Ya Heidegger

> The following was the occasion of the dream. Louise N., the lady who was assisting in my job in the dream, had been calling on me. "Lend me something to read," she had said. I offered her Rider Haggard's *She*. "A strange book, but full of hidden meaning," I began to explain to her; "the eternal feminine, the immortality of our emotions..." Here she interrupted me: "I know it already. Have you nothing of your own?"—"No, my own immortal works have not yet been written." ... The end of the adventure in *She* is that the guide, instead of finding immortality for herself and the others, perishes in the mysterious subterranean fire.
>
> —FREUD, *THE INTERPRETATION OF DREAMS*

Heidegger's example of a plane as the nonobject of technology (that is, as the last stand of objecthood brought to us by technology) is on the same reserve list on standby as the mummy conceived as cryogenic placeholder of return or, in Freud's manifest, as the identificatory control panel of projections. In short order, what Freud went on to address as group psychology, Heidegger located as the metaphysical emplacement of standing reserve *(Bestand)*. The mummy is not an object except in the mode of its concealedness. Revealed, it, like the plane on the runway, lies in wait as "standing-reserve, inasmuch as it is ordered to ensure the possibility of transportation" (Heidegger, "The Question concerning Technology," 17). Emptied of fuel reserves and thus of the possibility of flight, the plane, like the disinterred mummified corpse, embodies the object status that remains or returns at a loss.

"All attempts to reckon existing reality morphologically, psychologically, in terms of decline and loss, in terms of fate, catastrophe, and destruction, are merely technological behavior" (Heidegger, "The Turning," 48). Psychoanalysis, the owner's manual to our ongoing technologization, is also coextensive with the melancholic holding pattern that Heidegger would like to get over (or, in the mode of denial, inflict). In *verwunden* two German verbs briefly overlap in their conjugation: "to surmount or get over" (grief) and "to inflict a wound."

> For this reason the coming to presence of technology cannot be led into the change of its destining without the cooperation of the coming to presence of man. Through this cooperation, how-

> ever, technology will not be overcome *[überwunden]* by men. On the contrary, the coming to presence of technology will be surmounted *[verwunden]* in a way that restores it into its yet concealed truth. This restoring surmounting is similar to what happens when, in the human realm, one gets over grief or pain. ("The Turning," 39)

On the inside, the mummy embodies the *Gestell,* the techno-enframement that, Heidegger admits, "is also the name for a skeleton" ("The Question concerning Technology," 20). On the outside, the Egyptoid phantasm covers with the apparatus of projection the takeoff of "standing-reserve." The mummy propped up at the beginning of yet another version of the mummy phantasm in fact always concludes a process that began with a death that had to be placed (under wraps) in the reanimation ready position. At the beginning there is a dead person whose loss must be recircuited through the emergency sensurround of identification (containing the material loss or mummy) at one end and—at the other—projection (releasing the astral body, the double, the phantom telecommand).

Heidegger agrees. But then there is one's own death: it's the bottom line, ultimately, therapeutically, for one's capacity to "be with" "co-beings" (at which point Heidegger may be advancing an interplanetary—and multicultural and multispecial—range of reference).

> An elephant in an Indian jungle "is" just as much as some chemical combustion process at work on the planet Mars, and so on. (*An Introduction to Metaphysics,* 3)

The essence of technology, which is not technological or psychological (or psychoanalytic), comes down to one's own death alone, a being left—to one's own resources, on a scale of empty or full.

In *Being and Time,* the departure of the dead other is, at one extreme, still a way of being in the sense of the body-thing left behind. The end of one being alive is the beginning of the remainder (and the opening of the *Reste*-rant). But this too falls short of the phenomenological *Bestand* insofar as the remainder does not just represent a mere body-thing. Even the leftover corpse is, theoretically speaking, still possible object *(Gegenstand)* for pathological-anatomical study that seeks to understand from its orientation to the idea of life. More than a lifeless material thing, it is the unliving one thus encounters from which life has absconded. Heidegger invokes the reception area of mourning and burial to underscore the more-than-thing status of the deceased. But in this mode of being with the dead, the deceased himself is not in fact there. You can only be with a fellow being residing with you in the same world. The deceased has gone from the world and left it behind. From out of this world, the survivors can still be with him. This admission of relations of long distance with the long distant pulls up short-tempered before the bottom line. One is at best bystander at the other's death. The psychological fixation on the other's departure is diversionary; it keeps us from analyzing being gone and wholeness on the basis of the mode of being of *Dasein*. *Dasein* cannot be substituted for in this way, in the way of experiencing in or through the substitute what is not given to be originally experienced. On the occasions of everyday life, we indeed represent, stand in for, even "are," the other. But one cannot take away the other's dying (*Sein und Zeit*, 237–40). Put differently, "psychologically" perhaps, Heidegger begins to describe the way not to mourn and yet at the same time remain functionally with the world. The one painful remove of substitution is elided without, perhaps, the full consequences of a melancholic psychosis. Focus on one's own inconceivable death to the accompaniment of free-floating and unexamined anxiety can give protection in the trauma zone. Leave the dying to the other. Heidegger proposes a remarkably efficient mourning framed according to a rational cognition that, however, if it is to prove successful too, must fake out the striking power of trauma in love and war.

H. Rider Haggard's occult following or understanding of the endopsychic, techno-mummy complex in *She* and *Ayesha* turns on, in the alternation between projection and identification, a "nightmare" of *Gestell:*

> A draped form hovered continually, which, from revealing now the perfect shape of a lovely blooming woman, and again the white bones of a grinning skeleton, which, as it veiled and unveiled, uttered the mysterious and apparently meaningless sentence:—"That which is alive hath known death, and that which is dead yet can never die, for in the Circle of the Spirit life is naught and death is naught. Yea, all things live for ever, though at times they sleep and are forgotten." (*She*, 130)

But the mummy *Gestell* cannot prophesy the future accidents that must instead be perpetually anticipated. Mummy (her name is "Hi ya") must admit the one constitutive limit separating her from her pretechnological rivals who have cornered the markup that progress gives prophecy: "Nor can I tell the issue since to me, to whom power is given so freely, foresight of the future is denied" (*Ayesha*, 221). More crucial (in 1887 and 1904) is that "Hi ya" cannot project intervention along the same lines of live transmission that her surveillance commands. Thus although she has "intelligence" of her enemy's secrets at long range, only at the front in close combat can she use her eye beams as weapons. She can also simulate terrific storms that blow everything and everyone away. But she cannot aim a transmission of personalizable intervention. In the future and at long range there is only the group format of catastrophe. (The one-on-one belongs in the past of endless separation between reanimation and reincarnation.) "Hi ya" lacks air force and missile systems to intervene where she has intelligence—namely, behind enemy lines.

During his World War I service as radio operator and weather forecaster, Heidegger was in close near-missing connection and communication with airborne attempts to see the future—and the return. Haggard's "Hi ya" must forever fall short of the long-range precision of her death wish: the long distance of warfare can only be realized (in the era of flight based on sight rather than on frequency) as total or suicidal destruction or as the one-on-one encounter increasingly reserved, in the long range, for relations with hallucinations or phantoms.

But even as we close in on future accidents, we are propelled into the perpetual long distance of preparedness (the standing-reserve of catastrophe survival). On the screen of Hi ya's projections appears not only the present but also the past—but a past composed of the look-alikes of those viewing the current show. Otherwise the future-less screen is blurred by the shocks of (and identifications with) catastrophe in mass format:

> For a while confused pictures flitted rapidly to and fro across the vast mirror of the flame, such as might be reflected from an intelligence crowded with the memories of over two thousand years which it was too exhausted to separate and define.
>
> Wild scenes, multitudes of people, great caves, and in them faces, amongst others our own, starting up distorted and enormous, to grow tiny in an instant and depart; stark imaginations of Forms towering and divine; of Things monstrous and inhuman; armies marching; illimitable battle-fields, and corpses rolled in blood, and hovering over them the spirits of the slain. These pictures died as the others had died, and the fire was blank again. (*Ayesha*, 225)

When she shares her future plans for taking over the world, it is clear that like Germany in the two world wars, "Hi ya" lacks a certain standing reserve of resources: instead she alchemically produces magical replacements or transformations. When Heidegger talks about technology, he talks energy recycling that either passes directly from storage to distribution and back again or switches back and forth between the tracks of substitution and simulation. Like the repression word, according to Freud, *Ersatz* was another word "made in Germany"; it was the label covering lack brought to us by the German simulation industries that arose during the world wars: rubber, coffee, and sugar were among the everyday resources reconstituted in the *Ersatz* mode. Methadone was made in Nazi Germany as morphine *Ersatz*. The original name of the extended release from pain for the soldier boys: Adolfin.

> The revealing that rules in modern technology is a challenging which puts to nature the unreasonable demand that it supply energy that can be extracted and stored as such. . . .
>
> That challenging happens in that the energy concealed in nature is unlocked, what is unlocked is transformed, what is transformed is stored up, what is stored up is, in turn, distributed, and what is distributed is switched about ever anew. (Heidegger, "The Question concerning Technology," 14, 16)

But there was a limit to this runaway switching of channels—a limit that fits on a runway. The one thing that cannot be replaced through this transforming recycling is the fuel that keeps the plane from falling back onto the runway of decontextualized loss and stranded objecthood. It's the essence—or, to give the same word a French twist, *essence*—of technology that, if we erase Heidegger's denial, runs on unacknowledged empty. And it should be reread as the broadcast of a wish that is a command:

> Everywhere everything is ordered to stand by, to be immediately at hand, indeed to stand there just so that it may be on call for a further ordering. (17)

The refueling plane that stays on empty, dead on its wheels, just is not seen when Heidegger turns on the runway lights of "The Turning":

> The turning of the danger comes to pass suddenly. In this turning, the clearing . . . suddenly clears itself and lights up. . . .
>
> And yet—in all the disguising belonging to Enframing, the bright open-space of world lights up, the truth of Being flashes. At the instant, that is, when Enframing lights up, in its coming to presence, as the danger, i.e., as the saving power. ("The Turning," 44, 47)

In the broken record of Heidegger's life inside his academic CV, there's one more outburst of overdetermination to get stuck on, which was amplified throughout the rectory he occupied at the time, namely, his harassment of a certain Staudinger, a Freiburg University colleague in chemistry, who had made the headline way back at the start of World War I with the calculations he offered the authorities as free advice proving that Germany just didn't have the resources and reserve supplies to sustain a world war effort. The circuit that already blows with the world war supply preparedness the first time around helps press Heidegger's techno-readings, even though published as what's new in the fifties, into the vicinity of German war technology in the thirties and forties.

Same time, same station as Heidegger's work of technology, then, Klaus Conrad's psychiatric study of the schizophrenia he encountered as military psychiatrist on location on the front in 1942 could reduce the cases he was treating to depletion of a kind of psychic reserve fuel or energy, which is all your typical schizo soldier really lacks. Conrad—whose debt to Binswanger as adherent of (his own version of) the existential brand of psychoanalysis puts him on the one line of (dis)connection between Freud and Heidegger—published in the 1950s reflections on the etiology of schizophrenia, which he based on cases he treated from 1941 all the way to the season finale in Stalingrad. Back then he was part of the military recycling effort that sought to heal the soldiers who were no longer able or willing to fight. What had been diagnosed during World War I as traumatic or war neurosis (or psychosis) was recognized by Conrad the second time around as unconditional schizophrenia.

Every advance of gadget love supplies a missing link: this one comes between mummification, schizophrenia, and *Bestand* (that is, the running out of *Bestand*). Conrad will conclude that the psyches of his disturbed soldier patients required only a fuel-full of energy to be set back into action (Conrad, 139). Following the rebound that Heidegger released between "identity and difference," the bouncing bond of these connections touches down on (or returns to) the mummy's "vault" (at once crypt and takeoff), which, already in the beginning, performs on a corporeal scale what Heidegger warned against as coming soon (but Heidegger, a true gadget lover, could not see the future).

Being in Therapy

The traumatic and war neuroses stood model for the expanded psychoanalytic view of libido, which, in crisis and down the preexisting divide between its shifting teutonic plates, could also go for the ego and absorb shocks ultimately to one's self-esteem in a stricken, grief-stuck inner world where you start over, over and again, from scratch, from the traumatic scratch in the record. Narcissistic disorders, with melancholia and schizophrenia at the front of the line, could now be targeted in theory and practice. The war record of psychoanalysis, which opened up Freud's second system, was the only lasting victory of its time, one that had been won in the corridor wars between (at one end) psychoanalysis and the psychotherapies and (at the other end) the nontransferential or narcissistic sciences of psychiatry and neurology. The eclecticized (or reunified) mix of approaches marks the passage of psychoanalysis into the psychological and medical interventionisms not only in Nazi Germany.

The success psychoanalysis could claim for its treatment of war neurotics, which, taken together with the psychological-warfare victories of the Allies in World War I, had large-scale implications and applications for the promotion of all future war efforts, soon required that the resistant medical sciences start assimilating psychoanalysis and the psychotherapies. This move is so global, in fact, that the U.S. World War II effort had to take it from the Nazis that Freud's post–World War I reflections on group psychology should be sent to the new war front. Psychiatric treatment of civilian mental illness after the war (certainly in the United States) encountered a home front of hospitalized psychotics that required of therapies and theories the kind of rethinking of schizophrenia that holds its degree and pedigree from the war zones of psychological invention.

One more view of and from the history of theory and therapy of schizophrenia is taken from another front of the polemical exchanges around this disorder. Owing to the prestige psychoanalysis earned through its successful intervention in cases of war neurosis during and after World War I, psychiatry had to back off from its all-out attacks on, and attempted exclusions of, psychoanalytic and psychotherapeutic models. It was this success (and its implications for the promotion of the war effort) that contributed to the staying power of psychotherapy (and psychoanalysis) across the corridor from psychiatry even during the Third Reich. That's why the research in Nazi Germany does not exclude itself from the community and continuity of thinking about mental illness. The international standard, Freud's intrapsychic model, remained available throughout the Nazi military establishment. Its intactness in this context was completely remetabolized—as genuine influence—through psycho theory and therapy's mobilization for the waging of psychological warfare. But that too was a world affair.

The modifications Conrad introduced into Freud's transferential model to make it fit the schizo soldiers on the Nazi war front followed patterns Binswanger was the first to cut with Heidegger plus Freud. The German psychotherapies had all along (even before their reunion with psychoanalysis under the Nazis) been open to alliance prospects with the author of *Being and Time*. German psychotherapy journals would include reports even on Heidegger's academic career and routinely praise the therapeutic correctness of his investigation of *Dasein*. In 1947, for his part, Heidegger expresses in a letter to Medard Boss, his Swiss talk show host at the *Zollikoner Seminare* coming soon, his great interest, despite a lack of specialized knowledge of the most current research, in the "problems of psychopathology and psychotherapy from the perspective of principles" (Condiau, 22). In seminar Heidegger called into question the "fatal distinction between consciousness and the unconscious" (20) while advising the therapists in attendance (after a word of caution that he would not be making them over as philosophers) that he *could* call their attention to that which concerns man but to which man doesn't have easy access (17).

Theoretically and philosophically, Heidegger's Swiss seminars take up issues with the psychoanalytic view of transference that translate back into the conditions and contexts of the therapeutic model. In theory as in therapy, Heidegger's following interpersonalizes the other, in particular the psychotic one, who, through *Daseinsanalyse*, somehow has the feeling that he's not the only one. When Heidegger takes the example of blushing, he gives its relations a total that counts down at the psychotic end of experience: blushing is a gesture, not the expression of an internal process, but rather on its own an already particular relatedness to one's cobeings *(Mitmenschen)* (18–19). In Binswanger's words of gratitude:

> We have Martin Heidegger to thank for revealing to us the a priori of this ontological structure of the Dasein. Only since Heidegger is it possible to speak of a dis-order in the ontological structure of the Dasein and to show of what it can consist, to show, that is, which elements are to be made responsible for the fact that a particular structural order, so to say, "denies," that it exhibits gaps and that these gaps are filled again by the Dasein.

> With this we are closer to what is daseinsanalytically the central problem of schizophrenia and its solution. (Binswanger, "Introduction to *Schizophrenie*," 250–51)

The psychosis-compatibles, from Jung and Heidegger to Lacan and Deleuze and Guattari, have been advertising in and answering the anti-Oedipals, I mean, the interpersonals. But these are the columns that are made to close ranks against narcissism when one of the other two exiles (pervert or groupie) gets singled out. Narcissism is doubled and divided, divided and conquered, in the face-off between psycho and pervert (or group member). To this end, transference and the unconscious are dismissed out of mind as the exhaust of outmoded models, while total structures of psychotic experience can be installed in every backyard or backseat like those Orgone retooling sheds, more units that run only for the cover of cyberfantasy or out of fuel.

Daseinsanalyst Medard Boss summarizes Freud's schizophrenia position in a techno-analogue that, he suggests, along the lines of Heidegger's criticism of relations between psychoanalysis and technology, indicates a connection so coextensive that *technē* and psyche are essentially not addressed:

> When we read Freud's explanation of psychotic symptoms, the picture which readily comes to mind is that of binaural recordings. One track carries the replica of sensory stimuli emanating from the external, unnamed objects themselves—this would be the "representation of the thing." The other track carries acoustic vibrations caused by the sounds of the word which once had been heard in connection with the object, in Freud's language the "representation of the word." If the whole "representation of the object" is to become conscious, it is necessary that both tracks be synchronized. (Boss, *The Analysis of Dreams*, 214)

Instead Boss opens up the psychotic I's disclosures:

> In the case of a schizophrenic patient there is also . . . a deconstriction, a disclosing of ways of discovering phenomena and of relating to them which are completely covered up in the waking state of an average existence. Concealing something or disclosing it, however, is far from producing it or being its basis, its genesis, or its cause. (229)

A recording device comes to Boss's mind, while Freud gets called on the oceanic views of language versus nonlanguage implicated in the distinction he grants schizophrenics for operating only on the direct, literal, corporeal, or machinic emanations of the signifier. For Freud, it's the entry level at which language starts mediating that must separate the hysterics, for example, from the schizophrenics. Freud was not one to hold out against the seduction of an analogy. But when it came to schizophrenia, he was strict about emphasizing this disorder's fundamental difference from what it otherwise resembled. He rejected the candidacy of an analogy with schizophrenic thought still supported to this day: that of the dream. In dreams, thought intervenes in, tampers with, and rides out the things that words have been turned into down the regression track. In other words, the line of communication in dreams between words and things, between word cathexes and thing cathexes, is open, while in schizophrenia it has shut down: the thought aberrations work on words alone. Freud, according to the Boss, falls right into the false distinction he falls for. But psychoanalysis knows that there is no beyond of language (or rather of the trace) and therefore can, in theory, postulate differences between disorders on a sliding scale of language that need not recant each time it goes metaphorical. Psychoanalysis invented jargon or theoretical shorthand, and that means, at the same time, the allegorical relation between the code one immerses oneself in and its *transferential* implications or exclusions.

From Heidegger to Binswanger and Conrad (and back again), the unity of a structural configuration "resolves" the limitations of the psychoanalytic model or unit that can cross one's thoughts with Freud's words. Prospects thus open up, beyond transference, for going with the flow of that fantastic self-overcoming of fuel boundedness (via rockets, computers, or TV) that the automobilic technologies give rise to in their (nervous) breakdown. The bottom line is that the psychotic need not acknowledge any lack of fuel because that's all he lacks.

From 1933 on, references to the importance of Heidegger's work for psychiatry appear in Binswanger's research; by 1941 or 1942, Binswanger had put out the therapy shingle "*Daseinsanalyse*": one part Heidegger, one part Freud. The Freud part breaks down into different mourning prescriptions: in 1926 Binswanger and Freud swap grief stories concerning losses in the youngest ranks of their future generations. Freud gives therapeutic counsel and then self-discloses to Binswanger: his favorite grandson's death had brought about his current "indifference" regarding the dangers to his own life. "You are young enough to surmount your loss; as for me, I don't have to any more" (Binswanger, *Sigmund Freud,* 79). The other's death is left to another to mourn. Freud, for his part, devotes himself to not surmounting nor inflicting grief, the ambiguous condition that, in its active unfulfillment, Heidegger diagnosed as technologization.

In his 1930 study "Dream and Existence," Binswanger relocates those dreams of falling from the skies that one also gets a rise out of within language ("every man's spiritual homeland") and, more precisely, at the transference way stations of metaphor. "When, in a bitter disappointment, 'we fall from the clouds,' then we fall—we *actually* fall. . . . Our harmonious relationship with the world and the men about us suddenly suffers a staggering blow, stemming from the nature of bitter disappointment and the shock that goes with it. In such a moment our existence actually suffers, is torn from its position in the world and thrown upon its own resources. Until we can regain our equilibrium in the world, our whole existence moves within the meaning matrix of stumbling, sinking, and falling" ("Dream and Existence," 223). What falls on the downside of flying ("it can also signify liberation and the possibility of ascending" [224]) all the way down to our resources and reserves is (even etymologically) related to the work of mourning. That's why it's "no longer part of the dream," in other words, of metaphor or language, "but part of the patient's psychosis when he speaks of the dream as a turning point in his life and finds its emotional content so fascinating that he reverts to it in his daydreams to the extent that he actually tries to remove himself from life" (234). In the 1956 sequel entitled "Extravagance," which fixes its focus on in-flight emotion sickness, Binswanger charts the itinerary of rising upward, one that breaks with striding forth across a horizon that the sheer verticality has blown apart. Across this chronic axis, the genres of air-head psychosis can be separated out into distinct pockets. "Even schizophrenic insanity can, in my opinion, be understood only if it is taken initially as an *existential mode* of Extravagance. The same holds true for 'mass phenomena' of Extravagance" ("Extravagance," 344–45). Closest to the masses, mania represents elevation (without penetration), flightiness, volatility, *and* leveling. The manic takes flight to skip both the vertical axis of choosing oneself and the horizontal one of discursive continuity shots that aim for the common purpose or sense of community and communication: "He cannot take a stand or make a 'self-sufficient' decision. Love and friendship have, in these airy heights, lost their power. Human intercourse is reduced to the level of psychiatric treatment" (347).

Schizophrenia, to add more contrast to the beam across airwaves, "is no longer rooted in an excess of breadth (of 'leaping') and of the heights of mere *vol imaginaire* that outweigh the (authentic) heights of 'decision'" (347). Schizophrenics weigh in with a disregard of experience or discursivity that gets them up one rung of decision making and leaves them there, pealing the veil of the one side taken for the idea or ideology that had a certain ring to it. Psychotherapy must "bring the patient safely back 'down to earth' from his Extravagance" (349).

The 30 Percent Reich

In *The Analysis of Dreams,* Boss gives H. Schultz-Hencke, who's all alone with Erich Fromm under "'neo-analytical' dream theories," a fair shakedown, as another Heidegger student (pre the turning to therapy) who tried to extend "Freud's mechanistic philosophy" of instincts to the *experience* of them, too. He came up with a sampling of "instinctual experiences" that add up to more than the Freudian life or death doubles.

> Surprisingly, Schultz-Hencke concludes that "the fact that these 'existentialist,' 'psychic,' or 'universally human' factors originate in 'biological instincts,' in no way conflicts with their spiritual character." (Boss, *The Analysis of Dreams,* 61)

Biological experiences have a "transcending significance," lowering a bridge where otherwise it's a draw between "character and biological urges" (61). "Thanks to this 'transcending significance' of the biological instinctual experience, we could, for instance, coin the phrase, 'Anal processes too are of philosophical importance'"(61–62). Hi ya! Thanks a lot!

Schultz-Hencke's neoprimer *The Inhibited Man* was first published in Nazi Germany in 1940 and was reedited for publication in 1947. In the preface dated 1946, Schultz-Hencke points out the many changes he determined not to make. There's no Nazi version to which he or anyone else (except maybe the Nazi analytic colleagues) would need to have aversion. He did drop some of the neologisms that translated or transformed pieces of Freud (like *Desmolyse* for or instead of *Analyse*). But that's just the icing on a take that's still too Freudian in its mode of anti-Freudianism. Today all around the world it's not necessary to give that much attention to Freud. Freud is so outmoded at the moment that there's no point criticizing him as was necessary in 1940 owing to the still determining force of Freudian influence. Now Freud can be respected, like the ancestor, like whatever is "history." A fully developed assimilation (or digestion) of Freudian concepts is already under way in the works of Schultz-Hencke's Anglo-American colleagues. But regarding his 1940 "strident criticism of Freud and his school," Schultz-Hencke has decided to refrain from changing anything at this postwar historical moment, "because I want to show what it was after all possible to publish in the Third Reich, even under circumvention of the enforced censorship. To take on extensive revisions now would give the appearance of ridding the work of what was unacceptable in human terms so as to adapt to the current situation" (*Der gehemmte,* 7). The subtitle, which put the now abandoned neologism *Desmolyse* up in lights, is just about the limit of what he was willing to change. The basic project, the amalgamation of Adlerian, Freudian, and Jungian schools, is the same in word as in the deed, the legacy.

Psychoanalysis was in every sense a sensation: Freud sexualized concepts or senses to such an extent that you couldn't go "oral" or "anal" without being forced to imagine some analogous sex act. Plus what Freud calls sexuality became too general: Schutz-Hencke still prefers owing to sex, strictly understood, what is its due (32). For example, when he watches little kids playing, he sees sex only 30 percent of the time. But that still merits a call to Child Protective Services.

Inhibition is the new key that turns around to unlock what's "expansive" in men. But when Schultz-Hencke reconsiders ambivalence under his category of inhibition, he demonstrates only a pathologized one-way reception of Freud's key concept. Inhibition's parallel universal, ambivalence amounts to the failure to form one whole. Ambivalence, inhibition: the one so afflicted can't get out of the "vicious circle," which is what's under it all, rather than the multi-interpretable unconscious. The circle is in the family, taken systemically or interpersonally (but in a structural, not intentional sense of excluded relations). In this stretch Schultz-Hencke singles out schizophrenia as the one illness that is 100 percent psychogenic and analytic, but in his sense. "Among mental illnesses schizophrenia is the one area in which most definitely purely psychically conditioned afflictions occur" (299–300). Schizophrenia is the demo of what others may call "object loss" but could more correctly be addressed as what results from the progressive decrease through spread of inhibition of contact with what's still out there:

> At first he leaves out some connection. Thus his judgment of the world becomes one-sided. Then he sees even less and his judgment becomes seriously distorted. Finally he loses relations with whole segments of the world. And his judgment becomes delusional.... This not "seeing" is what one calls object loss. (301)

The "existential" association is made across this loss that isn't one: Mr. Inhibited is overafraid, overburdened with childish fears that propel him into death or, just as swiftly, away from it. "How should he prepare *[entwerfen]* for death, when his floating guilt feelings bind him against his will to mankind, as though they were his destiny, more so than they truly are or need to be. Here lies the essential significance of the totality and its consequences for man in general" (91). Schultz-Hencke thus prepares the way for an unambivalent or "existential" rapport with one's own death. But if you don't need anybody else around, the death invoked here seems already embodied as and by the other—not as death but as the dead. He tries to hold these differences beyond ambivalence, always moving into another kind of clearing.

The refrain or restraint that Schultz-Hencke would place psychoanalysis under keeps ticking off with images of "explosives." The basic concepts of sensation-hungry analysis are dynamite (28). But after the study has been progressing for quite some time, the remainder of what is inhibited, in the form of conduct and character *(Haltungen),* "could be called explosive bits of the unconscious, and one may refer to them thus, as long as one stops short of secreting inside this enigma anything speculative" (111). The detonations resounding in the concepts extend, endopsychically, to the double field of Freud's discoveries: repression and the unconscious. And because every so-called inhibition can turn around into the expansiveness it tries to contain, the inhibited man is truly volatile: "If this severely inhibited person gets exposure to a tempting situation, then what was inhibited breaks through the repression cover. The explosive charges of character or conduct blow themselves up out of all proportion and develop into crude life experiences" (293).

Healing cases or degress of inhibition can be made difficult because lifting the inhibition is not the cure. "Blinded by overexposure to certain theories, the patient will always and again believe that he has become acquainted with his whole childhood history, he has seen through the symbolism of his dreams, but he's still not healthy" (313). He gives the Jungian component of his amalgamated trinity the go-ahead for future reference, or for future generations to decide whether membership in a "'world of images' which human imagination has created over the centuries" might not give patients grounding, fulfillment, and sense of belonging through mythic, cultic, and esoteric modes of meaningfulness.

As he approaches adolescence, Schultz-Hencke recognizes the "yearning for the androgynous, for the magical" (209). But that's not a problem until the investment of this yearning comes into maturity after adolescence, with couplification. The only truly troubled adolescence is the kind that writes itself down. This is what then gets spread around. But it's not a problem of adolescence *during* adolescence. The problem teen is a certain inhibited type who's given to write himself out of the picture, "the picture of literature, as though man were really the way literature represents him"

(231). It's the type of suicidal journal-ism. Ever since Goethe's *Werther,* the Passion model of artist-heroism has been folding out as the teen Passion of the readership.

Only with postadolescent couplification does the "other sex have the role of revealing the limited character of life" (210).

> If you look over a number of human lives and you ask yourself, What appeared to them as the particular hardness of life, then one stumbles across, among other things, always and again the partner, the lover, as the prototype of what is so hard; that is, when it comes to life's hardness, a leading role is played by the hardness that the lover or partner "represents." (210)

The other sex is the other. That's how mother fixations offer a happier medium.

When Schultz-Hencke allows for the given indeterminacy of sexual orientation, it's time for another depth charge to go off. The young adult whose "sensitivity and feeling for life are spoiled by the explosives of anxiety, guilt feeling" will end up coupling with the "extremely maternal man, the maternal-masculine woman" (212). But woman isn't mother:

> In the sphynx and the vampire we hear the man bemoan the fact that woman, as partner and lover, is just not mother, but rather, compared to this unreachable ideal, is a dangerous beast of prey, a murderess who sucks energy and blood.
>
> Thus a circle closes itself. The mythic image of the yearned-for great mother and the simultaneously feared man-murdering woman gives symbolic expression to the distress of man's position in the world. (212)

Schultz-Hencke closes with a call to arms. In the original afterword, which is still part of the postwar edition, he calls on his "comrades" in psychotherapy to "fight for recognition today of depth psychology in the interest of perhaps half a million Germans who can be helped, but only with 'heavy artillery'" (315).

Hey Sullivan Man

In the big open book of the history of psychodynamic therapies, Harry Stack Sullivan, like Karen Horney, Erich Fromm, and Schultz-Hencke, counts as neopsychoanalyst. For the neo world war, he was fast-forwarded from his hospital strongholds to the national headquarters of the Selective Service to serve as psychiatric adviser. But outside the corridors of his interpersonal relations, the armed services were too vast, and never as preselected as his schizophrenics on the ward, for him to shrink down to interpersonal size. In one year and out the next, he urged ever more rigorous screening of selectees. Breakdown in the war was a guarantee he was willing to give in the many cases so far of poor selection. But rapid buildup of forces was the requirement, and constant friction sparked Sullivan's decision to resign in 1941. Sullivan saw fragility everywhere—which is a good thing when working with identified patients. He could be just the one it took to know one. One psychiatrist-biographer of Sullivan's life and work adds to the man's psycho rep the good rap of therapeutic rapport:

> Throughout his life Harry Stack Sullivan struggled with emotional problems and difficulties in his relationships with people, which had marked effects on the psychiatric concepts he evolved. . . . Sullivan's problems contributed to his sensitivity, insight, and diligence in dealing with psychiatric patients. . . . Some psychiatrists, including myself, feel that Sullivan's work makes him the most important figure in psychiatry in the last 100 years, and that his concepts and treatment techniques are much more valid and useful than those of Freud and many others. (Chapman, 17–18)

Schizophrenia was his specialty: he was one of the pioneer colonizers of the borderline inside psychosis. The two bookends of Sullivan's innovations were Bleuler and Freud. Bleuler, who took up schizophrenia (or dementia praecox) atheoretically, was already compatible with the at once eclectic and descriptive agenda of *DSM* up-to-dateness.

For Freud, schizophrenia would remain a philosopher's disease and, indeed, a philosophical one. Schizophrenia thus offered Freud and the immediate Freudians a kind of safety zone of speculation. Freud at one point even wagered that this psychotic disorder is transference proof and thus inaccessible to treatment; that way he didn't risk having to prove in practice what he was arguing in theory. But he ended up not limiting himself to this limit concept.

According to Freud, remember, dream and schizophrenia are not a match in the crisscrossing of identifications. Another station in the crossing-out of elimination is the distinction between hysteria and schizophrenia. What dictates the substitution and symptom formation (for example the hypochondriacal "organ speech") in schizophrenia is not a resemblance between the things somehow denoted by words but a sameness of the very words used to express things. On account of the noncoincidence of word and thing in schizophrenic thinking, the formation of substitutions or symptoms may seem so close to what goes down in the transference neuroses—but remains just as far away.

In 1931 Sullivan presented the "modified" use of psychoanalysis in the treatment of schizophrenia. First Sullivan proclaimed reversal of the Freudian banishment of psychosis from transferential precincts; in his view, schizophrenics presented no special difficulties when it came to transference reactions. (Although Freud referred only in passing to the seemingly nontransferential relationality of psychosis, the Freudians subsequently made of this mention one of the party line rules marking the limits of analysis.) Another notion Sullivan sought to correct, one that may be Freudian but was, once again, not one of Freud's set ways (Sullivan simply refers to "the literature"), is that libido has been fixed at some point in the past of the patient and that the release of this pent-up libido gives the cure. Sullivan views this cure-all through freeing of libido as "but a figure of speech for something that occurs in recovery under analysis" (Sullivan, 283). It is instead the reconstruction through the transference of the whole personality (otherwise parceled out in schizophrenia among dis-integrated tendencies) that remains the aim of schizophrenia's special treatment.

The other psychoanalytic view that Sullivan dismisses as philosophical is the one that says that full-blown schizophrenia represents an autorecovery state (of emergency) that the patient infinitely prefers to the preceding horror vacui of evacuation of libido and loss of the external world. In this view, social recovery only covers for the disease otherwise left intact through the cooperation between the patient who wants to remain sick and the psychiatrist who wants to see the patient resocialized.

So that Sullivan did not appear to be aiming too high, he added to his prescription supplementary applications of "sociopsychiatric" methods of socialization (with special emphasis on fortification of reality testing). Within a special habitat native to enlightened hospitals, the patient can develop the "interpersonal security" required for social recovery (287). Because the schizophrenic is forever on the lookout for ambivalence, Sullivan includes a checklist of personality types who should stay clear of the treatment of schizophrenia. Philosophical, resistant homosexual, reformer, and controlling types are among those unable to give the patient shelter in a reconstructed whole personality.

In addition to the modified use of the transferential relation as model for the kind of supportive environment the schizophrenic requires to keep on his way to social recovery, Sullivan also recommends the use of chemotherapeutic agents (notably ethyl alcohol) to impair the vigilance of one overamplified tendency and thus permit provisional functioning of another neglected and undeveloped tendency.

Right around the time he was losing his grip on the psychiatric advice columns of the Selective Service, Sullivan composed "Psychiatric Aspects of Morale." For Sullivan, "psychiatry" was "sufficiently broad a term, with enough lunatic fringes of meaning," to fit the corporate model of proper boundaries, one that collapses onto the crypt contours of melancholic incorporation. Capital, communion, technology, group psychology, unmourning are all the same moments down the tunnel vision of the history of trauma or identification.

> Psychiatry... is concerned with interpersonal relations, the processes that occur in integrations of more than one person—in two-groups, three-groups, and larger aggregations; all but one of the "members" of which integrations may be imaginary—i.e., personifications rather than real persons. (277–78)

Like Schreber, like Bion, like Ferenczi, like Sullivan: auto-analysis is neck and neck in the speed race against the vampiric libido drain of the psychotic break. For Sullivan, the field was interpersonal (in other words, he was struggling to hold onto the object): the "hypothetical entity" called psychiatry incorporated the given or data of only this field, which is then surveyed according to "how almost completely one is unknown to one's self, except as he observes himself or hears reports of himself as he is observed in interpersonal relations" (279). With this in mind, Sullivan gives us his sliding scale for morale treatment, which reaches its lowest point of "utter demoralization" in a panic. Here's the catch for Sullivan (and this is his interpersonal take or intake): panic is just like "being choked by someone" (280). But Sullivan can't just take a choke but focuses instead on a particular phase of choking, which he slow motions us to watch closely: "Interference with the free flow of air produces profound disturbance in the organism long before asphyxiature sets in. The mental state and the somatic concomitants are closely related to full-blown panic" (280). The severe mental disorders are a panic, but access was restricted to asylum ward psychiatrists. Now a related form is available for inspection on the battlefield when a soldier's safety lies in numbness.

> Real, fully developed panic is ordinarily confined to the unhappy experience of those who have to deal with severe mental disorders. It is the paralyzing prologue to almost unutterable terror which sweeps over some adolescents as they are passing into a schizophrenic state. Even with them it is short-lived, and they become catatonic shortly after the episode of panic.
>
> Finally, there is a "panic" which is related in its beginnings to actual panic, but consists in blind attempts to save one's self from something terrible. This is closely related to the "panic" that occurs in certain special circumstances among troops. (280)

Even a blind panic still permits soldiers in their terror state to take the emergency exit of acute psychoneurotic episodes. Panic's everyday psychopathology is getting rattled and all shook up until adaptive, constructive thought has been arrested. The degree of suggestibility is way up there and leaves you there, open to any simpler way out of an untenable decision.

A less-spectacular mode of demoralization, but most effectively devastating, are the varieties of discouragement and depression: "These states of discouragement grade up to the grave (and, fortunately, in this country thus far seldom seen) form of chronic demoralization—despair" (281). Grading up to the grave, Sullivan stacks up the dis-pair, the unpairing of the interpersonal relation: "There occurs a disintegration of interpersonal relations which may become quite as complete as is the case in the severe psychoses. People in despair, in general, rapidly become numb. . . . They engage in automatic sorts of behavior" (281). Despair collaborates with the success of the *Blitzkrieg:* "Great streams of them have littered military roads to the extent that supplies and reinforcements could not be gotten to the front" (281–82). (A thousand years fine for littering.)

The German experts instill despair by double-crossing the authority of the news media with the pseudoauthority of the false information the Germans were feeding back:

> They send out the unreliable news and then prove that it is unreliable. This is wonderfully effective in spreading demoralization, because once the mediate channels of communication are taken to be unreliable the people are actually isolated from their government and the way has been prepared for isolating them

> from immediate spoken communication. . . . Once the reliance on communications from the central government and its agencies is choked off, the psychiatric strategy can be directed at the individual communities. . . . Effort is made to widen all the cleavages that exist in the group. . . . Methodically cultivated anti-Semitism has been wonderfully useful in making people uncomfortable with one another. I was told very solemnly by one of the Nazi officials that I was entirely misguided in my views in this connection. Actually almost everyone that he had ever met was full of anti-Semitism. The people who insisted that they were not anti-Semitic were, of course, so anti-Semitic they did not dare to be aware of it. I was reminded of traditional psychoanalytic arguments. The point is that it does not matter whether you are anti-Semitic or not as long as you get to fretting about it. (289–90)

Because "our notions of ourself—i.e., the self we are always telling people about, including ourself—are full of fossils perpetuated by our primary educational system from philosophies and 'psychologies' of bygone days," and because there is a solid minority of people "simply incapable of full social life" (ranging among the absolutely psychopathic, the relatively detached, and the already temporarily demoralized), we are having difficulties lining up for those new formations of this war, which already belong to the future now (292). Democracy, for one, is not an acceptable army standard in the here and now, nor can its exchange rate be fully maximized for the civilians in total-war time zones. Self-reliance becomes less effective than "a realization of mutual dependence, a realization of mutual support and protection, and of cooperative, if not fully collaborative, effort" (293). The problem we face today is more total, but it is already always contained as standard exchange rate "in the conversion of conscripted or drafted troops into soldiers" (293). "Now that warfare has come to involve everyone, the same characteristics which make the new conscript—or, as we now call him, the new selectee—anything but a soldier also make the civilian population anything but people capable of the effort called for in total defense" (293). Whereas the dominant mode of self-reliance, competition, represents "an actual menace in modern warfare," the solo orbit of gadget-loving group-of-oneness represents the no-alternative plan of collaboration or cohabitation with technology: "Because now . . . the enlisted man controls more gunfire than did . . . a squad in the World War, troops, therefore, can often be spread thin and each soldier used, one might say, as a tactical unit" (293).

Troops must be trained free of the impulse to look out for themselves, or for the aggregate of this antiquated notion of self. Mental disorders belong in the hospital, which is where psychiatry follows their beat in peacetime. Now that psychiatry has a whole battlefield of experience out there, a new sense of where the home is for the mentally disordered (all those absolutely uninterpersonal and untreatable types), at least in wartime, may become available (it's not a democratic model, by the way): "In the nation at war the psychopathic personalities, among others, certainly might well be out of harm's way in a civilized version of the concentration camp" (294). Through aptitude for specialization testing, citizens can either be made to fit or retrofit efficiently into the total effort or may be removed "safely and humanely from harm's way" (295). The changeover back to peacetime conditions of democracy must also be given professional attention. There's no question that the total fight against National Socialism has projectively imposed antidemocratic standards on our own ability to win that fight. The highest selectivity of the American forces need not be a stigmatizing either/or within the new sensurround of sink out of harm's way or fit into the different functions of the total war effort. Nor is there the drawback that Sullivan has been hearing about, that by selecting out the "'cream' of our youth" for early dying, we are undermining the stock we take in America. But all the creaming of that youth is neither a loss nor a gain to lines of reproduction (at least as long as women are not yet being inducted). It's the women who "are still bearing children and presumably contributing half the chromosomes and at least three quarters of the early experience—which seems to a psychiatrist to have some significance for the future of America" (299). Besides, among the boys turned down for frontline service there are studly exemplars, good biological material. They've just been neuroticized by their wretched upbringing, no doubt "by some of these same stalwart Americans who are worrying about the 'eugenic aspects' of the program" (299).

Drama Psycho

J. L. Moreno was the kind of dyadic inventor (the adolescent kind) who never made it to the third basis of patent rights. All he could do was wait and see "who shall survive," the title of his autobiography, which is thus left to wait for him, by proxy:

> 1943, Paternity Syndrome
>
> I am like a fellow who makes daily deposits in the bank but whenever he gets a bank statement his account shows a deficit. He must suspect that the whole system of banking is wrong.
>
> When I was young I had the idea for a stage which is in the center, like the sun, round like the earth, vertical like the skyscraper, but someone imitated it and earned money and fame. Said I to myself: "Moreno, you have to live ten years longer than this fellow, in order to make up. You have so many ideas, you will have more success with the next idea. Keep on working." I invented a recording machine, a new graphic language, I kept on working and ten years later I saw the idea of group psychotherapy wandering off from one fellow to another. I humored myself again and said: "Well Moreno, you just have to live ten years longer than any of them, your time will come, have patience and keep on working." I kept on working and another ten years went by. And then I saw another idea which I had fathered, psychodrama, being distorted, and another idea, sociometry, being abused and then I said to myself, not without gloom but also not without fortitude: "Well, Moreno, you must live ten years longer, twenty years longer, thirty years longer. You have to survive them all, that is the only thing which is left to you. Some day recognition will turn up suddenly and unexpectedly, just keep on working." I am surviving them and maybe in anticipation I called this book "Who Shall Survive?" But I asked my demon: "Well, how much longer do you want me to live?" (*Who Shall Survive?* 78–79)

His inventiveness was all over the place, but the interdisciplinarian always loses the shoot-out for the one or third position that is solo-sized only. Harry Stack Sullivan? Moreno gave him his interpersonality, but Sullivan didn't go all the way with it, didn't take it two-way (52). When Moreno quotes one of his own 1932 lectures in which group therapy is defined in terms reminiscent of Bertalanffy—"Group therapy is a method which protects and stimulates the self-regulating mechanisms of natural groups" (47)—

it thus also already occupies one wavelength with the family systems cyber-theories that emerged in the forties. It's Moreno's special disappearing act: plagiarizing everyone in advance.

Kurt Lewin weighs in under the category of "The Counter-Helpers." Moreno switched Lewin's channel from the attention span of individual and *Gestalt* psychology to participation in group and action methods. But he was "psychologically too old to jump from the timeworn psychological laboratory into the open spaces of roleplaying, group dynamics and action research" (56). One of the "many undynamic people . . . found among the students of group dynamics," Lewin moreover (move over!) gave Moreno's techniques the air of artificiality, which was the one and only credit Moreno did receive as his over-due (56).

But although Moreno is always on the lookout for all-out institutional conflict to see who's got the longest influence, he spectacularly avoids the encoded corridor of world war, as though this were indeed the crypt that must be kept if his priority, in his own mind, is to remain intact. At one point he leaves the taxi meter running and thus manages, with the extra time and debt, to claim priority over himself: yes, even he was doing group work already in 1911 and again in 1913, but he's not counting that. Like Mesmer and all the other so-called precursors, his group efforts back then were without any theoretical group-level innovations. For that accomplishment, he assigns himself a date in 1931. But when it comes time to summarize his pioneer past, after he has thrown it all away in order to come in as uncontested founder of group therapy (twenty years later, according to his schedule, but as much as a decade before any other group-therapy-theory contestants who might come to mind but who go unmentioned), the date that's made for this disposable past is suddenly 1914 (49). Moreno's anecdote about the interest President Roosevelt expressed in psychodrama comes restricted in circulation to its applicability for New Deal domestic renovations of a depressed economy. Moreno's claim to the invention of psychodrama and sociometric systems in 1931, which is based on work he published at this time on analysis of prison groups, jumps the second gun, through his study of cell shock, of all the shell shock group therapies and theories devised during the Nazi and World War II years. What Moreno's calculations leave out too emphatically by half are the two sets of war years, which were victory years for all the other psychodynamic therapies and theories (individual, group, and family).

Nineteen thirty-one is also the date Moreno makes with "The Passing of the Psychoanalytic System, I" (*Who Shall Survive,* 35). He gives the first passing one year. Under "1932, the Passing of the Psychoanalytic System,

II" (43), Moreno charges psychoanalysis with having turned each discovery, more or less valid in itself, around to its downside, thereby constructing a virtual calamity chain, one that extended its helping "and" to the followers and even to some of the resisters.

> Adler's system started with another calamity, the inferiority of organs and the feeling of inferiority. Rank started with a different calamity again, with the trauma of birth. All therapeutic prescriptions in these three systems were made to overcome the initial calamity which the human actor encounters. (44)

> The key concept of the Freudian system is the libido. But Freud instead of associating sex with "spontaneity," associated it with anxiety, insecurity, abreaction, frustration and substitution. His system shows strong inclinations towards the negative and for negation, a tendency which grew stronger in him with age. Even sexuality, which owes to him its permanent elevation to a respectable and powerful agent, he studied in its negative rather than in its positive aspects. It was not the sexual actor and his warm up towards orgasm, it was not sexual intercourse and the interaction of two in its positive unfoldment, but rather the miscarriages of sex, its deviations and displacements, its pathology rather than its normality, to which he gave his attention. (44)

But even Moreno's in-large-part recollected polemical attentions belong to what psychoanalysis has by now become—history. "Freudian discoveries" have not disappeared but are now "part of more inclusive ones" (46). The focus of the makeover of the discoveries is the transference, the ultimate factor in a series of near misses that have culminated a new season of finales under Moreno's direction: "Tele has been discovered as the universal factor dominating interpersonal relations and social interaction; transference is a byproduct of tele structure" (46).

> The libido lives on in the sociometric system as a subform of creativity. The unconscious lives on as a by-product of the warming up process.... Free association is a limited and often artificial adjunct of acting out; spontaneous acting out is a universal function of human behavior, a sequel to the act-hunger of the infant; acting out, which appeared to Freud as a sign of resistance and a phenomenon to be forbidden in the couch situation, has become one of the steering wheels of therapeutic interaction.... Regression is a form of compulsive playing, a form of role playing.... Resistance is a function of spontaneity, it is due to a decrease or loss of it. (46)

In the audience attending Moreno's lecture "Existentialism, Daseinsanalyse and Psychodrama," as documented in the follow-up discussion that's also part of the record in volume 2 of *Psychodrama,* Medard Boss could be found asking appreciative, needing-to-know kinds of questions. Moreno answers:

> Existentialism as a movement predates psychoanalysis and has reached its high point in the psychodrama of our time. . . . Seen within the dynamics of the entire movement one can interpret even such phenomena as Van Gogh and Hitler as falling into the heroic existentialist trend, versus the intellectualistic trend represented by Heidegger, Husserl, Sartre and many others. . . . Far more than the Nazi doctrine and racist theory, there was characteristic for Hitler a self-realization drive, a hunger to live and to fill existence with himself to the limit, with the good and the bad which was in him, regardless of all values, including all the Germanic values. He was more of an existentialist than he was a Nazi. Existentialism, in order to be meaningful, should surmount analysis. The existentialist should reach a new level of naive creative living, able to live safely on a nonanalytic and superanalytic principle. (*Psychodrama,* 221)

In *Who Shall Survive?* Hitler is awarded a separate headline and section—"1938, Hitler's Spontaneity"—among all the other news flashes that count down the modern history of psychotherapy (as the emergence of psychodrama). Moreno recalls that already back then, when interviewed about the Hitler question, he had seen Hitler's losing of the war that had only just begun:

> The first style of Hitler's oratory was to come in shouting, a protagonist of the masses, it was all raw spontaneity. His method was to catch the spontaneity of the people and return their reverberations in a form of heightened violence. As long as he was in the here and now he imagined that God was on his side. But recently I heard that his style of oratory has changed, that he has ghost writers, and even that he is his own ghost writer. This indicates a profound change. He is afraid of the moment, he doesn't trust his spontaneity as he used to, he fears that it may fail him and he doesn't trust his empathy of the masses' wants. He has left the principle and the principle is leaving him. (*Who Shall Survive,* 68)

In the lecture right before "Existentialism, Daseinsanalyse, and Psychodrama" and Hitler, Moreno had already treated "Hitler" psychodramatically. A certain Karl comes to Moreno's stage at the beginning of World War II and claims to be the real Adolf Hitler; the other one is an impostor, thief, parasite. Act 1:

> Karl steps forward and makes an announcement to the German people, speaking over a public address system.... The group receives his proclamation with spontaneous applause. A few scenes follow swiftly; Hitler returns to Germany on a boat.... He ends the first session with a moving scene at the grave of his mother whom he lost at the age of eighteen. (*Psychodrama*, 195)

In the second act, Moreno introduces the "auxiliary egos," defined as "the crucial therapeutic agents": "They are assistants to the chief therapist, but simultaneously they are closely related to the world of the patient." If the auxiliary egos succeed, play their parts well, they "make the patient's hallucinations unnecessary" (195). The most successful auxiliary ego is the Göring player; they are soon on a first-name basis.

> They acted like pals; their relation was full of homosexual undertones. From then on Herman began to get an inside hold on Hitler's thoughts and feelings. We began to use this relationship as a therapeutic guide, for now Hitler was able to accept correction from Herman. (198)

The patient was able to make a "good social recovery." And, Moreno continues, he "returned to the fatherland a few years later. His case illustrates the hypothesis that 'acting-out techniques' are the choice treatment for 'acting-out syndromes'" (199). Through psychodrama, then, a connection could be established where prospects for one-on-one transference (or "rapport") had been unconditionally surrendered as unrealizable. According to Moreno's reading of the energy gauge, the real Hitler and all his auxiliary egos—the Germans—had been able to release a prewar upsurge of power that was a psychodramatic success. This was before Hitler lost his spark. But what helped Karl out onto the acting-out stage of recovery was his recognition in and through the group that "so many others... had the dream of becoming Hitler" (200).

Dichten Denken Tanken

Klaus Conrad's psychosis research has been brought up to mark an increase in psychoticization over neurotic conditions from World War I to the second one, and to measure the growing split, following Freud's discovery of the "internal enemy" of war neurosis, between war and neurosis. The latter split mixes well with the former observation that war neurosis had changed psychopathology channels and started breaking out in the psychotic patches of personalities. The hysterical brands, in other words, began putting in a disappearance. In the meantime it was the organ speech of hypochondriacal or borderline psychotic retroflection that was on the air. The sign-off of suicide was also on the rise, even or especially after war neurosis had met its match and maker in Nazi psychoanalysis. What had been condemned already pre–World War I as the insurance scam of simulation or malingering was by now doubly neuroticized in the analysis of broken-down soldiers, whose condition could not but confirm Freud's long-standing definition of neurosis as "flight into illness." Nowhere to hide.

It has become possible to observe this withdrawal into psychosis from 1920 to 1950 as the end result of "ideological separation, a splitting between war and neurosis, which is finally so total, that the concept of war neurosis, in other words, the conceptual convergence of war and psychiatric illness, itself appears obsolete" (Küchenhoff and Warsitz, 48). It seems that increasingly the reality of war gets bracketed out while the focus is on the patient. But the example of Conrad at least (and of his school in Marburg, which, according to the title pages of the dissertations he cites in his book, and which acknowledge him, he shared with Kretschmer) is continuous with the war and insurance contexts of the first military settings of neurosis on trauma. The critical duo must in fact lip-synch the refrains of *Daseinsanalyse* while invoking "being with," the "cohuman," and the interpersonal relation, which are altogether suppressed by too much intrapsychic consideration (Küchenhoff and Warsitz, 70). What's missing is the very possibility of "reflecting the relationship between external and inner reality, and to make it a component of one's theory" (69). But the structural analysis Conrad performs schedules inner-outer relations according to the dates of its primal and discursive history: one patient (case 64) overhears noises in pipes as the delusional sensurround of noises of many persons, including close family relations, being hanged and strangled around him, and senses, taking the wave of transferential excess, that their flesh is being served up to him at feeding time. Conrad addresses these "apocalyptic fragmentary experiences" by invoking Jungian archetypes and, by name, sadistic fantasy orgies "in the sense of Freud" (Conrad, 113). "This form of experience has of course close connections with the dream and one could, we are convinced, use *the contents of delusions psychoanalytically just as one does the contents of dreams.* They are formally psychologically the same: namely, *the release of what is qualitatively* Gestalt *through the influence of determining tendencies of the personality*" (113). Freud's name again holds the place of the missing entry—into war.

If Conrad enters the battlefield of greater psychoanalysis as field in theory, then he also enters an overlap between the scene he was making and the origin of Kurt Lewin's pioneer "field theory." But while Conrad kept inside the analytic field, Lewin was determined to go the social-studies distance in his exploration of the psychological spacing of groups (his first study in American exile in 1935 concerned the barriers that made minorities, like the Jews in pre-Nazi Germany, just like restless teenagers). According to Manfred Moser, Lewin's field trips into group dynamics (whereby he sought from the late thirties onward to motivate or program psychologically the democratic relation or disposition) began in 1917 when he first sketched the "peace landscape," on which "space of free movement," "time perspective," and so on would be based, based, that is, on the 1917 perspective of a field artillerist.

The psychotic transferential meat market of the Nazi wards strikes up connections with the outside in the form of at once genealogical and discursive intersections with the intrapsychic axis. At another inside-out juncture in Conrad's book, a footnote informs us of a setback on the corridor war front between eclecticized or reunified psychotherapy and psychiatry proper. Case 96, after his successful treatment in 1941, "fell ill again in '43, went from asylum to asylum, and then fell victim finally to the euthanasia movement" (Conrad, 47 n. 1). But the psychotherapy side scored, too: Conrad's case 108, who felt under pressure of thoughts crossing his mind at the time he was drafted in 1940, was, thanks to therapy, finally able to size up his premonitions of death (and his sense that the others see him as criminal, spy, deserter) as follows: "It's a darkly intuited anxiety, a devastation or excitement, about which one doesn't know where it comes from, in part no doubt it comes out of the subconscious" (37).

According to the endopsychic advantage that the psycho soldiers seem, just the same, to be having with the theory, analysis-compatible treatment at the delusional stage (at the latest) is the only outside chance the schizo has to get out from under the one-way course of his illness all the way to total depletion (right down to the bottom of the reserve tanks) of all libido or fuel supplies.

> With delusion as with no other disease does the outside environment, the situative field, including all reserves *[Bestände]*, from lighting and decoration of the space to gesture, voice, behavior and words of the persons have such decisive significance.... The delusional patient is pulled into the situation as an *oversensitive apparatus for registering essential properties* and responds with the wildest reactions to the slightest changes in the field. The more profoundly this basic tuning has progressd the more important is influence from the outside. That in this sense psychotherapy is possible with him I never doubted. At the time it was clear to me that extensive talks with friendly engagement of content was therapeutically effective with the majority of patients 16 years ago. (83)

Based on his psychiatric treatment and study of Nazi German soldiers who were no longer fit, no longer one size fits all, for the mobilization of the total war effort, Conrad developed what the war held in store for him: a theory of the stages of schizophrenia that includes recommendations for treatment. The view that Conrad transported to and from the front was that schizophrenia research was in a crisis that was shared with the theory and therapy of the human subject at large. In the psychiatric view, schizophrenia is incomprehensible and therefore approachable only via brain-pathological and other purely physical treatments. The other view, which Conrad free-associates in the 1958 publication with the philosophies of Bergson and Husserl, focuses on schizophrenia not as a disease but as a form of failure (as when one fails a test), a failure to sustain, withstand, or understand the crisis that comes one's way. But total allegiance to this phenomenological-anthropological perspective (which implies that many if not all pathological states are interchangeable) would require abandoning the science of psychopathology research for the work of the poet (5). So Conrad blazed a third way to go about the problem schizophrenia presents: he prepared his own mix and match of *Gestaltanalyse* and *Daseinsanalyse* (to be administered in that order) for the work of uncovering "the experimental structure of the fresh schizophrenic pulsion" *(Erlebnisstruktur des frischen schizophrenen Schubes)*. Thus he set out to break down the complete breakthrough of schizophrenia into phases or stages. Borrowing from the idiom of theater, Conrad called the first stage the *Trema*, which, on another stage, characterizes the anticipatory tension or stage fright an actor or academic regularly experiences. In the first case that Conrad paradigmatically unpacks (case 69), he analyzes how an unrealizable wish to be advanced up the ranks (a wish that presses on the patient via a complicated relay of injunctions and prohibitions) creates a jamming of energy that makes the "wish dynamic" exceed itself—and thus its boundaries—to the point that nothing else has any room alongside it. At the same time, the whole mechanism is predicated on tension and on the barrier that blocks fulfillment of the wish. This is how Conrad reconstructs his patient's double bind: "They want to make me an officer, but at the same time want to prevent it" (17).

The topology of the trema-producing situation describes a "total field" that is closed in on all sides by barriers, which Conrad compares to barbed wire fences. But for the schizophrenic suffering from delusions of persecution, even the reality of Nazi politics is an extraneous coincidence and not an exciting cause. Once, when this patient saw someone point to the door, he attacked the guards standing there; he thought he recognized one of them as the gentleman from the Reichs-business school who had told him all about concentration camps. Once the patient passed through his crisis and was admitted to the open floor of the psychiatric clinic, he no longer had the feeling that he was in a concentration camp. In crisis he had worried that they would give him a "role," his code word for getting tied to a tree or branded with the hammer-and-sickle logo (11–13).

Unlike the actor or exam candidate who can for the time being simply flee, the patient inside his trema has only two moves he can make to take himself out of the impasse: total victory or total defeat. The patient thus moves onto the next stage of schizophrenia dominated by his delusional intake of the environment as sensurround of revelatory or ominous significance organized around his own total war effort. This is the stage of apophany *(Apophänie)*. On this stage the delusional patient comports himself like someone on a receiving line to revelation. The sense that case 69 had of being teleguided via thought transference and hypnosis reflected the apophanic experience of his own thoughts: "Only now can we speak of an apophany of the complete field" (21). The apophanic experience technologizes the body right down to its reserve supplies, or *Bestände*. The psycho soldiers were being jolted with electricity, shot up with poison, zapped by a wave apparatus, and, ultimately and ahead of their time, run by remote control *(Fernsteuerung)*, a coinage and concept not so common, Conrad assures us, back then. (It was in fact current in Hans Dominik's science fiction in the twenties.) But you always saw it first with the psychos, who "were there," unprotected by the sublimational, subliminal veil otherwise thrown over our intimate relations with technology. More often than not while reading, patients will start to hear voices dictating correctly or incorrectly.

It's like whispering, or like someone transmitting via radio (95). It's a kind of "sensual thinking" experienced apophanically (97). Case 60 hears the whispered running commentary intended only for him while flying his fighter plane.

In apophany the environment has been transformed into a highly significant setup often recognized by the patient to be in fact a theater production or a film set in which he is to be trapped or tested. This is in keeping with the remarkable, noteworthy quality invested equally in every detail. Everything out there, right down to the reserves and supplies *(Bestände)*, is apophanically illuminated (53). Given the military complex these psychotics shared, the espionage theme was a readily available development for this projective stage (87, 92, 106, 107, 112, 118, 120). And inside and out, it's again the reserves and supplies in which the covert operations take a controlling interest. Case 42's crisis was set off when the coal rationing card he was in charge of keeping was needed by the officer in command and taken from the patient's desk in his absence (42).

Case 10's spy movie paranoia began as a dispute at the military gas station where he was responsible for rationing. When a couple of soldiers came to tank up, but without the required forms to fill out, the patient refused outright to dispense the necessary gas. But even when the soldiers brought the paperwork, the patient began having misgivings, which finally landed him in psychiatric treatment (52). But already the night before he had gone to another soldier's quarters to go over the gas station ledgers. When he found the door locked, he was convinced that everything had been set up to test whether he would notice. He knocked at another door, entered, and came across a soldier lying on a cot. The patient noticed right away that this had all been planned to make allusions that would go without saying about the fact of his being homosexual. Like the gas-rationing misunderstanding on the morning after, the transgressive understanding in the barracks was just a test (51). As in Freud's rereading of the Prometheus story, this primal scene of technologization already shows the man defending the community's energy source against the wipeout of his own homosexual flooding.

In 1941 Reinhard Wendiggensen presented Conrad's case 10 as the central study of his doctoral thesis on Schreberesque psychosis meets *Daseinsanalyse*. The patient was first overwhelmed in 1937 by espionage suspicions: soon the war started, and he was drafted into a fueling unit. During the homo or fuel test that sent him into treatment, the patient also caught and was caught by sight of secret documents, *Geheimakten*, lying about at the intersection of espionage and inversion: *Akt* can also refer to a "nude."

In the Paris clinic, he followed the first act with his attack on a fellow patient for making "homosexual suggestions" (Wendiggensen, 15). But although homosexual thoughts indeed go into this patient's mix and makeup, they do not necessarily exceed the measure of ingredients listed on the back of normalcy. In fact, the uncontrolled release of these thoughts at the crisis point reflects less on his position in the projection booth than on the general metabolism of psychosis. Yes, there is a "reversal" in the barracks scene, but it's not that his homosexual rapport with the comrade in bed has been projectively rewired to circuit break it. The reversal consists in the immediate experience of the impulse or thought as highly significant, "whereby it entered automatically into the testing situation: I am being tested to see if I react homosexually" (29–30). "The schizophrenic change in structure functions here much as would a one-sided intense lighting which all of a sudden emphasizes strongly, at the same time through the diagonal shadow of the beam, the very fine impulses which were never clearly articulated in consciousness" (30). That's why it's no contradiction that with this intense focus on whatever crosses his mind, the patient at the same time complains that his concentration powers are weak: main and side thoughts intersect and pass each other without boundary (39).

In addition to the light show, Wendiggensen is attracted to another analogy for the structuring of his patient's experience. The patient's new system of reference or relations resembles a "force field," "which realigns all objects taken up at the moment as theme within the magnetic field like iron shavings. What was formerly neutral, that is, nonmagnetic is now changed in the sense of a charge and points automatically to the 'center' or, better yet, the fulcrum of the force field" (33). A form of experience has installed itself to the extent that "between the subject and the supplies *[Bestände]* of his field *[Umfeld]* a kind of 'magnetic field' has developed, which brought about the subject's sense of himself as though surrounded by the circle of a spell *[Bannkreis]*" (35). The third point of comparison linking these one-on-one analogies "is the process of 'becoming whole,' that is, of 'becoming system'" (35). The theory of the structure of (psychotic) *Dasein* is what in fact happens to the psychotic right down to his own reception of what's happening.

In the analogy contest inside the therapeutic relationship, the patient gives in to the apparatus but refuses Wendiggensen's "tone" or "voice" to describe his sense of being remote controlled. Earlier the patient had declared the force, the force that's with Hitler, for example, to be spiritual or psychic and not machinic: "Now the patient does think of an apparatus from which the whole thing emanates, a type of wave machine *[Wellenapparat]* which somehow could be adjusted to a stronger or weaker frequency" (15). This apparatus puts him in the unique position of being teleguided *(ferngesteuert):*

> One could steer planes and submarines by remote, but that one could also teleguide a human, that is something so monstrous that it has decisive significance,—for politics in general—in order to keep entire peoples checkmated. And these are only the preliminary trial experiments. (18)

But steering or guidance by remote does not follow from a voice he hears. Not only the Nazi German therapeutic community insists on the voice or speaker (the führer function turns it up full blast in group-psychological contexts). In the intrapsychedelic changeover the patient has undergone, whereby he becomes one with his experience, everything, according to Wendiggensen, has taken on the "ego tone" (41). But the patient says it's like a direct order, a wish that has him at its command: he just does it. That he is neither hearing nor obeying the voices, while bad for the transferential therapy, is consistent with the daseinsanalytic view of the complete transformation of the psychotic's form of experience. "Supplies *[Bestände]* of the figure (the separate experiences) are no longer referred to the figure as a sharply bordered and raised *Gestalt* but to a whole which equally comprehends former figure and background" (43–44). This transformation is not the kind of doubling that leaves the doubles intact:

> One should remember in this connection that it is not some unchanged imaginary ego standing outside experience which has other experiences, which at the same time looks on changed objects with otherwise intact "functions"; rather the ego itself in its *Bestände* [its substance and staying power] is under attack, is no longer the same ego. (44)

The new form of experience doesn't depend on "the *Bestände* of the thematic field, in other words, of the experiential background" (45). But something new (like a form of experience no longer dependent on supplies) still comes down to something that's getting old in the register of loss. What's teleguided *(ferngelenkt)* is also "alien-guided" *(fremdgelenkt).* Everything is at the same time automatically "made" "foreign": "With our patient the entirety of all sequences of movement receives a completely new quality, namely that of foreignness, in such a way as though the movement were not his intention but transpired without his participation, were in fact automatic" (38). Following and joining each other "like clockwork," the automatically foreign experiences belong to the foreign body, the unburied corpse:

Following the "spot light theory" of attention one could say that whatever the light beam of his attention was directed towards was transformed in appearance much as when one places quartz glass in front of the light it results in everything the light beam illuminates taking on a "corpse color." (32)

Only One Thing Missing

> A French Aviator who followed the profession of Airline Pilot for Eight Years offers the American edition of this book in homage to the Airline Pilots of America and their Dead.
>
> —ANTOINE DE SAINT-EXUPÉRY, *WIND, SAND, AND STARS*

To say out loud what he thinks—that everyone inside there knows his thoughts—would amount, case 56 admits to Conrad, to treason (92). How does the military read the thoughts of these patients? He doesn't know exactly what the machines look like, but one patient wagers that it must be connected with light (91). Because everyone took him to be someone he wasn't, case 54 conceded that it could easily have something to do with espionage (81).

In the face of this stockpiling of a significance meant for the schizophrenic only, a kind of literalization (and shutdown) of reflection imprisons experience inside the ego. This is the other side of the patient's inability to "cross over." "He can no longer forget himself and simply be with things, that is, with the other" (79). Conrad calls this other side of one and the same structural transformation of experience in schizophrenia *Anastrophe:* "Wherever there is apophanic experience the ego must also at the same time transform itself anastrophically and vice versa" (80).

Both outer and inner worlds are apophanically experienced in schizophrenia. A sudden idea gets transformed into an inspiration, a dictation or command. The broadcasting of thoughts and the hearing of voices follow this line of development. In this register of delusion, Conrad regularly encountered a psychotic conviction that the war effort could be personally influenced, often by writing letters to Hitler. This latter activity must not have been uncommon; in the case histories of these patients, the military personnel seem instantly to recognize these letters as symptoms and immediately send the letter writers to the nearest neurological clinic. But before this referral, the delusion displays a double register characteristic of psychosis (versus neurosis). The patient is both inside ("in Kafkaesque manner") and outside the dictated order in which he is being tested and in which he can as observer also intervene: "We see from this description how 'personality-removed,' that is to say, how non-neurotic are the experiences the patient registers. He simply looks on in surprise" (75).

The epidemic extent of letter- and petition-writing activities up and down the ranks is another latecomer to the original insurance context and differential diagnosis between simulation and neurosis that traumatic and war disorders either entered or introduced. *Querulantenwahn*, the diagnosis reserved for such complainers, corresponds to all three: psychopathy, schizophrenia, and mania. In 1944 Rudolf Müller, another Conrad student back in Marburg, wrote up the case of a boxer (case 20 in Conrad's book) who in 1939 came down with his first "wave of querulousness" (Müller, 30), and in 1940 received his first diagnosis: "querulous psychopathic personality" (31). He tried to pull the emergency brake and start over again in 1940 by volunteering for the air force, but his nerves didn't pass the test of selection. Without relief, then, the cycle of punishment and protest escalates until in 1942 he composes an endless letter to Hitler and goes on hunger strike to enforce fulfillment of his request for reinstatement of his honor in the eyes of his führer. At this limit he is brought to Müller for a battery of tests (Rorschach, Wartegg, picture postcard selection, among others).

The tension he suffers from is episodic and in that sense wavelike; it's an alternation between "wave valleys" and "wave peaks." Müller tries to shift the machine-scape onto transferential groundedness. The patient does admit that things went wrong in the past, too; he was a spendthrift, and his relations with his father were wasted (42). In 1941, while riding out one of his "waves" of querulousness, he had a fit of jealousy concerning the message he was picking up from his brand-new wife's glances. Add to that she's pregnant, and the patient must break up and leave her. He goes by train but then gets off at the next station and has the local doctor check his ability to engender children. When his capacity checks out, he goes back to his wife, and they make up. To contain this patient's acting out, Müller grows expansive, along intrapsychic lines, and asserts that even the simulation of shell shock or railway spine is still neurotic. The patient's illness is his obsession with the idea of being mentally disturbed.

> This idea, that he is nervously disordered, shows in its development traits very similar to the other ideas of the patient. It immediately takes on an overvalued quality, dominates his entire thinking, more and more moments of experience are brought in to support it from the supplies *[Beständen]* of experience, whereby every critical perspective is missing and only whatever is useful in the sense of the idea is summoned. (42)

Something must have happened in December 1939, something the patient hasn't mentioned or remembered yet, to set off his "justice neurosis" *(Rechtsneurose)*. Suddenly a transvaluation or overvaluation of himself and his position was under way.

> One does not at all have the impression that at first he suffered an injustice *[Unrecht]* and as a reaction to it the justice neurosis emerged, but rather that at first there arose a structural change of the personality and through this and the transformation of the ego-world-relation that followed from it the justice neurosis was set into motion. (44)

Indeed, the neurosis makes him act as though he had all kinds of rights in the Nazi military: not only does he protest unfair punishment, but he refuses to sign any release or settlement forms whenever he's given a show of arbitration. It was the "style" of the patient's oeuvre of protest, however, that alerted his judicial correspondents to there being something not quite right in his head (36). But Müller argues that the patient's writing remains translatable, thus giving entry into his patient's "agrammatical disturbance" (57), which he can chart as curable, transference style.

Conrad extends the coverage to several cases of the genre of querulous re-petition. When case 12 was en route back home from the Russian front in December 1941, he heard the führer's speech on the radio. Instantly a new wish to communicate with the führer overpowered him. In Berlin he and his letter were turned away by the SS lieutenant at the Chancellery. Unable to hand the letter over in person, the patient did the next best thing: he sent a telegram. On the train back from Berlin, a strong "relational delusion" possessed him, ending finally in (guaranteed) fatal catatonia (Conrad, 34). "A few days later Case No. 43 announced in the clinic that the newspapers were saying that he's supposed to be shot; someone should write to Hitler to plead for him" (43). Case 21 was convinced that he "stood in connection with Adolf Hitler who had given him special powers. All of M. could now be leveled at his command. The innocent would suffer along with the guilty" (75). When case 53 was drafted at the start of the war, he had just completed his book of heaven-sent prophetic writings with which he hoped to apply for the mediator role and thus restore peace to Germany. (Case 48 felt he had already been advanced to the position of top führer of the army; he was now only ventriloquizing Hitler [75].) Sometimes case 53 stood in spiritual rapport with Hitler; when drowsy he would feel as though he had been with the führer with tears in their eyes (86). But when he heard Goebbels's radio talk right before the invasion of Czechoslovakia, the urge came over him to do something to prevent war: "There was boiling inside me a rage such that if someone had crossed my path I would have had to kill him" (85). Should he go to the prison camp and speak out from there, something inside him wondered. But he knew they would write him off as crazy. So he rushed into the local police station and cried out, "I believe in

God," whereupon he was seized and returned home in his wife's custody. He knew that if he didn't finish writing down the prophetic messages he was receiving, Germany would be in danger. He felt increasingly, as the jolts of electricity he was also feeling were on the rise, that he was writing in Germany's defense. The first thing he did when he joined his regiment was to tell the commanding officer that he was not allowed to use weapons. The officer informed him he would be shot if he ever said such a thing again. Next he gave the officer his completed book of prophetic messages to read. (He also told him about some recent visions, for example that "someone would lay cables bearing a liquid flammable substance from England" [87].) The officer seemed to understand now; he asked the soldier to come to him and only to him any time he had anything else to share. By the time the soldier finished traveling with his troop to France, he was completely exhausted. His closing effort before he was sent to Conrad's clinic was, one, to tell England, via an English chaplain, to put down all weapons and surrender; two, to represent the führer in the peace effort; and three, to announce that Christianity proper could now begin with the end coming soon of history, which had all along been only a history of wars.

This case was already contained in Karl-Heinz Steffen's 1942 dissertation (at the University of Marburg) entitled "Initial Schizophrenic Structural Transformations as Prophet Delusion." Conrad sets this date to underscore that one of the prophecies was in fact synchronized with coming events: the patient saw a yellow cloud that appeared suddenly only to spring back into the sky like a red ball. This could not yet have reflected, Conrad assures us, the impact of the first atomic bomb (85, 85 n. 1).

In Steffen's study, this patient too hears no voices but is given and driven, first to return to Germany in 1934, then to write verses and letters of prophecy. He wants to be a mediator so that he can keep forwarding the conflict. In all the letters the schizos are writing to Hitler, it is in the "transference" *[übertragung]* from the handwriting to the typed record, and from desktop to publishing house, that Wendiggensen's, Steffen's, and Conrad's patients contain their particular disturbance. When Steffen's patient is informed by one publisher that the führer alone knows what he has to do, the patient's cottage industry shuts down for treatment. Given the postal networking of transferences that have the Nazi hierarchy covered, Steffen frames the case with a version of the patient's own view that Hitler is his apostle or messenger.

> We know... that in such states of initial schizophrenic experience it's possible for senseless murders, yes even mass murders

> to be committed, even if not by personalities of the type of our patient. But his case precisely makes the deeds of others, who express themselves less about it, but are that much more likely to enact it, more understandable. (31)

For Conrad, this case of schizophrenic psychosis demonstrates an exceptionally long-term social adjustment on the outside (until, of course, the full-scale outbreak or breakdown in sync with the coming of war). Before that he for the most part restricted his apophanic experience to the inner world, which would spill out during drowsy, in-between states. What can be observed already here for a change is otherwise under way in the complete picture of schizophrenia taken during the *Trema* phase. The sudden idea that pops into one's head (in German the word for this surprise thought, *Einfall,* also means "invasion") can no longer be dismissed: it has turned into a dictated inspiration or revelation (Conrad, 90).

While observing case 69, the one modeling his paradigm, Conrad noted that certain "experiential supplies" *[Erlebnisbestände]* were forming themselves into "asyntactical images which no longer permitted recognition of a continuity of meaning" (22). One step further, and the situation's continuity of sense would have been busted wide open, and asyntactic, archetypical images would have rushed in, over, and out. This phase is called *Apocalypse.* Case 69 ran up against but did not cross over into this phase (it's where catatonia tends to go). If the final outcome of the schizophrenia is death, a "terminal stage," in which toxic coma takes over, has also been occupied on the way. But there's no form or content of experience to be addressed here (22).

The final phase more often attained in schizophrenia than not is that of *Consolidation,* the residual phase or legacy of the encounter with full-blown schizophrenia. The shift from the apophanic and apostrophic phase of schizophrenic experience to consolidation is the way to go for case 28. On the way to the psychiatric clinic, for example, he was urging on the velocity of his transportation with cries of "Faster! Faster!" It turned out that he was convinced that he was at all times participating in the entirety of the war effort. Somehow or other he was there, everywhere. When he urinated at night, he had the sense that he was determining that at that moment bombs would fall on England. Back in bed, lying on his stomach, he was at the same time flying in a plane across English airspace. He's the guardian or god of the bomber planes flying over England (74). He thus exhibits a characteristic reciprocity of effects in apophanic/apostrophic experience: "Effects the world and its supplies have on the ego—which the delusional perception thoroughly analyzes—are recircuited through a reverse direction of effects from the ego back to the world. There is reason to believe that where there is full blown delusional experience both directions are experienced always at the same time" (76). During consolidation, the influence he was phantasmatically exercising over the war and over the weather was gradually given up by the patient. At first he still felt that he could "hypnotize" the weather even though he now chose not to exercise his "divine capacity." But over time he came to recognize in his weather reports coincidences instead of any fulfillment of his wish power. And one day the patient suddenly realized that "the feeling of being able to influence the war was in truth the same feeling he also had had with the weather" (74).

The "uniformity" of the "uniformed" population of nearly two hundred psychotics Conrad treated from 1941 to 1942 gave him his inside view of schizophrenia right at its onset. For his part, Conrad recognizes "the uniformity of psychosis or better yet: that which is typical about these psychoses *in uniform*" (108). He can thus also see through the view of schizophrenic psychosis as growing out of an immediate conflict. With the uniformity and uniforming of military life there is no real opportunity for conflict in the strict sense (40). Uniforms order what is typical of an illness to march forward; that which is more typical of the individual in turn steps back (156). The uniformity of Conrad's study population, in which the psychotic soldiers presented a unified image and each psychosis resembled the other (130), requires rigorous border patrolling between external, extraneous political issues and the intrapsychic conflict. It is just a test case of therapeutic correctness versus the political kind. It's not so easy to view these soldiers who are no longer able to fight as psychotics. For example: when case 28 resisted the ritual abuse of military discipline, he was on his way to the acute outbreak of psychosis two weeks later. Conrad insists that the patient's run-in with discipline represented the kind of incomprehensible move that signals the onset of schizophrenia. When the patient simply covered his ears, turned around, and walked away from the superior officer who was shouting at him, he demonstrated a "total destruction of the structure of the situation" that was at this point of crisis his only remaining "option for dealing with the rise in tension": "a short circuit in the true sense of the word occurred, perhaps in order to prevent a catastrophic conflagration" (33). Thus when another case suddenly took his subordinates on tours of Paris to "teach them respect for the culture of our enemies," he, Conrad emphasizes, made "two disparate situational fields communicate; again barriers were torn down and showed themselves to be ready to go" (35).

What Conrad calls barriers are not literally so but are "realities, which have a not meager importance in our lives as the concrete resources or reserves *[Bestände]* of our current field."

> What appears especially in the frame of the military situation mostly as transgression against discipline, is in reality expression of an emergency reaction which apparently is supposed to help realize a barely maintained integration into the structure of the situation in the very moment of its being endangered. Always a destructive process has already taken up a position, the expression of which is the tense underlying affectivity, so that a slight increase of pressure can have as consequence the breakdown of the barriers, and that brings with it the senseless behavior. (35)

The breakdown of barriers or limits that signals the outbreak of schizophrenia is therefore connected to the progressive depletion of resources and reserve supplies in the course of the illness. The lack of barriers leads to a boundary blending of thoughts that keeps it all prehistoric: "Everywhere we can see clearly that the thought doesn't make it into a clear formulation in language but rather prematurely gets stuck in an immature stage and then and there agglutinates with the following thought" (101). But before reaching the bottom of mixed thinking, Conrad pulls the emergency brake on his own discourse. It's schizo alert. "A precise analysis of this disturbance would however surpass the demarcated frame of an experiential analysis of schizophrenic experience during the fresh schizophrenic thrust or outbreak" (101). The phenomenological line he is pursuing is something he can keep the faith with and thus keep certain dimensions of his own line of questioning off limits. "Of course every one of our psychiatric case studies takes us to a limit and could seduce us to transgress it" (37).

During the consolidation a reverse movement sets in that dismantles the apophany. At this point the delusion can be corrected, and reality testing restored through transferential psychotherapy. But the patient does not then return to the starting point belonging to some pre-illness integrated personality. Following the frenzied preparedness and exhausted collapse there remains, not only in the case of Steffen's patient but as a rule of development of schizophrenia, only low-impact energy distribution: "With complete stealth the total sum of energy of the personality often decreases" (Steffen, 43). Indeed, in each case under Conrad's treatment, the schizophrenic psychosis had irreversibly reduced and depleted the patient's "energetic potential." The structural transformation that goes down with schizophrenia always sets itself up as enduring (Conrad, 128). With consolidation the patient typically complains of a loss of energy, power, or excitement. Case 85's only remaining pleasure was to go to the movies, which gave him back a certain suspense. Conrad has his number: the patient now needs some push from the outside because the inner one is gone (123). There was never any talk of this lack of energy during the psychosis. In their excited state, the patients exhibited often enormous amounts of willpower. But even already during the psychosis, the patient was all along experiencing a reduction of energy and was thus attempting as a kind of last stand "to mobilize all reserves of the will"; but the patient always "left the fight as a changed person, one impoverished, depleted of energy" (125).

The "energy potential" talked about here, Conrad admits, is "comparable to the 'war potential' of a country which in peace time as during a war, in other words at a time of heavy use of war materials, remains a constant quantity" (126). Conrad breaks the cases of psychosis down according to the degree of energy potential lost or depleted by the time of recovery or stabilization. Only the nonschizophrenic psychoses kept this loss to a minimum. Conrad therefore concludes that the loss is what defines schizophrenia (143). Whereas those suffering from "anxiety psychosis" *(Angstpsychose)* could, following treatment, be sent back to the front, those who were afflicted with "dementia simplex," for example, suffered a depletion of energy potential that was so great "that the patient for this reason falls out of the social structure of the *Wehrmacht*" (129).

> If one could only discover some energetic substitute which could be given the patient from without—analogous to a missing hormone—then one would have in the true sense of the word "healed" his schizophrenia, for the patient lacks nothing else at this stationary stage of his process. As severely disturbed as the catatonic asylum patient appears, he lacks nothing but the fuel *[Treibstoff]* which could put the psyche back into gear. (139)

When Conrad reckons the uniformity of his uniformed study population as a distinct advantage in the understanding of psychosis, he crosses the border into Freud's view of the role of endopsychic perception in delusion and hallucination. In 1941 Conrad asked a patient in the course of the diagnostic interview what his opinion was regarding the current state of the war.

> "It's as though there were war inside the country."
> [Why?]

> "In economic matters and so on, there was a lot that caught my attention."
>
> [Like what?]
>
> "Outside in nature and everything, in the construction business and the economy and building matters and all the rest, everything has changed."
>
> [Humans too?]
>
> "Yes, in character they've all changed." (134)

While intrapsychic conflict is bigger than life, the reserve or *Bestand* structure (which, according to Heidegger's forecast, will pick up where humanity left off) puts everyone, one by one, on standby. The fuel tank inside the soldiers Conrad analyzes is what they represent in the bigger picture of total mobilization. Here we touch down again on the runway where Heidegger parked his techno-example of the plane that even when stationary is still in the ready position for takeoff. The plane on the runway modeling the standing reserve or *Bestand* that's the essence of technology is what Heidegger comes up with as though in denial of the fuel-bound half-life of the German mobilizations of world war technology.

But with the takeoff of the final phase of total war on the automatic plane of realization, renewed applications of feedback propelled a new rocket age away from the earthbound dependency of automobilic technologies on the reserve fuel tank. At the same time, this science fiction front of survival was set up on the borderline inside psychosis. The zone of nontransferential disconnection otherwise set aside as melancholia or schizophrenia was a new frontier for future colonization through the evolving super or survivor body growing out of equal machine and human parts up and down the axis of intrapsychic airspace. The V-1 and V-2 "miracle weapons" *(Wunderwaffen)* follow Daniel Paul Schreber's psychotic or cyberspatial trajectory from the wound *(Wunde)* of loss and separation (or takeoff) to the wonder or miracle *(Wunder)* of a new sci fi world that must be colonized in place of the one that has been lost. But whereas Nazi research worked this outer-space experience to the max in the encounter with the enemy (including the enemy within), when it came to the home base of operations there was only the one way to go of inoculation (which doesn't get you out of the groove of the fix you're in between transference and narcissism).

References

Abraham, Karl. "Psychoanalysis and the War Neuroses." In *Clinical Papers and Essays on Psychoanalysis.* Vol. 2. Ed. Hilda Abraham. Trans. Hilda Abraham and D. R. Ellison. 1919; New York: Basic Books, 1955.

Adorno, Theodor W. "Bemerkungen über Politik und Neurose." In *Gesammelte Schriften,* ed. Rolf Tiedemann. 1954; Frankfurt a/M: Suhrkamp Verlag, 1972.

Alexander, Franz, and Gerhard J. Piers. "Psychoanalysis." In *Progress in Neurology and Psychiatry,* ed. E. A. Spiegel. Vol. 2. New York: Grune and Stratton, 1947.

Anderson, R. C. "The Motivations of the Flyer and His Reactions to the Stresses of Flight." *Aviation Medicine* 18 (1947): 18–30.

Bateson, Gregory. "Section of Psychology (18 January 1943)." *Transactions of the New York Academy of Sciences,* 2d. ser, 5, no. 1 (November 1943): 72–78.

———. *Steps to an Ecology of Mind.* San Francisco: Chandler, 1972.

Becker, Werner H. "Psychotherapie bei Geisteskranken." *Psychiatrisch-Neurologische Wochenschrift* 45–46 (1943): 275–77.

Beinhorn, Elly. *Berlin–Kapstadt–Berlin.* Berlin: Militärverlag Karl Siegismund, 1939.

Beinhorn-Rosemeyer, Elly. *Ich Fliege um die Welt* [I Fly around the World]. Berlin: Ullstein, 1952.

Benary, W. "Kurzer Bericht über Arbeiten zu Eignungsprüfungen für Flieger-Beobachter." *Zeitschrift für angewandte Psychologie* 15, nos. 3–4 (1919): 161–310.

Beumelburg, Werner. *Ypern 1914.* Vol. 10 of *Schlachten des Weltkrieges,* ed. George Soldan. Berlin: Stalling, 1925.

Billeb, Eberhard. "Geopolitische Auswirkungen der Luftfahrt" [Geopolitical Effects of Air Travel]. *Zeitschrift für Geopolitik* 12 (1937): 996–1004.

Billings, Edward G., et al. "Comparison of One Hundred Army Psychiatric Patients and One Hundred Enlisted Men." *War Medicine* 4 (1943): 283–98.

Binswanger, Ludwig. "Dream and Existence." In *Being-in-the-World: Selected Papers of Ludwig Binswanger,* trans. Jacob Needleman. 1930; New York: Basic Books, 1963.

———. "Extravagance." In *Being-in-the-World: Selected Papers of Ludwig Binswanger,* trans. Jacob Needleman. 1956; New York: Basic Books, 1963.

———. "Introduction to *Schizophrenie.*" In *Being-in-the-World: Selected Papers of Ludwig Binswanger,* trans. Jacob Needleman. 1957; New York: Basic Books, 1963.

———. *Sigmund Freud: Reminiscences of a Friendship.* Trans. Norbert Guterman. New York: Grune and Stratton, 1957.

Bion, Wilfred R. "Emotional Turbulence." In *Borderline Personality Disorders: The Concept, the Syndrome, the Patient,* ed. Peter Hartocollis. New York: International Universities Press, 1977.

———. "Experiences in Groups: I." *Human Relations* 1, no. 3 (1948): 314–20.

———. "Experiences in Groups: II." *Human Relations* 1, no. 4 (1948): 487–96.

———. "Experiences in Groups: III." *Human Relations* 2, no. 1 (1949): 13–22.

———. "Experiences in Groups: IV." *Human Relations* 2, no. 4 (1949): 295–303.

———. "Experiences in Groups: V." *Human Relations* 3, no. 1 (1950): 3–13.

———. "Experiences in Groups: VI." *Human Relations* 3, no. 4 (1950): 395–402.

———. "Experiences in Groups: VII." *Human Relations* 4 (1951): 221–27.

———. "The Leaderless Group Project." *Bulletin of the Menninger Clinic* 10 (1946): 77–81.

———. "Psychiatry at a Time of Crisis." *British Journal of Medical Psychology* 21 (1948): 81–89.

———. "The 'War of Nerves': Civilian Reaction, Morale, and Prophylaxis." In *The Neuroses in War*, ed. Emanuel Miller. New York: Macmillan, 1940.

Bion, Wilfred R., and John Rickman. "Intra-group Tensions in Therapy: Their Study as the Task of the Group." *Lancet*, 27 November 1943, 678–81.

Blundell, Nigel, and Roger Boar. *The World's Greatest Ghosts.* New York: Berkeley Books, 1988.

Böhme, Albrecht, with M. Staemmler, E. Lange, F. Ziegler, and H. Peter. *Psychotherapie und Kastration: Die Bedeutung der Psychotherapie als Erziehungs- und Ausscheidungsmethode für sexuell Abwegige und Sittlichkeitsverbrecher, dargestellt an Fällen aus der Kriminalpraxis, unter Heranziehung der Graphologie als Hilfswissenschaft.* Munich: J. F. Lehmanns Verlag, 1935.

Bond, Douglas D. *The Love and Fear of Flying.* New York: International Universities Press, 1952.

Boring, Edwin G. *Psychology for the Armed Services.* Washington, D.C.: Infantry Journal Press, 1945.

Boss, Medard. *The Analysis of Dreams.* Trans. Arnold J. Pomerans. New York: Philosophical Library, 1958.

———. *Psychoanalysis and Daseinsanalysis.* Trans. Ludwig Lefebre. 1963; New York: Da Capo, 1982.

Braceland, Francis J., and Howard P. Rome. "Anxiety and Fatigue." *Connecticut State Medical Journal* 7, no. 12 (December 1943): 827–31.

Brady, Robert A. *The Spirit and Structure of German Fascism.* London: Victor Gollancz, 1937.

Brecht, Karen, et al., eds. *"Here life goes on in a most peculiar way . . ." Psychoanalysis before and after 1933.* Trans. Christine Trollope. Hamburg: Kellner Verlag, 1985.

Bresler, J. "Gibt es nationale Psychotherapie?" [Is There a National Psychotherapy?]. *Psychiatrisch-Neurologische Wochenschrift* 2 (1940): 12–14.

Buchner, Hans. *Im Banne des Films: Die Weltherrschaft des Kinos* [Under the Spell of Film: The World Domination of Cinema]. Munich: Deutscher Volksverlag, 1927.

Caidin, Martin. *Ghosts of the Air: True Stories of Aerial Hauntings.* New York: Bantam, 1991.

Chapman, A. H. *Harry Stack Sullivan: His Life and His Work.* New York: G. P. Putnam's Sons, 1976.

Chasseguet-Smirgel, Janine. "'Time's White Hair We Ruffle'—Reflections on the Hamburg Congress." Trans. Philip Slotkin. *International Review of Psychoanalysis* 14 (1987): 433–44.

———. "Überlegungen zum Hamburger Kongreß." *Jahrbuch der Psychoanalyse* 20 (1987): 89–113.

Cocks, Geoffrey. *Psychotherapy in the Third Reich: The Göring Institute.* New York: Oxford University Press, 1985.

Condiau, Gion. *Sigmund Freud und Martin Heidegger: Daseinsanalytische Neurosenlehre und Psychotherapie.* Freiburg: Universitätsverlag, 1992.

Conrad, Klaus. *Die beginnende Schizophrenie: Versuch einer Gestaltanalyse des Wahns.* Stuttgart: G. Thieme, 1958.

Console, William. "Psychiatric Reactions to Aerial Combat and Their Sequelae." *Connecticut State Medical Journal* 10 (30 January 1946): 900–902.

Creel, George. *Rebel at Large: Recollections of Fifty Crowded Years.* New York: G. P. Putnam's Sons, 1947.

Crinis, M. de. With Christel H. Roggenbau. "Therapie der psychischen Erkrankungen" [Therapy of Psychic Illnesses]. In *Die Therapie an den Berliner Universitäts-Kliniken,* ed. Heinz Kalk. Berlin: Urban and Schwarzenberg, 1945.

Debenham, Gilbert, et al. "Treatment of War Neurosis." *Lancet,* 25 January 1941, 107–9.

Deegener, ———. "Sonderlinge unter tauglichen Rekruten." *Soldatentum* (1936): 69–72.

Derrida, Jacques. *Specters of Marx: The State of the Debt, the Work of Mourning, and the New International.* Trans. Peggy Kamuf. New York: Routledge, 1994.

Despiau, Charles. *Arno Breker.* Paris: Flammarion, 1942.

Dietsch, W. "Über Funkveranlagung." *Zeitschrift für angewandte Psychologie,* supp. 72 (1936): 140–48.

Dillon, Frederick. "Neuroses among Combatant Troops in the Great War." *British Medical Journal* 2 (8 July 1939): 63–66.

Dirks, ———. "Über den Kampfgeist der Panzerabwehrtruppe" [On the Fighting Spirit of the Tank Defense Troops]. *Soldatentum* (1939): 11–17.

Eichberg, A. "Der Intellektuelle als Rekrut" [The Intellectual as Recruit]. *Soldatentum* (1938): 65–68.

———. "Der tölpische Mensch als Rekrut." *Soldatentum* (1937): 243–48.

Engels, ———. "Über den Kampfgeist der Panzerabwehrtruppe." *Soldatentum* (1939): 75–78.

Erikson, Erik Homburger. "Hitler's Imagery and German Youth." *Public Opinion Quarterly* (winter 1943): 475–93.

Fairbairn, W. Ronald D. "The Repression and the Return of Bad Objects (With Special Reference to the 'War Neuroses')." In *Psychoanalytic Studies of the Personality.* London: Routledge and Kegan Paul, 1952.

———. "The Treatment and Rehabilitation of Sexual Offenders." In *Psychoanalytic Studies of the Personality.*

———. "The War Neuroses ——— Their Nature and Significance." In *Psychoanalytic Studies of the Personality.*

Farago, Ladislas, ed. *German Psychological Warfare: Survey and Bibliography.* New York: Committee for National Morale, 1941.

Farber, Leslie, and Leonard Micon. "Gastric Neurosis in a Military Service." *Psychiatry* 8, no. 3 (August 1945): 343–61.

Fenichel, Otto. *The Psychoanalytic Theory of Neurosis.* New York: W. W. Norton, 1945.

———. *Rundbriefe.* 23 January 1941–15 March 1943. Bancroft Library. University of California–Berkeley. Collection Number 88/2z.

Ferenczi, Sandor. "Die Psychoanalyse der Kriegsneurosen" [Psychoanalysis and the War Neuroses]. Internationale Psychoanalytische Bibliothek no. 1. Leipzig: Internationaler Psychoanalytischer Verlag, 1919.

Finck, H. "Volksgesundheit und Liebesleben" [*Volk* Health and Love Life]. *Ziel und Weg* 8 (1934): 287–94.

Fischer, ———. "Die Bekämpfung des Panikproblems im zivilen Luftschutz" [The Fight against the Panic Problem in Civilian Air Defense]. *Soldatentum* (1939): 18–23.

Flik, Gotthilf. "Psychische Vorgänge beim Funken, im besonderen die subjektiven Umformungen" [Psychic Processes during Broadcasting, in Particular Subjective Transformations]. *Zeitschrift für Psychologie* 150, nos. 4–6 (1941): 320–83.

Freud, Anna. *The Ego and the Mechanisms of Defense.* Trans. Cecil Baines. New York: International Universities Press, 1946.

Freud, Anna, and Dorothy Burlingham. "Infants without Families: Reports on the Hampstead Nurseries (1939–1945)." In *The Writings of Anna Freud,* vol. 3. New York: International Universities Press, 1973.

Freud, Sigmund. *The Standard Edition of the Complete Psychological Works.* Ed. James Stachey. London: Hogarth Press, 1953–1974. Cited in the text as *SE.*

Fromm, Erich. *Escape from Freedom.* 1941; New York: Avon Books, 1969.

Gade, Hans-Georg. "Zur Psychotechnik des Flugzeugführers." Von der technischen Hochschule der freien Stadt Danzig zur Erlangung der Würde eines Doktor-Engenieurs genehmigte Dissertation. 1928.

Gerathewohl, ———. "Eigenart und Behandlung des Einzelgängers" [The Special Nature and Treatment of the Loner]. *Soldatentum* (1938): 163–68.

Gillespie, R. D. *Psychological Effects of War on Citizen and Soldier.* New York: W. W. Norton, 1942.

Glover, Edward. "Notes on the Psychological Effects of War Conditions on the Civilian Population." *International Journal of Psychoanalysis* 23 (1942): 17–37.

———. "The Return of War-Neuroses." *War, Sadism, and Pacifism: Further Essays on Group Psychology and War.* London: George Allen and Unwin, 1946.

Göring, Matthias H. "Grundlagen der Psychotherapie" [Foundations of Psychotherapy]. *Deutsche Medizinische Wochenschrift,* (17 September 1937): 1442–46.

Gordon, Don E. *Electronic Warfare: Element of Strategy and Multiplier of Combat Power.* New York: Pergamon, 1981.

Grinker, Roy R., and John P. Spiegel. *Men under Stress.* Philadelphia: Blakiston, 1945.

———. *War Neuroses in North Africa: The Tunisian Campaign (January–May 1943).* Air Surgeon Army Air Forces. New York: Josiah Macy, September 1943.

Grunwaldt, Hans-Heinrich. "Das erotische Moment im Rekrutenleben" [The Erotic Moment in the Life of the Recruit]. *Soldatentum* (1937): 31–36.

———. "Über die psychischen Bedingungen des Luftschutzes" [On the Psychic Conditions of Air Defense]. *Wissen und Wehr* 6 (1937): 394–99.

Haggard, H. Rider. *Ayesha: The Return of She.* New York: Grosset and Dunlap, 1904.

———. *She: A History of Adventure.* New York: Books, 1886.

Hanse, A. "Zur volksbiologischen und wertphilosophischen Begründung einer deutschen Psychotherapie." *Medizinische Klinik* 8 (23 February 1934): 286–88.

Hantel, Erika. *Brücken von Mensch zu Mensch: Erfahrungen einer Betriebspsychologin.* Stuttgart: Hippokrates-Verlag Marquardt, 1953.

———. *Verborgenes Kräftespiel: Seelenpflege in der Industrie.* Stuttgart: Ferdinand Enke Verlag, 1947.

Hattingberg, Hans von. "Ehekrisen ärztlich gesehen" [Marriage Crises from the Medical Point of View]. *Deutsche medizinische Wochenschrift* 66 (1940): 909–12.

———. "Zur Entwicklung der analytischen Bewegung (Freud, Adler, Jung)." *Deutsche Medizinische Wochenschrift* 59 (1933): 328–33.

Heidegger, Martin. *An Introduction to Metaphysics.* Trans. Ralph Manheim. 1953; Garden City: Doubleday, 1959.

———. "The Question concerning Technology." Trans. William Lovitt. In *The Question concerning Technology and Other Essays.* New York: Harper Torchbooks, 1977. ["Die Frage nach der Technik." In *Vorträge und Aufsätze.* Pfullingen: Günther Neske, 1954.]

———. *Sein und Zeit* [Being and Time]. 1926; Tübingen: Max Niemeyer Verlag, 1986.

———. "The Turning." Trans. William Lovitt. In *The Question concerning Technology and Other Essays.* ["Die Kehre." In *Die Technik und die Kehre.* Pfullingen: Günther Neske, 1962.]

Helwig, Paul. *Charakterologie.* Leipzig: B. G. Teubner, 1936.

Herzog, Edgar. *Erziehungsschwierigkeiten im Schulalter* [Difficulties in Rearing School-Age Children]. Würzburg: Konrad Triltsch Verlag, 1940.

Hodges, Andrew. *Alan Turing: The Enigma.* New York: Simon and Schuster, 1984.

Horney, Karen. *New Ways in Psychoanalysis.* New York: W. W. Norton, 1939.

———. *Self-Analysis.* 1942; New York: Norton, 1972.

Janis, Irving L. "Psychodynamic Aspects of Adjustment to Army Life." *Psychiatry* 8 (May 1945): 159–76.

Johansson, Warren, and William A. Percy. "Homosexuals in Nazi Germany." *Simon Wiesenthal Center Annual* 7 (1990): 225–63.

Jones, Ernest. "Die Kriegsneurosen (war-shock) und die Freudsche Theorie." In *Zur Psychoanalyse der Kriegsneurosen.* Internationale Psychoanalytische Bibliothek no. 1. Leipzig: Internationaler Psychoanalytischer Verlag, 1919.

———. "Psychology and War Conditions." *Yearbook of Psychoanalysis* 2 (1946): 169–94.

Jordan, ———. "Der geborene Soldat" [The Born Soldier]. *Soldatentum* (1937): 114–19.

Kahn, David. *The Code-Breakers: The Story of Secret Writing.* New York: Macmillan, 1967.

Kecskemeti, P., and N. Leites. *Some Psychological Hypotheses on Nazi Germany.* Washington, D.C.: Library of Congress. Experimental Division for the Study of War Time Communications, Harold D. Laswell, Chief. Document no. 60, 30 July 1945.

Kemper, Werner. "Der seelische Anteil an der Sterilität" [The Psychic Component in Sterility]. *Deutsches Ärzteblatt* 72 (1942): 397–99.

Kirkpatrick, Clifford. *Nazi Germany: Its Women and Family Life.* Indianapolis: Bobbs-Merrill, 1938.

Klein, Melanie. *Narrative of a Child Analysis*. New York: Basic Books, 1961.

———. "Some Psychological Considerations: A Comment." In *The Writings of Melanie Klein*, vol. 3. New York: Free Press, 1975.

Kreipe, ———. "Der Rekrut der allgemeinen Wehrpflicht" [The Recruit of the General Service Requirement]. *Soldatentum* (1936): 94–98.

Kreipe, Karl. "Die Bedeutung der Sinneswahrnehmung (insbesondere des Sehens und Hörens) für den soldatischen Dienst" [The Significance of Sense Perception (in Particular Seeing and Hearing) for the Soldierly Service]. *Soldatentum* (1934): 9–14.

Kris, Ernst. "The 'Danger' of Propaganda." *American Imago* 2, no. 1 (March 1941): 3–42.

Küchenhoff, Joachim, and Peter Warsitz. "Psychiatrie und Psychoanalyse nach den Weltkriegen. Wiederholen oder Durcharbeiten?" In *HardWar/SoftWar: Krieg und Medien 1914 bis 1945*, ed. Martin Stingelin and Wolfgang Scherer. Munich: Wilhelm Fink Verlag, 1991.

Künkel, Fritz. "Seelenheilkunde" [Soul-Healing Knowledge]. *Süddeutsche Monatshefte* 33 (1936): 294–300.

Künkel, Fritz, and Elisabeth Künkel. *Die Erziehung deiner Kinder: Hilfsbuch für Eltern und Erzieher* [The Raising of Your Children: Manual for Parents and Educators]. Berlin-Schildow: Falken Verlag, 1936.

Kunz, Josef L. *Kriegsrecht und Neutralitätsrecht* [War Rights and Neutrality Rights]. Vienna: Verlag von Julius Springer, 1935.

Lacan, Jacques. "The Direction of the Treatment and the Principles of Its Power." In *Êcrits: A Selection*, trans. Alan Sheridan. 1961; New York: W. W. Norton, 1977.

———. "The Mirror Stage as Formative of the Function of the I as Revealed in Psychoanalytic Experience." In *Êcrits: A Selection*.

———. "Psychoanalysis and Cybernetics, or On the Nature of Language." In *The Seminar of Jacques Lacan. Book II: The Ego in Freud's Theory and in the Technique of Psychoanalysis, 1954–1955*, ed. Jacques-Alain Miller. Trans. Sylvana Tomaselli. New York: W. W. Norton, 1988.

———. *Télévision*. Paris: Editions du Seuil, 1974.

Lamarr, Hedy. *Ecstasy and Me: My Life as a Woman*. N.p.: Bartholomew House, 1966.

Langer, Walter C. *The Mind of Adolf Hitler: The Secret Wartime Report*. New York: Basic Books, 1972.

Laqua, Carsten. *Wie Micky Maus unter die Nazis fiel: Walt Disney und Deutschland*. Reinbek bei Hamburg: Rowohlt Taschenbuch Verlag, 1992.

Lasswell, Harold D. "Political and Psychological Warfare." In *A Psychological Warfare Casebook*, ed. William E. Daugherty and Morris Janowitz. Baltimore: Johns Hopkins Press, 1958.

Lindbergh, Anne Morrow. *North to the Orient*. New York: Harcourt, Brace, 1935.

Lipmann, Otto. "Die psychische Eignung der Funkentelegraphisten." *Zeitschrift für angewandte Psychologie* 15, nos. 5–6 (1919): 301–40.

Lucke, Viktor. "Einzelne Fragen zur Psychologie der militärischen Erziehung" [Some Questions regarding the Psychology of Military Training]. In *Bericht über den*

Kongress der Deutschen Gesellschaft für Psychologie, vol. 14. Tübingen, 1935. The piece also appeared in *Soldatentum* in July 1934.

Ludwig, Walter. "Beiträge zur Psychologie der Furcht im Kriege." *Beiheft zur Zeitschrift für angewandte Psychologie* 21 (1920): 125–72.

Lüderitz, ———. "Selbstwertglaube und Unterordnung" [Belief in Self-Worth and Subordination]. *Soldatentum* (1937): 67–72.

Mahler, Margaret. "On Infantile Precursors of the 'Influencing Machine' (Tausk)." In *The Selected Papers of Margaret S. Mahler.* Vol. 1, *Infantile Psychosis and Early Contributions.* New York: Jason Aronson, 1979.

Mahler, Margaret, with Manuel Furer. *On Human Symbiosis and the Vicissitudes of Individuation.* Vol. 1, *Infantile Psychosis.* New York: International Universities Press, 1968.

Mayers, Albert. "Dug-Out Psychiatry." *Psychiatry* 8, no. 4 (November 1945): 383–89.

Meeks, Fleming. "'I guess they just take and forget about a person.' Hedy Lamarr, Hollywood sex goddess, was also a brilliant inventor: She got paid for her movies, but not for her invention." *Forbes,* 14 May 1990, 136–38.

Meerloo, A. M. *Total War and the Human Mind: A Psychologist's Experiences in Occupied Holland.* Published for the Netherlands Government Information Bureau by George Allen and Unwin, 1944.

Meier-Welcker, ———. "Gedanken über Gehorsam" [Thoughts on Obedience]. *Soldatentum* (1938): 68–73.

Menninger, William C. *Psychiatry in a Troubled World: Yesterday's War and Today's Challenge.* New York: Macmillan, 1948.

———. "Psychosomatic Medicine on General Medical Wards." *Bulletin of the U.S. Army Medical Department* 4, no. 5 (November 1945): 545–50.

Metz, Paul. "Die Eignung zum Flugzeugführer als Anlagenproblem" [The Aptitude for Flying as Problem of Disposition]. *Zeitschrift für Psychologie* 143 (1938): 12–14.

———. "Funktionale und charakterologische Fragen der Fliegereignung" [The Functional and Characterological Questions of Flying Aptitude]. *Zeitschrift für angewandte Psychologie,* suppl. 72 (1936): 153–72.

Mierke, Karl. "Gefährdete Kameradschaft" [Endangered Comradeship]. *Soldatentum* (1939): 130–41, 188–97.

———. "Versageranalyse bei Funkern." *Archiv für die gesamte Psychologie* 55 (1938): 297–370.

Minski, Louis. "Psychological Reactions in the Wounded." *British Medical Journal* (31 March 1945): 444–45.

Mohr, Fritz. "Aus der Praxis der Psychotherapie." *Medizinische Klinik* 42 (1917): 1116–19.

———. "Brief an eine durch Fliegerangriffe stillunfähig gewordene Mutter" [Letter to a Mother Who Became Incapable of Nursing through Air Attack]. *Hippokrates* 43 (1940): 1016.

———. "Einige Betrachtungen über Wesen, Entstehung und Behandlung der Homosexualität." *Zentralblatt für Psychotherapie* 15, nos. 1–2 (1944): 1–20.

———. "Das Leib-Seele-Problem (vom Standpunkt des Psychotherapeuten aus)" [The Body-Soul-Problem (from the Point of View of the Psychotherapist)]. *Münchener Medizinische Wochenschrift* 86 (1939): 61–64.

Moreno, J. L. *Who Shall Survive?* New York: Beacon House, 1955.

———. *Psychodrama*. Vol. 2, *Foundations of Psychotherapy*. New York: Beacon House, 1959.

Moser, Manfred. "Im Felde. Die Aktionsforschung, ihr Bewegungsraum und ihr Mensch-Medium." In *Hard War/Soft War: Krieg und Medien 1914 bis 1945*, ed. Martin Stingelin and Wolfgang Scherer. Munich: Wilhelm Fink Verlag, 1991.

Müller, Roland. *Beate Uhse: Vom Mut einer Frau*. Schwedt: Kiro Verlag, 1994.

Müller, Rudolf. "Querulantenwahn, psychopathische Entwicklung oder schizophrener Prozess." Inaugural-Dissertation zur Erlangung des Doktorgrades in der Gesamten Medizin der Hohen Medizinischen Fakultät der Philipps-Universität Marburg (Lahn), 1944.

Müller-Braunschweig, Carl. "Psychoanalyse und Weltanschauung" [Psychoanalysis and Worldview]. *Reichswart* (22 October 1933): 22.

Münnich, K. "Der Mensch als Unfallsursache bei Flugzeugunglücken. Eine Untersuchung an Hand der Flugunfallstatistik des amerikanischen Bedarfsluftverkehrs" [Man as Cause of Accident in Plane Wrecks: A Study Based on the Plane Accident Statistics in American Air Traffic]. *Industrielle Psychotechnik* 16, no. 1–3 (1939): 1–8.

Nitzschke, Bernd. "Psychoanalyse im Nationalsozialismus. Aktuelle Konsequenzen einer historischen Kontroverse: der 'Fall' Wilhelm Reich." *Psychotherapie, Psychosomatik, medizinische Psychologie* 49, nos. 3–4 (1999): 131–37.

Otto, ———. "Frontsoldatentum und Religion im Weltkrieg" [Soldierhood at the Front and Religion in World War]. *Soldatentum* (1935): 59–69.

Plänker, Tomas, and Ernst Federn. *Vertreibung und Rückkehr: Interviews zur Geschichte Ernst Federns und der Psychoanalyse*. Tübingen: Edition Diskord, 1994.

Quinn, Seabury. "The Man in Crescent Terrace." In *Mummy Stories*, ed. Martin H. Greenberg. 1946; New York: Ballantine, 1990.

Rees, John Rawlings. *The Shaping of Psychiatry by War*. New York: W. W. Norton, 1945.

Reitsch, Hanna. *Flying Is My Life*. Trans. Lawrence Wilson. New York: G. P. Putnam's Sons, 1954.

Riefenstahl, Leni. *Memoiren, 1902–1945*. Frankfurt a/M: Zeitgeschichte, 1987.

Rodley, Chris. "Introduction: Leo Marks Interviewed by Chris Rodley, 1998." In *Peeping Tom*, by Leo Marks. London: Faber and Faber, 1998.

Rohden, Herhudt von. "Betrachtungen über den Luftkrieg" [Reflections on Air War]. *Militärwissenschaftliche Rundschau* 2 (1937): 198–214; 3 (1937): 347–61; 4 (1937): 504–17; 5 (1937): 623–31.

Roudinesco, Elisabeth. *Jacques Lacan and Co.: A History of Psychoanalysis in France, 1925–1985*. Trans. Jeffrey Mehlman. Chicago: University of Chicago Press, 1990.

Sachs, Hanns. "The Delay of the Machine Age." Trans. Margaret J. Powers. *Psychoanalytic Quarterly* 11, nos. 3–4 (1933): 404–24.

Saint-Exupéry, Antoine de. *Wind, Sand, and Stars*. Trans. Lewis Galantière. New York: Reynal and Hitchcock, 1939.

Sayers, Janet. *Mothers of Psychoanalysis.* New York: W. W. Norton, 1991.

Scherbening, ———. "Der Kompaniechef und seine Soldaten" [The Company Leader and His Soldiers]. *Soldatentum* (1938): 168–71.

Schmideberg, Melitta. *Children in Need.* London: Allen and Unwin, 1948.

Schreber, Daniel Paul. *Memoirs of My Nervous Illness.* Ed. and Trans. Ida Macalpine and Richard A. Hunter. Cambridge: Harvard University, 1988.

Schroetter, Hermann von. "Zur Psychologie und Pathologie des Feldfliegers" [On the Psychology and Pathology of Pilots]. *Wiener Medizinische Wochenschrift,* 1919. The study appears in seven parts or installments beginning with no. 12 of the weekly. References are to the installment number and the page number as counted within that installment.

Schultz, J. H. *Das Autogene Training (Konzentrative Selbstentspannung).* 1932; Leipzig: Georg Thieme Verlag, 1937.

———. *Geschlecht, Liebe, Ehe: Die Grundtatsachen des Liebes-und Geschlechtslebens in ihrer Bedeutung für Einzel-und Volksdasein* [Gender, Love, Marriage: The Basic Facts of Love and Sex in Their Significance for the Individual and for the People]. 2d ed. Munich: Reinhardt, 1941.

———. "Das Leib-Seele Problem in der Heilkunde." *Süddeutsche Monatshefte* 33 (1936): 289–94.

———. *Neurose, Lebensnot, äretliche Pflicht* [Neurosis, Life Crisis, Medical Duty]. Leipzig: Georg Thieme, 1936.

———. "Psychopathie und Neurose." *Forschungen und Fortschritte* 17 (1941): 228–29.

———. "Der seelische Schutz des Gesunden in den verschiedenen Lebensaltern." *Medizinische Klinik* 36 (1940): 213–16.

———. *Die seelische Gesunderhaltung unter besonderer Berücksichtigung der Kriegsverhältnisse* [Maintaining Psychic Health under Specific Consideration of the War Conditions]. Berlin: E. S. Mittler und Sohn, 1942.

———. "Seelische Gründe der Unfruchtbarkeit" [Psychic Reasons for Infertility]. *Europäischer Wissenchafts-Dienst* 16 (1942): 22–24.

———. "Seelische Reaktionen auf die Verdunklung" [Psychic Reactions to Blackout]. *Deutsche medizinische Wochenschrift,* no. 21 (1940): 564–67.

———. *S. Freud's Sexualpsychoanalyse: Kritische Einführung für Gerichtsärzte, Ärzte und Laien* [S. Freud's Sexual-Psychoanalysis: A Critical Introduction for Court Physicians, Physicians, and Lay Persons]. Berlin: Verlag von S. Karger, 1917.

———. "Vom Seelenleben der Jugend" [On the Psychic Life of Youth]. *Ziel und Weg* 5 (1943): 88–92.

Schultz-Hencke, Harald. *Der gehemmte Mensch: Entwurf eines Lehrbuches der Neo-Psychoanalyse* [The Inhibited Man: Outline for a Textbook of Neopsychoanalysis]. Stuttgart: Georg Thieme Verlag, 1967.

Seversky, Alexander P. de. *Victory through Air Power.* New York: Simon and Schuster, 1942.

Sharpe, Ella Freeman. "From *King Lear* to *The Tempest.*" In *Collected Papers on Psychoanalysis,* ed. Marjorie Brierley, 214–41. London: Hogarth, 1950.

———. "A Note on 'The Magic of Names.'" In *Collected Papers on Psychoanalysis,* ed. Marjorie Brierley, 107–8. London: Hogarth, 1950.

Siewert, Wulf. "Flugzeug und Erdraum" [Airplane and Earth Space]. *Zeitschrift für Geopolitik* 8 (1935): 508–16.

Simoneit, Max. "Die allgemeine Wehrpflicht als psychologisches Problem" [The General Military Service Requirement as Psychological Problem]. *Soldatentum* (1936): 58–62.

———."Ehre und Ehrhaftigkeit in der soldatischen Lebensform." *Soldatentum* (1934): 118–22.

———. "Soldatentum als Lebensform." *Soldatentum* (1934): 65–69.

———. *Wehrpsychologie: Ein Abriß ihrer Probleme und praktischen Folgerungen* [Defense Psychology: A Summary of Its Problems and Practical Consequences]. Berlin: Verlag Bernard und Graefe, 1933.

———. "Zum Panik-Problem." *Soldatentum* (1937): 63–65.

Staabs, Gerdhild von. "Der Sceno-Test: Beitrag Zur Erfassung unbewusster Problematik bei Kindern und Jugendlichen." *Zentralblatt für Psychotherapie* 1943, suppl. 6.

———. *Wie begegne ich den Erziehungsschwierigkeiten beim Kleinkind?* [How Do I Deal with Difficulties in Rearing the Young Child?]. Würzburg: Konrad Triltsch Verlag, 1940.

Steffen, Karl-Heinz. "Initialer schizophrener Strukturwandel als Prophetenwahn" [Initial Schizophrenic Structural Transformations as Prophet Delusion]. Inaugural-Dissertation zur Erlangung des Doktorgrades in der Gesamten Medizin der Hohen Medizinsichen Fakultät der Universität Marburg, 1942.

Stevenson, Burton E. *A King in Babylon*. London: Hutchinson, 1918.

———. *Little Comrade*. London: Hutchinson, 1917.

Strauß, H. "Über die seelischen Einwirkungen bei Minensprengungen" [On the Psychic Effects of Mine Detonations]. *Soldatentum* (1937): 60–64.

Sullivan, Harry Stack. "Psychiatric Aspects of Morale." *American Journal of Sociology* 47, no. 3 (November 1941): 277–301.

Tausk, Victor. "Über die Entstehung des 'Beeinflussungsapparates' in der Schizophrenie" [On the Origin of the "Influencing Machine" in Schizophrenia]. In *Gesammelte psychoanalytische und literarische Schriften*, ed. Hans-Joachim Metzger. Vienna: Medusa Verlag, 1983.

Theweleit, Klaus. *Buch der Könige*. Frankfurt am Main: Stroemfeld/Roter Stern, 1988.

Thorner, H. A. "The Treatment of Psychoneurosis in the British Army." *International Journal of Psychoanalysis* 27 (1946): 52–59.

U.S. Air Force, prepared under the auspices of the Surgeon General. *German Aviation Medicine: World War II*. Vol. 1. New York: Scholium International, 1971.

U.S. Army. "Combat Psychiatry: Experiences in the North African and Mediterranean Theaters of Operation, American Ground Forces, World War II." *Bulletin of the U.S. Army Medical Department* 9, suppl. (November 1949).

U.S. Army. *Neuropsychiatry in World War II*. Vol. 1, *Zone of Interior*. Washington, D.C.: Office of the Surgeon General, 1966.

U.S. Army. *Neuropsychiatry in World War II*. Vol. 2, *Overseas Theaters*. Washington, D.C.: Office of the Surgeon General, 1973.

U.S. Army. "Psychotherapy with Pentothal Narcosis." *Bulletin of the U.S. Army Medical Department* 4, no. 2 (August 1945): 133.

Villinger, Werner. "Psychiatrie und Wehrmacht" [Psychiatry and the Armed Forces]. *Münchener Medizinische Wochenschrift* 88 (1941): 437–42.

Walther, Rudolf Hermann. "Ansätze zu einer Psychologie des Kraftfahrens und Fliegens" [Preliminary Reflections on a Psychology of Truck Driving and Flying]. *Soldatentum* (1934): 14–22.

Watkins, J. G. *Hypnotherapy of War Neuroses.* New York: Ronald Press, 1949.

Weinberg, S. Kirson. "Problems of Adjustment in Army Units." *American Journal of Sociology* 50, no. 4 (January 1945): 271–78.

Weiner, Ed. "Tribute: Hedy Lamarr." *TV Guide,* 25–31 March 2000, 8.

Weizsäcker, Adolf. *Das stille Kind* [The Quiet Child]. Würzburg-Aumühle: Konrad Triltsch Verlag, 1940.

Wendiggensen, Reinhard. "Zum Problem des initialen schizophrenen Strukturwandels." Inaugural-Dissertation zur Erlangung des Doktorgrades in der Gesamten Medizin der Hohen Medizinischen Fakultät der Universität Marburg, 1941.

Winnicott, D. W. "Anna Freud." In *Psychoanalytic Explorations,* ed. Clare Winnicott, Ray Shepherd, and Madeleine Davis. 1969; Cambridge: Harvard University Press, 1992.

———. "Berlin Walls." In *Home Is Where We Start From.* New York: W. W. Norton, 1986.

Winnicott, D. W., and Clare Britton. "Residential Management as Treatment for Difficult Children: The Evolution of a Wartime Hostels Scheme." *Human Relations* 1, no. 1 (1947): 87–97.

Wuth, Otto. "Das Psychopathenproblem in der Wehrmacht nebst Besprechung einiger einschlägigen Fragen." Lecture held at the Militärärztlichen Akademie Berlin on 9 and 10 March 1939.

Yealland, Lewis R. *Hysterical Disorders of Warfare.* London: Macmillan, 1918.

Filmography

Berge in Flammen [Mountains in Flames]. Dir. Karl Hartl and Luis Trenker. Globus-Film, 1931.
Casablanca. Dir. Michael Curtiz. Warner Bros., 1942.
Hitlerjunge Quex. Dir. Hans Steinhoff. UFA, 1933.
Jud Süß. Dir. Veit Harlan. Terra Filmkunst, 1940.
Olympia. Dir. Leni Riefenstahl. Tobis Filmkunst, 1938.
Peeping Tom. Dir. Michael Powell. Anglo-Amalgamated Productions, 1960.
Snow White and the Seven Dwarfs. Dir. David Hand. Walt Disney Pictures, 1937.
SOS Eisenberg. Dir. Arnold Fanck and Tay Garnett. Universal Pictures, 1933.
30,000 Kilometer Aalleinflug über Persien Siam u. Indien [30,000 Kilometers Solo Flight over Persia, Siam, and India]. Dir. Elly Beinhorn-Rosemeyer, 1939.
Victory through Air Power. Dir. James Algar et al., Walt Disney Pictures, 1943.

Index

Laurence A. Rickels is professor of German and comparative literature at the University of California–Santa Barbara, and adjunct professor in the art studio and film studies departments. He is the author of *The Vampire Lectures* (Minnesota, 1999), *The Case of California* (Minnesota, 2001), and *Aberrations of Mourning*, and the editor of *Acting Out in Groups* (Minnesota, 1999). He is a therapist as well as a theorist, and has appeared on the Web in this double capacity as Dr. Truth.

Benjamin Bennett is the Kenan Professor of German at the University of Virginia. He is the author of many books, including *Theater as Problem: Modern Drama and Its Place in Literature* and *Beyond Theory: Eighteenth-Century German Literature and the Poetics of Irony.*